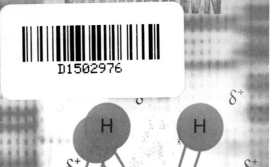

LIVING

FASCINATING, EVERYDAY CUSTOMS and
TRADITIONS from the people of the Bible

THE
EVERYDAY SERIES

Everyday Living: Bible Life and Times

Copyright © 2006 by Thomas Nelson, Inc.

Published in Nashville, Tennessee, by Thomas Nelson, Inc., Publishers.

All Scripture quotations are from the New Century Version® of the Bible (NCV), Copyright © 1987, 1988, 1991 by Word Publishing, a Division of Thomas Nelson, Inc. Used by permission. All rights reserved.

Interior design and typesetting by Katherine Lloyd, The DESK, Sisters, Oregon.

ISBN 1-4185-0566-8

Library of Congress Cataloguing-in-Publication data available on request.

1 2 3 4 5 6 7—10 09 08 07

TABLE OF CONTENTS

N othing makes the pages of Scripture come to life more than under-standing the world in which they were written. *Everyday Living: Bible Life and Times* takes a lively tour of the world of the Bible. Glimpses into the ancient world are presented with a modern twist, com-paring them with day-to-day living right now.

Beginning with the overall setting, the land and climate are consid-ered. Did you know that Israel boasts its own tropical rain forest? Would you believe that some areas in Palestine depend upon the dew to water their crops?

Then come the plants and animals. Date palms were so vital to ancient life there were as many uses for the palm tree as there were days in the year! Also, what was the topic of the lively discussion between Bal-aam and his donkey?

The next chapters introduce you to the people of the Bible—Who were they? Where did they live? What did they do everyday? Did you know that most families lived in the same building as all their livestock? Would you believe that vendors at the coliseum sold souvenir glasses with pictures of gladiators on them?

Many people think that folks in Bible times wore bathrobes, so a chapter on "Their Style" has been included to set the record straight. Did you know that ancient women painted their fingernails and toenails? Would you believe that oily hair was considered a good thing!

Have you ever wondered just what was on the ancient dinner table? A chapter on their food gives a peek at the Bible-time menu. What was Rebekah's trick for making goat meat taste like venison? Did you know that a desert nomad is credited with the invention of cheese?

A vast array of jobs and trades are mentioned throughout the

Scriptures. Do you know what a fuller did? Guess why New Testament Christians had to be careful about their choice of butcher?

A chapter is dedicated to the discussion of ancient culture, art, music, and literature. Did you know that there is a copper scroll that has sent hundreds of people on treasure hunts? What kind of education did Moses receive in the land of Egypt?

Worship was an integral part of ancient life. This book covers some of the pagan practices and gives insight into the worship of the one true God. You'll never guess why the priests in the Temple at Jerusalem always went barefoot!

War was a very real part of the world during Bible times. Do you know what the first long-range missiles were? Would you believe that Roman soldiers took most of their pay in salt?

Every topic is linked with a passage from the Bible. You will see these manners and customs played out, and new nuggets of truth will enhance your appreciation for the lives that were lived so long ago.

—The Publishers

CHAPTER ONE

THE LANDSCAPE

Mark Twain, who visited Israel in 1867, described it as: "… [a] desolate country whose soil is rich enough, but is given over wholly to weeds—a silent mournful expanse… **A desolation is here that not even imagination can grace** with the pomp of life and action. There was hardly a tree or a shrub anywhere. Even the olive and the cactus, those fast friends of the worthless soil, had almost deserted the country."

THE "FERTILE CRESCENT"

There is a curving stretch of land that extends from Egypt in the south to the mountains in the north. It is bounded by the coastline of the Mediterranean Sea and two great rivers, the Tigris and the Euphrates. In all, this parcel is well-watered and sufficiently irrigated to make the land productive. It has become known as the "Fertile Crescent." Compared to the surrounding territories, it was a lush paradise. This attracted the attention of jealous neighbors, and the greedy gaze directed towards a pretty piece of property led to many a war through the years. The Israelites had to guard themselves from the encroachments of their enemies.

A HANDLE FOR THE HOMELAND

The land of Palestine has so many handles that it's easy to get confused. That little area between the Mediterranean Sea and the Arabian Desert has been called by many names through the centuries. When the Israelites first came to their land (Ex. 3:8), it was called Canaan. The land was then divided up, and each section was known by the name of the tribe that occupied it. That's why we hear phrases like "in Dan" (1Kin. 12:29) and "from Asher" (Gen. 49:20). After Solomon's reign, when the land divided, there was the kingdom of Israel and the kingdom of Judah (1Kin. 12:17). In New Testament times, the Romans divided the homeland into several regions, giving us new names like Judea and Galilee to reckon with.

LIMESTONE LANDSCAPING

The land of Palestine is full of limestone, which lends the landscape some distinctive characteristics. On the surface, limestone develops into stretches of hard-baked, cracked pavement. Great for hopscotch, bad for farming. Over time, limestone is influenced by

DID YOU KNOW?

- The name "Palestine" derives from the Philistines, who invaded the land in about 1200 BC.

- Early settlements in Palestine were normally established close to springs, or in places where a well could be sunk to reach the water.

the flow of water, and underground caves and streams are formed. Limestone became a favorite building material in Bible times. Not only was it plentiful, but it was soft and easy to work with. Limestone could be cut in any direction without splitting or shattering. When Solomon was having his Temple built in Jerusalem, he had the masons cut and finish the stones at the quarry. That way there was not noise of hammers and chisels to annoy the citizenry in town during construction (1Kin. 6:7).

DESERT

The deserts of southern Palestine are windswept, barren places. The face of the earth is covered with sand, flint, or even salt (Jer. 17:6). Nothing much could grow in such inhospitable soil. Yet someday these same deserts would bloom like a rose (Is. 35:1). Beneath the shifting sands is the bedrock, laid bare by the forces of wind and water. After centuries, the wind scoured this desert rock into unexpected shapes. Rare downpours of rain gouged out deep valleys, with outcroppings of rock overshadowing narrow passes. Heat rippled during the day and the nights brought a bone-chilling cold. The only ones to call these desert places home were jackals, ostriches, wild goats, owls, and the nomads in their goatskin tents. The children of Israel wandered through this desert wilderness for forty years (Num. 14:33).

ISRAEL HAD A JUNGLE?

When you think of Israel, you think of sifting sands as far as the eye can see, not the lush growth of a jungle. Amazingly, Israel did have its jungle. The Jordan River valley was a deep gorge, filled with a jungle of plant life and swarming with flies. Not unlike the tropical rainforests, heat combined with humidity, and moisture dripped from the overhanging branches. The underbrush in this lowland area concealed lurking predators. Though they are gone today, lions were a danger during Old Testament times. David had to protect his flocks from them (1Sa. 17:34), and Samson confronted one as well (Judg. 14:6). The Lower Jordan Valley provided one of the most fertile growing area in the world, since its tropical climate produced an abundance of fruit.

DAVID

Hiding in Caves

Saul had called David to his home in order to enjoy the young man's talent with the harp. While the music soothed his troubled spirit, Saul took a liking to the youngster, and he made David his own armor bearer. David was never far from Saul's side, and became the best of friends with his own son, Jonathan. After the David and Goliath episode, Saul even made the young man from Bethlehem his son-in-law, giving him Michal's hand in marriage (1Sa. 18:27). But suddenly, everything changed! Saul's feelings did a one-eighty, and his hatred for David grew. He even threw his spear at David one evening, barely missing him. Dominated by envy, jealousy, and rage, Saul made plans to kill David. In fear for his life, David escaped the palace and headed for the hills.

For months, David and his close friends played hide and seek with Saul's troops in the Shephelah, the foothills of the Judean mountains. By moving his few men quickly, David avoided the three thousand men in the royal army (1Sa. 24:2). He and his men found refuge in the hills and valleys, the limestone caves, hidden caverns, and underground streams.

Saul finally got close to the Rocks of the Wild Goats. Finding a spacious cave in which to rest, Saul ordered his men away and prepared to take a little snooze. Sheltered from the heat of the day, he thought himself perfectly safe and fell asleep. Little did he know that David and his men shared the shelter with him, hidden further in the cavern. David's men wanted to kill Saul, but he held them back, insisting that none try to harm God's anointed. Instead, he crept forward and silently, cut the hem of Saul's cloak, then eased back into the shadows. Saul awoke, looked about sleepily, then

moved to join his men outside. When David called to him from the mouth of the cave and showed him the torn cloth, Saul was ashamed. David had proved himself to be faithful, and Saul relented in his pursuit (1Sa. 24:17–19).

THE COASTAL PLAIN

Along the Mediterranean Sea were smooth, sandy beaches. The Coastal Plains were the slopes that made their way from the hillsides in the east down to the sea. Some of these plains were quite fertile, and farmers planted their wheat fields and citrus groves there. These prosperous areas were the home of the Philistines. In fact, that stretch of land is called The Plain of Philistia. Their strongholds there included the city of Gath, from which Goliath hailed (1Sa. 17:4). Most of the plains, though, were rather unattractive for settlements. A ridge of sandstone and dunes followed the coastline. They prevented water from draining out of the hills to the east. The lower plains became covered with lagoons and swampy forests.

THE SHEPHELAH

There is a long strip of land in the low hills, just eight miles wide, between the coastal plains and the Judean hills. It is called, in Hebrew, the Shephelah, meaning "lowlands." This district was once covered in forests of sycamore trees. The chalky hillsides there are dotted with caves, and whole communities have been discovered within the subterranean passages. David took refuge in some of these caves (1Sa. 22:1). Samson's hometown was in the Shephelah (Judg. 13:24-25). Five valleys led through the Shephelah, into the Judean hillside. These lowlands were in frequent contention, and the routes through them were well-guarded. One of these valleys was where Joshua commanded the sun to stand still in the sky so that the Israelites could prevail in battle (Josh. 10:12). David faced the giant Goliath in another valley of the Shephelah (1Sa. 17).

MEGIDDO

The plain of Megiddo is roughly triangular, with each side being fifteen miles long. It's located on the ancient superhighway, the *Via Maris*—the Way of the Sea. This roadway connected Egypt with the major cities of the north and east, and both traders and armies used it. The fortress at Megiddo was located next to a narrow pass, and control of the fortress meant control of nearly all the region's transportation. Joshua was able to kill the king of

Megiddo when he entered the Promised Land, but the Israelites did not control the city itself until David's reign. King Solomon used Megiddo as one of his major defense cities. He stocked it and fortified it to serve as a military outpost along the borders of his kingdom (1Kin. 9:15).

THE SEA OF GALILEE

In a region where there was not a whole lot of water, the Sea of Galilee was huge. Still, it is not terribly large. The lake is about six miles wide, and fifteen miles from north to south. A hike around its circumference was thirty-two miles long. The lake has gone by several different names throughout its history. It is called the Lake of Chinnereth in the Old Testament. In the New Testament it was known as Lake Gennesaret (Lk. 5:1), the Sea of Tiberias (Jn. 6:1), or most often as the Sea of Galilee. The Sea of Galilee was the lake upon which Jesus calmed the storm (Mk. 4:39), and it was the water on which he walked (Mt. 14:25).

COUNTRY BUMPKINS FROM GALILEE

Galilee was an area filled with trade routes, linking it with the outside world. There was a lot of coming and going, and the community was culturally diverse. Jesus spent his childhood in Nazareth in Galilee, where Jews made their living by farming or by fishing on the lake. The citizens of Galilee kept up with happenings within the Roman Empire, and understood the politics of the times. Jerusalem seemed to be a world away. There, in the capital city, the Jewish people kept themselves aloof from the goings-on of the world. They were more mindful of the Law and of Tradition. In fact, they thought that the Jews from Galilee were nothing more than country cousins, and bumpkins at that! This attitude was reflected in Nathanial's words: "Can anything good come out of Nazareth?" (Jn. 1:46). It didn't take long for Jerusalem Jews to peg a hill-country Galilean, for they had a different accent (Mk. 14:70).

THE LAND OF OBSCURITY

The northwestern area of Palestine includes the rugged country of Upper Galilee. The land is full of mountains and sharp cliffs, so few people

MOSES

On the Mountaintop

When God prepared to give his Law to his people, He called Moses to join him on a mountaintop. Moses had been a shepherd in this area for years, and it was in this region that Jethro had welcomed him into his home and later given him Zipporah's hand in marriage. When God had spoken to him through the burning bush, he had told him that he would be back (Ex. 3:12). Instead of leading a rag-tag flock of sheep up the slopes, though, he was leading the entire congregation of Israel. As Mount Sinai came into view, the people made camp and Moses awaited God's instructions. According to the Lord, a few precautions had to be taken. The people were commanded to bathe and wash their clothing in order to consecrate themselves. They were to come towards the mountain when the trumpets gave the signal on the third day hence. Markers were set up around the base of the mountain to keep the curious back. God had warned them that if any man or animal touched the base of the mountain while God was on it, they would die (Ex. 19:12). On the third day, Moses prepared himself for the long hike up the mountainside. The trumpets sounded, and all eyes turned upwards as dark smoke descended upon the peak of Mount Sinai. Thunder and lightening crackled, reverberating through the ground, and shaking the very earth. The children of Israel trembled in fear as the voice of God beckoned Moses to come. As Moses climbed, the people put some distance between themselves and the smoking mountain. They dreaded to hear God's voice, fearing that they would die if they did so (Deut. 4:33). Only Moses and Aaron were allowed to enter the churning darkness. The heat of the flames blackened the top of the granite peak. And God used his own hand to write his Law upon tablets of granite there (Ex. 24:12).

settled there. In fact, most of its citizenry were people on the run, or refugees who were not welcome elsewhere. King Solomon, who was on amicable terms with King Hiram from the north, made a gift of twenty cities in this area to his comrade. Hiram was pleased by the gesture, and came down from his palace in Tyre to tour his new holdings. Hiram was far from pleased with all he surveyed. He seemed to think that Solomon had granted him a kind of white elephant gift. "What cities are these that you have given me?" He nicknamed the area *Cabul*, which can be roughly translated "obscurity" (1Kin. 9:12–13). King Hiram's scorn strained his relationship with his new mountain-dwelling subjects. Nonetheless, Hiram called the area The Land of Obscurity for the rest of his days.

THE RIVER JORDAN

The Jordan River served as an effective natural boundary to Canaan, holding back any invaders from the east. It was the border of the Promised Land. The head of the river itself is near Mount Hermon in the north, and it flows through two lakes on its way to the Dead Sea in the south. As the Jordan leaves Lake Galilee, it enters a very deep valley. The valley's steep sides are lined with overhanging cliffs, and the river further cuts the floor itself. Crossing this rift was very difficult in ancient times. To make matters worse, the valley was filled with jungle-like vegetation, and inhabited by wild animals (Jer. 49:19). The few places where natural fords were formed for crossing the Jordan River were heavily guarded as strategic outposts. Both Ehud (Judg. 3:28) and Gideon (Judg. 7:24) spoke of gaining control of the fords from their enemies.

THE TRANSJORDAN

Transjordan is a term that means "on the other side of the Jordan." There are mountains in the Transjordan that leap up into the skyline, higher than those across the river in Palestine. The land is well-watered and fertile, making it ideal for both agriculture and pasturage. It was here, on the other side of the Jordan that the tribes of Rueben, Gad, and the half-tribe of Manasseh chose to settle (Num. 32:33). They saw all that good pastureland for their livestock and dug in their heels. They didn't want to go any further. God allowed them to stay put, so long as they crossed over the Jordan to help the rest of the tribes fight against the Canaanites (Josh. 4:12).

BASHAN

Bashan was a kingdom in the area of the Transjordan, but it was unlike all its counterparts. Bashan was high country, and received plenty of rain and snow. Its rich soil produced plenty of grain, and in New Testament times, Herod made Bashan's wheatlands the granary of the Near East. Even more famous, though, were the cattle of Bashan. The huge bulls and well-fed cows of Bashan were known worldwide (Eze. 39:18). Og was king of Bashan, and he was a giant of a man, sleeping in an iron bed that measured thirteen feet long and six feet wide (Deut. 3:11). When the children of Israel conquered that area, the cities and surrounding countryside of the kingdom of Bashan were given to Gad, Reuben, and the half tribe of Manasseh as their inheritance (Num. 32:33).

ROLLING HILLS OF HOME

When the children of Israel entered the Promised Land, they settled in the central hill country. The various cities perched on hilltops in this area were strategically important, for they made good defense points. Still, these rolling lands stood a little apart from the rest of the world. Most nations avoided the ups and downs of the central highlands in their everyday comings and goings. The Jews were able to maintain their own little world there. Jerusalem sat atop Mount Moriah in this hill country. From there the land generally sloped slowly to the sea in the west, and dropped abruptly towards the Jordan in the east. These rolling hills made good pasture for the many flocks of the Jewish people.

VALLEY OF HINNOM

There is a valley on the southwest slopes outside the city of Jerusalem. It is called the Valley of Hinnom, or *Gehenna* in Greek. In ancient times, pagans used the Valley of Hinnom for evil purposes. Children and babies were burned alive as sacrifices to false gods like Baal and Molech (2Kin.

23:10). One corner of this valley was called Tophet, which meant "fire-stove." Even as time passed and human sacrifices in the valley went by the wayside, the Valley of Hinnom remained a yucky place. The Jews turned it into the city dump! Anything unwanted or unclean was pitched into the valley, including the bodies of executed criminals. Fires burned there around the clock to incinerate the trash, so the valley was filled with smoke and fire. This made the place a good object lesson in Jesus' teaching about hell (Mt. 10:28). Judas Iscariot committed suicide in this valley (Mt. 27:5).

MOUNT MORIAH

Many of the most famous stories in the Bible mingle together at Mount Moriah. It was there that Abraham brought Isaac in order to sacrifice him (Gen. 22:2). It was the traditional sight of Jacob's dream of a stairway to heaven (Gen. 28:12). Mount Moriah was known as the hill of Jerusalem, where Mel-chizedek reigned as priest and king of Salem. When the Jebusites lived in its fortified city, they called it Zion. Later, David conquered the city, making it his capital city and renaming it "The City of David." Solomon's Temple was built on Mount Moriah (2Chr. 3:1). Traditionally, the very summit of the mountain, called the Foundation Stone, was the sight of the Holy of Holies inside the Temple. The stone was used as a threshing floor (2Chr. 3:1). It was there that the ark of the covenant rested (1Kin. 6:19).

FORESTS

Back in Bible times, the land was not rocky and desolate. The hills were heavily wooded with lush forests—sycamores, cedars, and oaks. There were shrubs and other bushes. Orchards were cultivated by the inhabitants—citrus trees, figs, pomegranates, and bananas. When Deuteronomy describes the land as the Hebrews found it, it says that it was "a land of wheat and barley, of vines and fig trees and pomegranates" (Deut. 8:7–8). However, after years of warfare, overproduction, and misuse, most of the trees were stripped from the land. It was common for invaders to chop down trees, burn orchards, and destroy crops.

SPRINGS OF WATER

The children of Israel, wandering in the barren wilderness, dream of the land that God has promised will be theirs. He told them it would be a good land, which meant that it would have water—"a land of brooks and water, of fountains and springs, that flow out of valleys and hills" (Deut. 8:7). Springs really do show up in valleys. Underground streams that flow through limestone passages sometimes hit a mass of stone that will force the water upwards. When it finds an outlet on the surface, a spring bubbles up. All the earliest settlements in Palestine would grow up around these springs, for they were a dependable source of water. When a city was utterly destroyed, the invaders would stop up the springs of water so that they could not flow anymore (2Kin. 3:25).

DEW

Along the coastal plains, dew did most of the watering during the summer months. The quiet mists that rolled in were called "the dews of heaven." The farmers depended upon this early morning condensation to keep his crops alive during the hot, dry months of summer. Some coastal areas have dew fall on two hundred nights a year. For those areas, the dew provides as much as a quarter of their annual moisture. Even today, dew in the hill country and coastal plains will roll off a tent like an early morning rain. The absence of dew was considered a sign of God's disfavor (Hag. 1:10).

MINERAL DEPOSITS

The lands of the Bible were rich in minerals (Deut. 8:9). From the earliest descriptions in the Bible, we read that in the lands surrounding Eden, there is gold, bdellium and onyx (Gen. 2:11–12). Copper was in use very early, with mines in full swing near Israel's naval port on the Gulf of Aquaba during King Solomon's time. There were silver mines and gold refineries (Job 28:1). When the Philistines arrived on the coast of Palestine, they brought with them the secret of working with iron. They charged other people to come to their blacksmiths to have their tools sharpened (1Sa.

13:20). An astonishing array of jewels is described: sardius, topaz, diamond, beryl, onyx, jasper, sapphire, turquoise, and emerald (Eze. 28:13). Marble was polished, and used in walls and floors. The other resources of the land came in the form of pitch, clays, and salt. In the areas around the Dead Sea, evaporation left thick layers of salt along its banks.

DID YOU KNOW?

• Fiercely hot and dry winds blow from the south, out of Arabia. These are the siroccos or the *hamsin*, well-known to the people of Palestine.

FIRE AND BRIMSTONE

When God set out to destroy something, he did a thorough job. This was the case with Sodom and Gomorrah, and the other cities of the plain there. Because of their great sin, God decided to do away with them and their inhabitants. God rained fire and brimstone down from the skies onto the cities (Gen. 19:24). Archeologists have found the ashen remains of ancient cities that are littered with balls of sulfur the size of golf balls. The whole land became brimstone, salt, and burning cinders (Deut. 29:23). When the land burned, the smoke went up like the smoke of a furnace (Gen. 19:28), and its perpetual desolation made the land uninhabitable forever (Zeph. 2:9; Jer. 49:18).

SIROCCOS

Winds were an important factor in Palestine. They could both help and hurt. In the hot summer months, evening breezes blew off the Mediterranean Sea, cooling the land and bringing the morning mists. Everybody loved the relief they brought. However, there were also the siroccos. These were the hot winds that blew in from the desert. In September and October, the farmers dreaded their arrival. Siroccos could last from three days to a week. They raised temperatures as much as twenty degrees, and humidity plunged with their arrival. A prolonged sirocco could destroy crops, leaving them withered in the fields (Is. 27:8; Eze. 17:10; Hos. 13:15; Lk. 12:55).

September
Monday 1
Tuesday
Wednesday 2
Thursday 3
Friday 4
Saturday
6 7 8 9 10 11

CHAPTER TWO

THE PLANTS

A s they say, **"time began in a garden."** Much of the vegetation found throughout Israel is unfamiliar to us. The Bible is full of interesting trees and shrubs, grasses and herbs, fruits and vegetables. This chapter unearths some interesting facts about the plants found in the pages of Scripture.

ACACIA

This tree and its wood are mentioned in Scriptures often. It seems to have been the local building material of choice. The Hebrews used its hard wood for boards, pillars, tables, and altars when they built their tabernacle in the wilderness. Acacia trees grow to be fiifteen to twenty feet tall and have long thorns all over them. In the spring, they have yellow flowers which later produce pods.

ALMOND TREES

Just as we might watch for the first robin to signal the arrival of spring, the people of Palestine watched for the blossoms of the almond tree. In the Holy Land, the almond tree blooms as early as January with a profusion of pink flowers, signaling the end of winter. The almond tree's blossoms were favored by artists, and many of the temple buildings were ornamented by their beauty. The Israelites call the almond the "wake up tree" (Jer. 1:11–12).

ALOE

There were two sorts of aloe mentioned in the Bible, and both were handy sources of moisturizer. The first was the true aloe, a member of the lily family. It's long spikes were filled with a fresh-smelling green goo, great for dry skin and sunburn. The second sort of aloe that is referred to in the Bible wasn't really an aloe at all. The aloe referred to was actually a large tree. Resin was extracted from its wood, and this aromatic substance was then used to make perfume (Ps. 45:8; Prov. 7:17). It was mingled with fragrant spices, like those mentioned in Song of Songs 4:14. "Fragrant henna with spikenard, spikenard and saffron, calamus and

DID YOU KNOW?

- Rue was an herb with clusters of yellow flowers and a very strong odor. It was used as a disinfectant, for medicine, and as part of the temple tithe (Lk. 11:42).

- The "lilies of the field" described by Jesus in Matthew 6:28 were probably anemones, whose red and purple blooms would cover the hillsides.

cinnamon, with all trees of frankincense, myrrh and aloes." Aloes were also among the oils and spices used in embalming the dead. Nicodemus brought a hundred pounds of aloe and spices along with the linen strips to wrap the body of Jesus (Jn. 19:39).

SOOTHING BALM

Balm was great stuff. The very word brings up thoughts of soothing relief. Even today we use lip balm, bag balm, and even Balmex diaper rash ointment! There was balm in Bible times too. Like aloe, it was a resinous substance that was extracted from wood. Balm came from the evergreen balsam trees, which grew in abundance on the hillsides in Gilead (Jer. 46:11). That's where the phrase "balm of Gilead" comes from. This balm was sticky and a soft yellow color. Some folks burned it as incense. In order to make a medicinal balm, it was combined with the oils from bark, leaves, and berries (Jer. 8:22; 51:8). Balm was a hot item on the trade routes. It was exported south, to the Egyptians (Gen. 37:25). Jacob sent a little balm along with other valuable gifts with his sons when they returned to Egypt to trade for wheat (Gen. 43:11).

BROOM TREES

In the open places of the wilderness, there is little relief from the heat of the sun. The only patch of shade to be found might be under the branches of a broom tree. Where nothing else grows, the broom tree thrives. Nomads used the twigs and roots of the broom tree to kindle their fires (Ps. 120:4). In times of desperation, the bitter roots served up an unappetizing meal (Job 30:4). The broom tree has twiggy branches that are almost leafless. In the spring, clusters of pink flowers brighten their appearance. Shepherds will catch a nap under the limbs of the broom tree. Elijah sat under a broom tree when he was on the run from Jezebel (1Kin. 19:4).

BASKET IN THE BULRUSHES

From the time we are very small, we hear the story of the baby in the basket, floating along the river Nile while big sister watches from the

THE GIFTS OF THE MAGI

A Royal Baby Shower

As the Magi traveled across the distances from the East to see the newborn King of the Jews, they carried with them a precious cargo of gold, frankincense, and myrrh (Mt.. 2:11). Gold was a gift fit for a king. But just what were frankincense, and myrrh? Why were these gifts added to their royal baby shower?

The frankincense tree was beautiful, with its pink flowers, but its true glory lay hidden beneath its bark. The bark was cut or peeled back to force the resinous sap to ooze out. Once the liquid came in contact with the air, it solidified into tear-shaped lumps in shades of amber or burnt orange. These little golden nuggets gave off a sweet scent when held in the warmth of one's hands. The smell of frankincense was warm and woody, with light lemony under-tones. The Hebrew name for the tree meant "incense." Indeed, frankincense was burned as incense and used in the anointing oils for the Holy Place (Ex. 30:34).

Myrrh came from a shrub-like tree with bushy little limbs that bore a plum-like fruit. Myrrh was collected in much the same way as frankincense. Its prickly branches were cut to allow the oily, yellow resin to seep out and harden into reddish-brown teardrops the size of walnuts. The surface of these semi-transparent nuggets was rough and powdered. Myrrh was brittle, and shattered into granules easily. It was a main ingredient in many perfumes, includ-ing those used by women (Est. 2:12; Song 3:6), in the temple (Ex. 30:23), and those used to anoint the dead (Jn. 19:39). The Hebrew name for myrrh meant "bitter," and in ancient times, myrrh was

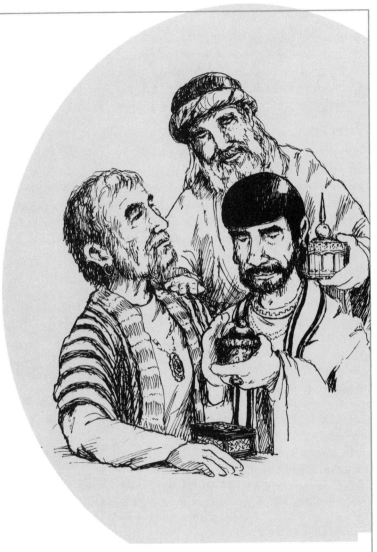

valued as much for its medicinal uses as for its aroma. Myrrh was also used as a painkiller, which is why it was mixed with wine and offered to Jesus on the Cross (Mk. 15:23).

bulrushes. Bulrushes are actually papyrus plants. Those were the same leafy reeds that the Egyptians used to make paper. Interior bark was cut into strips and sewn together. Once it dried in the sun it was ready to write on. Papyrus grew all along the length of the Nile, and Egyptians used them to make braided cords, baskets, clothing, shoes, boats, and sails.

CAROB PODS

Carob trees are tall and evergreen. In the spring they are covered with clusters of small flowers, and as the fruit begins to mature, there are eight-inch pods dangling from its branches. These pods are thick, broad, and brown, and there are beans inside of them. Carob pods are quite edible, being packed with vitamins and minerals. They're sweet too. Some people like to think that John the Baptizer ate these carob pods with honey, so the fruit is sometimes called "Saint John's bread." In Bible times, farmers didn't let such nourishing stuff go to waste, so the dried pods were gathered and used for cattle feed. Pigs loved them, and the prodigal son looked on with envy as the herd consumed mounds of them (Lk. 15:16). These are the same pods that are ground up to make carob powder, the health food store's chocolate substitute.

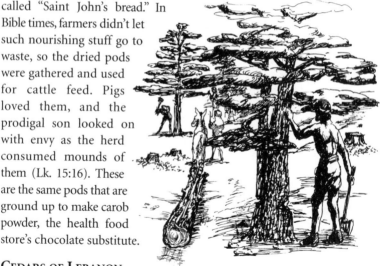

CEDARS OF LEBANON

In ancient times, the mountains of Lebanon were covered with the most magnificent of cedars. They are legendary. These trees were eighty feet tall, with branches that spread over one hundred feet. The trunks of these giant trees were thirty or forty feet around. The timber was strong and durable, so it was used for building the houses of kings (2Sa. 7:2; 1Kin. 7:12) and for constructing ships (Eze. 27:5). Carpenters loved working with cedar, for it is red in color, fragrant, and free from knots. Fragrant sap exudes from the trunk and cones (Ps. 104:16; Song 4:11). After forty centuries of logging, very few of the magnificent trees remain.

DATE PALMS

The Date Palm flourished in the lands of the Bible. Cities were even nicknamed after the number of date palms in their vicinity. Bethany was called the "house of dates" and Jericho was called "the city of palm trees." The Bible describes palms as being upright (Jer. 10:5), and they have become a symbol of righteousness (Ps. 92:12). They grow to be eighty feet tall, and can live over two hundred years. The palm tree was useful for many reasons. In fact, the Arabs say that the date palm has as many uses as there are days in the year. For instance, the shoots that would sprout up around the base of the trunk were cut off, dried, and braided to form ropes, sandals and baskets. The best product of the palm, though, was its fruit. The palm bears most of its dates between its thirtieth and eightieth years. Solomon's Temple is decorated with carvings of the date palm (1Kin. 6:32, 35). Palm branches were waved in the air and spread before Jesus when He entered Jerusalem (Jn. 12:13).

EBONY

Ebony and ivory have always been side-by-side, even in the Bible. Traders from Arabia brought ivory tusks and ebony (Eze. 27:15) to the wealthy in Tyre. So what is ebony? The Hebrew word for it was literally "stonewood," and wood is just what ebony is. Ebony trees have white flowers in the spring, and they bear small edible fruits. The ebony tree has a whitish gray bark, but at its heart the wood is black. This beautiful black wood is easy to carve and can be polished to an almost metallic sheen. In Bible times, ebony was used for making musical instruments and for decorative inlays on furniture.

FIG TREES

The fig tree is not a particularly tall tree, but its large leaves and branches spread out to make a large shady patch underneath. The Hebrew word for this tree even means "to spread out." The children of Israel, wandering in a barren wilderness, looked forward to the day when they would have permanent homes and a fig tree to call their own (Deut. 8:8). Sitting in the shade of your own fig tree was equated with peace and prosperity (Mic. 4:4; Zec. 3:10). During the reign of Solomon, the entire kingdom lived in peace, with each man sitting in the shade of his fig tree (1Kin. 4:25).

FLAX

Flax was another plant that grew well in Egypt. It grew about three feet high, and was covered in pretty blue flowers in the springtime. The fields of flax that lined the Nile River Valley clothed the nation. This plant was the source of the fabric called "linen." Egyptians had the most comfortable linen in the world, and they kept their flax-processing methods a deep dark secret. The Egyptians added an extra step to the usual process to help soften the fibers of the flax. Stalks of flax were anchored in river water and soaked until they started to rot. The smelly mess was then dried in the sun. To separate the fibers that would become the threads of the linen cloth, the stalks were beaten. Egyptians preferred to wear linen that was natural in color, so most folks wore white and off-white clothing.

Sometimes a band of purple or red was added at the border, denoting importance or royalty.

GOPHER WOOD

Everybody knows that Noah built the ark out of gopher wood. Nobody knows what gopher wood is! Some scholars suggest that gopher wood refers to the cypress tree. Cypress trees have beautiful red wood that smells out of this world. It is durable, suitable for building, and grew abundantly throughout Noah's neighborhood. However, scholars do like to bicker over such things, and many other suggestions have been made as to the true identity of gopher wood. Many varieties of trees are suggested: oaks, pines, firs, and even a huge, carved out cedar tree! Others suggest that the word translated "gopher" isn't a kind of tree at all. They think it refers to the method of preparing the wood: planed wood, squared beams, woven branches, laminated planks, or pitch-coated. It is all speculation, so, many translations of the Bible just call it "gopher wood."

DID YOU KNOW?

- The Israelites cherished memories of eating garlic in Egypt (Num. 11:5), where it was used to flavor breads.

- Mint grew like a weed in Palestine, and was one of the least important herbs even though it was used as a tithe at the temple.

- Saffron is a precious herb that comes from the stigmas of a crocus.

- One of the many nicknames given to the Holy Land is "the land of the grapes" because of the numerous vineyards here.

GRASS

Grasses in Bible times were not the emerald green, manicured lawns that we think of today. Grass was defined in a more basic sense, as the herbs and grains that fed folks (Prov. 27:25). Wheat, rye, and barley—all of these came from the grasses men planted in their fields. Some grasses were intended for men, and others were meant to become cattle fodder (Ps. 104:14). Grass was fragile stuff. It sprang up quickly after the rain (Ps.

92:7), but withered just as easily in the heat of the sun (Is. 15:6). Grass was used to symbolize the brevity of man's life on earth (Ps. 90:5; 103:15–16).

HYSSOP

Common hyssop is a sweet-smelling plant that is related to mint. It grew vigorously all over Palestine, even springing out of walls (1Kin. 4:33). The little bushes were about two feet tall, had small, pointed leaves, and carried flower spikes in several different colors. We see it first used to spread the blood of Passover lambs on the doorposts of the homes of the Hebrews in Egypt (Ex. 12:22). The Jews used hyssop in several of their ceremonies (Lev. 14:4–6). The bushy branches were dipped into water or blood and then shaken, to sprinkle the stuff about (Heb. 9:19). Hyssop was associated with cleansing. David prayed, "purge me with hyssop, and I shall be clean" (Ps. 51:7 KJV). Just before Jesus died, he cried out for a drink. Sour wine was placed in a sponge on the branch of hyssop and held to his lips (Jn. 19:29).

LOVE POTION

Rachel and Leah fought over some mandrakes that young Reuben had found while out in the fields during the wheat harvest. Since Reuben was Leah's boy, Leah had first dibs on them! The mandrake roots often were shaped like a little person, and so it was once believed that the plant had special powers to boost fertility. The sisters were fighting over an aphrodisiac, and both hoped to coax Jacob into their own bed for the night. Both sisters were in a race to bear the most children, and Leah was ahead. Rachel hoped that the mandrakes would give her an edge over her sister so that she could conceive that month. The Hebrew word for the mandrake is connected with the verb "to love."

MUSTARD

All through Palestine, and along the shores of the Sea of Galilee, a tall plant waves its yellow flowers in the breezes. The black mustard is an herb that grows wild. It grows as tall as eight feet, and is sturdy enough for birds to build their nests in it (Mt. 13:31–32). The seeds are small and black, and used to flavor fruit and vegetables. Birds also flock to the mustard plants, for they find the seeds to be tasty as well. Many people were amazed that such a large plant could grow from such a tiny seed (Mk. 4:31). Jesus used this comparison in his parables (Lk. 13:19) and to describe the power of a small amount of faith (Mt. 17:20).

OAKS IN BASHAN

Bashan was a country located across the Jordan River from Israel. The land slopes up quickly east of the Jordan, and the cities of Bashan are located high up in the hillsides. Since they get plenty of rain, the people of Bashan enjoy prosperous farms. Like Texans, they grow things big in Bashan! Their cattle are famous for their size and strength (Ps. 22:12). Their king, Og, was so tall that he slept in a bed that was thirteen feet long (Deut. 3:11). And, mighty oaks grew in Bashan. Isaiah mentioned "all the cedars of Lebanon...all the oaks of Bashan" (Is. 2:13). Though Lebanon's cedars were more highly prized than Bashan's oaks, the Israelites used the timber and even exported it. According to Ezekiel, the oaks of Bashan were used to make oars for Phoenician ships (Eze. 27:6).

OLIVE GROVES

Olive trees are mentioned way back in the beginning of Genesis (Gen. 8:11). Groves of the olive trees were planted throughout Palestine, mainly for the precious olive oil they provided. The Israelites used olive oil for just about everything. They cooked with it, poured it in their hair, rubbed it into their skin, and used it to light their lamps. A mature olive tree is approximately the size of an apple tree, and produces beautiful clusters of white flowers. It takes fifteen years until an olive tree is old enough to bear fruit, but they live for hundreds of years. Some of the oldest trees in Palestine are olive trees. Olive wood is sometimes used for building things. Solomon utilized the wood of olive trees in the construction of his Temple (1Kin. 6:23, 31–33).

AN ORCHARD OF POMEGRANATES

Pomegranate trees were found throughout Bible lands, and their fruit and flowers were greatly admired. The ten men who spied out the Promised

Land for Joshua brought back pomegranates along with some of the other fruit that was in season then (Num. 13:23). Later, they kept orchards of them (Song 4:13). The artists who worked on the tapestries of the Tabernacle and on the garments of the high priest embroidered them into the fabric as a decoration (Ex. 28:33–34). The two great pillars of Solomon's Temple each had two hundred pomegranates carved onto their capitals (1Kin. 7:20). The pomegranate tree has bright red flowers, and its reddish-maroon fruit is filled with glistening jewel-like seeds.

STRAW AND STUBBLE

When the farmers of Palestine finished their harvest and threshed their grain, the straw that was left behind was used to feed their cattle. A good host would provide his guest with feed and straw for his pack animals (Gen. 24:25). Straw had other useful purposes. In Egypt, straw was mixed with clay in order to make bricks (Ex. 5:7). When Pharaoh refused to give the Hebrew slaves any more straw, they were forced to gather stubble in the fields and chop it for straw (Ex. 5:12). Stubble was considered useless to the Jews, and when it was fully dried, it was usually burned (Is. 47:14; Joel 2:5).

SPIKENARD

One of the most precious spices of the Bible was spikenard. The pound of perfumed oil with which Mary anointed Jesus' feet was the extremely expensive oil of spikenard (Mk. 14:3–4). The perfume that was poured out was worth three hundred denarii, or nearly a whole year's income (Mk. 14:5; Jn. 12:5). She brought it in an alabaster flask (Mk. 14:3), and the fragrance of it filled the whole house (Jn. 12:3). Spike-

DID YOU KNOW?

- The plant mentioned in Gen. 37:25 and 43:11 was probably a shrub known as the "rock rose." It produces very fragrant pink flowers and is valued for its perfume.

- The box tree is mentioned as one of the "glories of Lebanon." The hard, highly polished wood of the box tree was used in Solomon's temple (Is. 60:13).

- The bitter wood of the cedar tree resists rot and repels insects, allowing the trees to live hundreds of years.

nard was imported from India, for it grew high in the Himalayan Mountains. The roots of the plants would push up several small spikes, each bearing pink blossoms. These spikes produced the perfumed oil.

UNDER THE TEREBINTH TREES

Terebinth trees were common enough in Palestine. They had long, spreading branches that made them pleasant to sit under. Abraham pitched his tent under the terebinth trees in Mamre (Gen. 13:18), and later bought the land there in order to bury Sarah (Gen. 23:17–19). Gideon met an angel under the branches of a terebinth tree (Judg. 6:11–12). The terebinth produces clusters of red berries that are eaten as a condiment in Palestine. Since terebinth trees could get quite large, they often served as landmarks in ancient times (Gen. 12:6). Villages would bury their dead under a terebinth tree, so they were honored and respected (Gen. 35:8). Terebinth trees were often considered to be sacred, and associated with the pillars and groves of idol worship (Judg. 9:6).

VINEYARDS

The climate and the soil in the Holy Land are perfect for growing grapes, so the hillsides are lined with prosperous vineyards. Back in the Old Testament, the children of Israel were astonished by the size of the grapes brought back by a scouting party (Num. 13:23). In Egypt, grapes had been rather small, but Palestine could produce a single grape the size of a plum! After forty years in the barrenness of the wilderness, such fruit must have seemed truly miraculous. After the ark came to rest, Noah became a farmer and planted vineyards (Gen. 9:20). Ahab coveted the vineyard belonging to Naboth (1 Kin. 21:2). Jesus used the vineyards in his parables (Mt. 20:1) and even compared His relationship with his followers to the vine and its branches (Jn. 15:5).

WILD FIGS

There is a tree in the land of Palestine that has many aliases. It is most famous for being the sycamore tree—the one that Zacchaeus climbed in order to get a good view (Lk. 19:4). The tree's large spreading branches made it a great climber. Its leaves resemble the heart-shaped leaves of a mulberry tree. So, the tree also goes by the wild fig tree, the fig mulberry tree, or the sycamore fig tree. The small yellow fruit forms in clusters close to the branches, and is similar to the common fig. Amos gathered the fruit of this tree for a living (Amos 7:14).

CHAPTER THREE

THE ANIMALS

Talking donkeys, rampaging bears, and tamed lions. The stories of the Bible give us fascinating accounts that involve the local wildlife of Palestine. **Animals were named by Adam** (Gen. 2:19–20) and rescued from the flood in Noah's ark (Gen. 6:20). A man who studied the ways of the animals found lessons for his own life (Prov. 6:6) and reason to praise God for his creation (Ps. 104:24–30).

TAME ANIMALS

Men depended upon their livestock for some of the most basic necessities of life. Just think! Food, drink, clothing and shelter could all be gotten from a herd of goats! Then there were all the critters that we place around our nativity scenes at Christmas—the donkey and the ox, the sheep and the camel. All familiar to the people of the Bible.

SHEEP

Mentioned about seven hundred fifty times in the Scriptures, sheep are the most biblical of creatures. Sheep were kept in flocks and watched over carefully by their shepherds. The ewes were milked. Lambs were kept as pets. The sheep's wool made wonderful clothing. Sheep were considered clean animals, and so mutton was found on the dinner table more than other meats. Once a year the sheep were rounded up for shearing time. This was a chance for all the locals to gather together for a good visit and to celebrate. Shearing time could be raucous, and the noise could cover all kinds of mischief. Jacob gathered up his family and holdings and made a run for it while Laban was busy with the shearing (Gen. 31:17–21). It was also at shearing time that Absalom killed his brother Amnon (2Sa. 13:23–29). Even Judah got into trouble during shearing time, because that's when he mistook his daughter-in-law, Tamar, for a harlot (Gen. 38:13–15).

DID YOU KNOW?

• In the Bible, "cattle" was a general term referring to livestock in general. Cattle could refer to donkeys, mules, horses, and camels.

• Arabs prized camels as all-purpose animals. They rode them, milked them, and ate them. Their soft hair provided clothing, and their dung was burned for fuel.

GOATS

The Jews prized goats as all-purpose animals. Though they were strong-willed and stinky, goats were invaluable to ancient people. Often the daughters of the household were given the job of milking the family nanny goat. Their milk provided the butter, yogurt, and cheese that were staples of mealtime. The meat of a goat was tasty, especially in the young animals. The flavor was similar to that of venison, which is why old Isaac was fooled by his wife's cooking (Gen. 27:9). Goat's hair was combed out of its coat and gathered to weave into a coarse cloth. The skins of goats were made into bottles, and the leather came in handy too. Even ram's horns were useful. Horns were made into everything from musical instruments to drinking cups.

SHEEP VS. GOATS

When a shepherd brought his flocks into the hillsides to graze, he usually tended a combination of sheep and goats. Though the two animals were very different from each other, their needs were basically the same. There are a few distinctions though. Sheep were generally white, and goats were generally black. Sheep preferred the smooth pastures of flat valleys, but goats seemed to enjoy scampering along the rocky mountainsides. Sheep eat grass, grass, and more grass. Goats will eat almost anything. The shepherds would often cut off small branches from the trees that he passed for the goats to eat. Sheep lie down in the shade during the heat of the day (Song 1:7), but goats will continue to graze all day long.

SCAPEGOAT

Goats were useful creatures, but they didn't win any popularity contests with people. One reason was the goat's role in the annual Day of Atonement. All of the sins of the people were symbolically transferred to a scapegoat. The high priest would lay his hands on the head of a goat, confess the people's sins, and then send the goat out into the wilderness where it was abandoned to die. Goats were also destructive. They cropped the grass of their pastures so closely that it couldn't grow back. The "goats" were divided from the flock and reserved for destruction in Jesus' description of His return (Mt. 25:33, 41).

DONKEYS

When a trip was big enough to warrant baggage, then the bundles were bound to a pack animal. For the overwhelming majority of people in Bible times, the pack animal of choice was the donkey. They were compact. They weren't fussy eaters. And they were sure-footed. The humble donkey could help out around the house, too, when travel plans were not in the making. The females were often ridden, and could be milked if the owners so chose. Donkeys could pull plows in gardens and fields. Lots of folks in the Bible used donkeys. Abraham packed one for his trip to sacrifice Isaac (Gen. 22:3). Jacob's boys used donkeys on their trip down to Egypt to get grain (Gen. 42:26). Abigail rode a donkey when she came down to dissuade David from attacking her husband's farm (1Sa. 25:20). Even Jesus rode a donkey when he rode into Jerusalem for the Passover celebration (Mt. 21:5). This was his triumphal entry, foretold by the prophets (Zec. 9:9).

HORSES

Horses never really caught on in ancient Israel. They were just too hard to keep up. Horses were fussy eaters. They needed specialized care and training. They had to be exercised. They were also very expensive to import! Other nations kept horses for their chariots, but Israel had been commanded by God not to multiply horses to themselves (Deut. 17:16). Even so, King Solomon started collecting them, and he had so many that entire cities had to be built to stable them (1Kin. 10:26).

MULES

For the record, a mule is a crossbreed. Its daddy is a donkey and its mama is a mare. The Israelites were not allowed to mess with gene pools in this way (Lev. 19:19), so the mules that showed up in the Bible were probably shipped in from Egypt. Mules did combine some favorable traits from their mixed parentage. They were stronger than donkeys, but more sure-footed than horses. King David kept mules for riding through the city (1Kin. 1:33). Absalom was riding on a mule when he was caught by his hair in the branches of an overhanging oak tree (2Sa. 18:9).

CAMELS

A camel was not exactly a family's pet. The camel was considered to be a dull-witted and cranky pack animal. Not only that, they would complain loudly when a load was strapped onto them. Still, when it came to long journeys across desert territory, the camel was ideal. Its big feet would pad across the sands, and its long eyelashes screened out blowing dust and glaring sun. A rider, perched nearly seven feet off the ground atop his packs, practically sailed across the land (Jer. 2:23). Well, lurched is probably a better word, but he would make very good time—up to ten miles an hour. Camels did not have to stop to refuel very often, but when it was time to water them, they would drink like a camel! A thirsty camel could drink twenty-five gallons of water in five minutes flat. Rachel must have been hard put to keep up with Eliezer's camels when she offered to water them for him (Gen. 24:19).

CATTLE

Oxen were the draft animals, used by Israelite farmers to pull their plows and draw their carts. Young cattle were sometimes butchered for a special celebration (Lk. 15:23). For the most part, though, oxen were too valuable for slaughter. It was rather shocking for Elisha to sacrifice both of the oxen he was using to plow (1Kin. 19:19). Only the wealthy kept many cattle at all, because they could eat a small farmer out of house and home. They were larger animals, and needed big pastures to keep them strong and healthy. The land of Bashan, east of the Jordan, was well-watered pasturage. The cows from this region were famous for their size and girth. The Psalmist compared his enemies to these great beasts. "People have surrounded me like angry bulls. Like the strong bulls of Bashan they are on every side" (Ps. 22:12).

BALAAM

Talking to His Donkey

Donkeys were making themselves useful to folks since the beginning. Most donkeys came in drab shades of gray and brown, but once in a while the breeders contrived to produce a white donkey. These blue-eyed critters were startling among their dark-eyed siblings, so they were reserved for royalty. Kings were willing to pay a pretty penny for these unique steeds. A donkey was like a pet, and with a lifespan of up to forty years, it became a lifelong member of the ancient family. Balaam had likely owned his little female—a jenny—since he was old enough to "drive," and had probably been traveling companions for decades already when this little incident in Numbers occurred. Balaam had been hired by Moabites to put a curse on the Israelites, who were passing through on their way to the Promised Land. With the flattery of princes and the prospect of cash on delivery, Balaam made plans to join the Moabite king. Since a donkey could be saddled, Balaam hopped on board his little jenny and set off at a trot. Little did he know that death stood in his path. Donkeys like to do what is good for the donkey, not necessarily what their rider thinks is best. That is where Balaam ran into trouble. All of the sudden, she balked. It wasn't unusual for a donkey to freeze on a trail with a drop-off, or refuse to get its feet wet, but Balaam couldn't see a thing to make her skittish, so he tried to urge her back onto the trail. He hit her, but she turned aside again, this time crushing his foot against a stone wall. Madder than blazes, he hit her again. Then, when the path narrowed, so there was nowhere to turn, his jenny simply laid down under him. Seething in pain and frustration, Balaam struck his donkey again. Then, suddenly, his donkey spoke up! "What did I ever do to you?" Apparently too steamed to

be startled, Balaam barked back at her "You hurt my foot! If I had a sword instead of this stick, I'd kill you now!" The donkey, showing amazing skill in reasoning with her enraged master said, "Haven't we been together since I was little? Have I ever done this to you before?" Balaam gave a grudging, "Well, no." At that moment, Balaam saw the Angel in the path, and quickly joined her in the dust of the road. Face down beside his faithful companion, he learned that his little jenny had just saved his life!

Dogs

The dog was a man's best friend from the earliest of days. Job mentions his dogs (Job 30:1), and the woman from Canaan spoke of the little pet dogs that begged for crumbs under the dinner tables (Mt. 15:27). Greyhounds were kept by kings, to run alongside them during the hunt (Prov. 30:31). Not every dog was a good dog, though. Lots of the dogs that roamed the streets of ancient cities were half-wild scavengers. These were the mangy mutts that ate whatever came their way. They lapped up the blood of King Ahab as it dripped from his chariot (1Kin. 22:38), and they ate the body of Queen Jezebel after she was thrown from an upstairs window (2Kin. 9:35–37).

Like a Dog

Dogs were not especially honored animals in ancient times. In fact, being compared with a dog was a rather nasty insult. Persecutors of God's people (Ps. 22:16) or Gentiles in general were called dogs (2Sa. 16:9). When a man felt insulted, he could exclaim, "Am I a dog?" to emphasize his disbelief at some statement (1Sa. 17:43; 2Sa. 3:8). On the other hand, a man might refer to himself as a dog in order to emphasize his lowly state or humility. "I am just a dead dog!" (1Sa. 24:14; 2Sa. 9:8).

Keeping Chickens

By New Testament times, women started keeping their own small flocks of chickens. Eggs were prized, and carefully collected for cooking or for setting. The picture of a mother hen gathering her chicks under her wings was a familiar one to the Jews (Mt. 23:37). Some women brought their carefully hoarded

DID YOU KNOW?

- Jews turned up their nose when offered a camel burger by their Arab neighbors, for camels were considered unclean animals (Deut. 14:7).

- To prove to the people that Solomon was King David's choice for an heir, he was urged to ride his father's mule through the town (1Kin. 1:33).

- Sparrows were the little birds that could be found in abundance throughout Bible lands. Not one of these little chatterers was beneath the notice and care of God (Mt. 10:29).

eggs to sell in the markets. In Rome, women could even own stalls where they sold eggs, poultry, and vegetables to the public. A hard-boiled egg became a traditional part of the Passover meal.

WILD ANIMALS

Lions and tigers and bears, oh my!
The wild animals found in the Bible range from the roaring lions to the soaring eagles. Their presence in the heights and hills made the protection of a shepherd vital to the lives of his sheep. The countryside was filled with all manner of bird and beast, reptile and insect!

LIONS

Lions are mentioned more than any other wild animal in the Bible. They symbolized power, courage, and royalty. Jesus is called "the Lion of the tribe of Judah" (Rev. 5:5). The people of Palestine had a healthy fear of "The roaring of the lion, The voice of the fierce lion, And the teeth of the young lions" (Job 4:10–11). Lions were a menace if they came up out of the hills and valleys (Jer. 49:19). A few brave souls were able to ward off lions single-handedly. David was able to rescue a lamb from the mouth of a lion, and strike it dead with his club (1Sa. 17:35–36). Samson actually ripped one in two with his bare hands (Judg. 14:5–6)! More often, though, lion hunts were a group endeavor, enjoyed by royalty. Ezekiel 19:1–9 speaks of the pits that were dug and the nets that were used in capturing this fierce prey. It was not unusual for kings to keep lions on their estates. Daniel was tossed into the den of lions that Darius of Persia kept on hand (Dan. 6:16–23).

BEARS

During Bible times, bears roamed all the land. These animals had light colored fur and enjoyed dining on sheep and goats. Shepherds

DANIEL

In the Lions Den

The ancients had an ongoing fascination with the lion. Some cultures admired its strength and courage. The Romans used the lion as the insignia for their legions. Many cultures viewed the lion as the king of all beasts, being wise and just. For this reason, the Egyptians and even Alexander the Great were depicted with lion's heads. The lion even became a popular symbol in Christianity, since one of Christ's titles was "the Lion of the tribe of Judah" (Rev. 5:5). Lions were powerful, having courage and dignity. They were great hunters, and in turn made for challenging prey.

The Assyrians, who lived to make war, did have to spend some time at home. When away from the field of battle, the Assyrians entertained themselves in extreme sports. Big game hunting was near the top of the list of favorite pastimes. Wild boar was plentiful, but nothing matched the challenge of hunting the big cats. Since the lions were so wily, tracking them could cover many miles and take days. Preferring to hunt on their own schedules instead of waiting on the lions, the Assyrians began keeping wild animals in kennels. On the day of a hunt, the prey could be selected and released. If the king felt like roast pork for supper, then they released a boar before the men. If he felt like a real challenge, they released a lion! This became popular in many kingdoms, including the kingdom of Babylonia. That is why King Darius had a den of lions handy on the premises in which to throw Daniel (Dan. 6:16). Poor old Daniel found himself on the wrong side of a stone slab, faced by a captive pride of lions. All night long he prayed, and when morning light came, he was untouched. However, when his accusers were cast into the same pit the next day, all their bones were broken and they were torn to shreds before they hit the floor (Dan. 6:24).

had to be on the watch for them, and David claimed to have killed a bear after rescuing a lamb from it (1Sa. 17:35–36). When Elisha was being mocked by a rowdy group of young people, his curse called down two female bears from the nearby hillsides. The she-bears mauled forty-two youths that day (2Kin. 2:24). Even then, there was nothing madder than a mother bear protecting her cubs. "A bear robbed of her whelps" was a favorite way to describe someone in a state of blind rage.

Foxes

The foxes found in the lands of the Bible were cunning little creatures that lived in holes or in second-hand burrows (Mt. 8:20). These little dog-like creatures with their pointed noses helped to keep down the mouse population in farmers' fields. However, they often had a taste for certain kinds of fruit. That is why the Song of Solomon 2:15 tells of the little foxes that spoil the vines. The fox was known even then for its clever nature. Jesus called the scheming Herod a fox (Lk. 13:32). Samson went through the countryside and caught three hundred foxes, then tied torches to their tails and set them loose in his enemy's fields (Judg. 15:4–5).

Wild Poultry

Partridges and quail were easy to catch, for they hated to take flight. A pursuer just needed to chase the little bird down until it became exhausted, and hit it over the head with a stick. Of course, this was a lot of running around, but the tender meat was something of a delicacy and worth the effort. David felt as if he was a partridge, pursued as he was in the wilderness (1Sa. 26:20). The children of Israel, complaining over the lack of variety in their diet, craved after meat. God gave them what they asked for on a grand scale by blowing a huge flock of quail into their camp. Quail were not especially strong fliers, and when they came to land in the Israelite camp, they were so exhausted that the Israelites were able to just scoop them up. There were enough little birds to last the whole passel of them for a month!

DOVES

The cry of the dove was described as a soft moaning (Is. 59:11). These cooing birds were placid little things. Doves did not resist their enemies or retaliate when pestered by boys who climbed among the rocks to capture them. Doves were clean birds, and could be used by the poor as a sacrifice when a lamb couldn't be afforded (Lev. 5:7) For the convenience of the people, doves were sold right in the Temple courtyards (Mt. 21:12). Joseph and Mary brought a pair of doves to the Temple when they brought baby Jesus to be dedicated (Lk. 2:24). These gentle creatures were equated with a defenseless and innocent people (Ps. 74:19) and became a lasting symbol of peace. Jesus urged that his followers be as harmless as doves (Mt. 10:16). The dove also symbolizes the Holy Spirit, who is said to have descended upon Jesus at his baptism "like a dove" (Mk. 1:10).

EAGLES

Eagles were admired for their strength and power. They were swift, they swooped down on unsuspecting prey (Job 9:26), and they could soar high into the heavens (Obad. 4). The eagles built their nests on cliffs, where the nests would be undisturbed. Obadiah said that the nests of eagles were set among the stars. Eagles showed considerable care for their fledglings, catching up the youngsters and guiding them through the air as they learned to fly (Deut. 32:11). Periodically, an eagle would molt its feathers. When the new feathers grew out, the bird looked young again, filled with the strength of its youth (Ps. 103:5).

DID YOU KNOW?

• King Solomon imported exotic animals every few years, like apes and monkeys (1Kin. 10:22).

• There are about eighty mammals listed in the pages of the Scriptures, but this is not an exhaustive list of the animals that lived in Palestine.

BIBLICAL INSULTS 101

"Sticks and stones may break my bones, but names will never hurt me!" Name-calling has been around a very long time. Some of the best insults in the Bible compare people with animals in an unflattering fashion. When the Pharisees came to hear the teachings of Jesus, he rebuked them for coming out, calling them a "brood of vipers" (Mt. 12:34). "Dog" was a term of derision. If you really wanted to insult someone, you called him a "dead dog" (2Sa. 16:9). In New Testament times, "dog" stood for a false teacher or a sinner (Phil. 3:2; Rev. 22:15). Amos called a bunch of women who were living in the lap of luxury "cows of Bashan" (Amos 4:1). A woman lacking discretion is compared to a swine (Prov. 11:22).

A WHALE OF A TALE

The Scriptures do not say exactly that a whale swallowed Jonah. The Hebrew word is more appropriately translated "really big fish." However, that's not to say that there are no whales in the Mediterranean. In fact, over the centuries whales have periodically visited the waters off Palestine's coast. Sightings of humpback whales and fin whales have been recorded. A sperm whale could have swallowed a man whole as well. The bones of a great toothed whale were kept in a temple in Joppa, though they were touted as the remains of a great dragon-like monster.

BUSY BEES

According to the wisest of proverbs, ancient people admired bees. Bees cooperated together to get their work done, and they were always on the move. No shirkers were allowed in the hive! Women who hoped to have such industrious daughters would name their baby girls Deborah, which meant "bee." Of course, the best thing about bees was the honey that they produced. Honey was precious stuff in a land where there was no sugar. If a man had a sweet tooth, he had better build a beehive in his backyard! Wild bees were known to stash the sweet stuff just about anywhere. Samson came across a swarm of bees putting their combs into the carcass of a lion (Judg. 14:8). Jesus was served a piece of honeycomb along with His broiled fish after his resurrection (Lk. 24:41–43).

LOCUSTS

A swarm of locusts was nothing but trouble. These insects were about three inches long and traveled in huge swarms. Their wings would carry them up into the skies, where they would catch the wind and sail together in an ominous cloud. With a

good tail wind, locusts can travel as many as one hundred dred miles before having to drop down. At night, they descend onto trees and grasses, and when the sun warms them up in the morning, the feasting begins. A locust eats just about anything, and an entire tree or field can be laid bare in a matter of minutes. A plague of locusts was one of the ten judgments brought down on Egypt (Ex. 10:4–15). Oddly enough, locusts are edible (Lev. 11:22). Apparently, people dry them, store them in bags like potato chips, and bring them out when the family gets the munchies!

UNEQUALLY YOKED

Every young person has heard the warning "Do not be unequally yoked together with unbelievers" (2Cor. 6:14 KJV). The yoke was a curved wooden bar used to harness two animals together. Their combined efforts made pulling a plow through stubborn soil easier. Elisha is first found in the fields with a team of oxen (1Kin. 19:21). At other times, the animals were yoked together to pull a cart. The Philistines yoked a pair of cows together to pull the cart that returned the ark of the covenant back to the Israelites (1Sa. 6:7). It was actually forbidden for a team of animals to be unequally yoked. God told the Israelites not to team up an ox with a donkey (Deut. 22:10). Though it might seem common sense, since the donkey's strength and size were no match for the ox's, there was a different reason for the law. The ox was a clean animal, used for both meat and for sacrifices by the Jews. The donkey, though a reliable mode of transportation, was an unclean animal. God did not allow His people to mix and match when it came to clean and unclean!

CHAPTER FOUR

THE PEOPLE

Although the Jews were chosen by God to be his own people, **He did not exclude other nations** when giving us the Scriptures. There is a wonderful variety in the cultures and backgrounds of the people who populate the pages of our Bibles. Even within the nation of Israel itself, there were several different groups that distinguished themselves for religious or political reasons.

PEOPLE OF PALESTINE

Although surrounded by a wide variety of nations and *often overrun by the political maneuvers of other countries, Israel really was an out-of-the-way place. You could say that they were "off the beaten path." As far as Jews were concerned, they were God's chosen people and that was that. All the others were merely Gentiles, and not worth any further distinction.*

STATURE

The Israelites were a little self-conscious about their height. They considered themselves to be much smaller than the Canaanites when they were looking over the Promised Land. The spies came home with stories of giants, saying "The people are greater and taller than we" (Deut. 1:28).

Archeologists have studied the skeletons of adult Israelites, and they found that their height was between 5'3" and 5'7" on the average. This smaller stature was due in part to the poor food supply caused by drought and plagues.

SMALL, BUT WIRY

Although the Israelites may have been smaller and thinner than their contemporaries, they were not weaker. Everyone worked hard, even the girls. Every day, young women filled their water jugs at the local well and carried them home on their heads. When filled with water, each jug weighed as much as fifty pounds. Preparing grain for food was another strenuous and backbreaking task. An ideal wife of that day was one with strong arms (Prov. 31:17).

SOCIAL STRUCTURE

There were three kinds of people in the Middle East. There were the country-folk, who lived in small villages and worked the land. There were the city-folk, who lived comfortably within walled cities. And there were the desert-folk, who wandered with their flocks through barren reaches and lived in tents. These classes of people weren't necessarily on friendly terms, and rarely met for social events. Although they lived near each other, their lives were worlds apart.

THE BEDOUIN

The Bedouin were the nomads and herdsmen of the desert. They raised sheep, goats, and camels. Bedouins knew how to ride their camels across the desert sands, and how to milk their goats in order to make yogurt and butter. They navigated the deserts with ease, and lived their simple lives in the midst of its barrenness.

HOUSES OF HAIR

The name that the Bedouin used for his home is literally translated "houses of hair." The long, rectangular Bedouin tents were made from cloth that was woven from the hair of goats. The long black hair of the goats they raised was shorn in the spring, and the women wove the cloth themselves. The roof, the walls, and the dividing walls inside the tents were all made from this fabric. In the heat of the summer sun, the outsides of these tents were hot to the touch, but the inside remained bliss-

DID YOU KNOW?

• The name that the Bedouin used for their tents is literally translated "houses of hair," because they were made from a cloth woven from black goat's hair.

• Fellahin families were quite large, because they included all the relatives. These extended families lived under one roof together.

fully cool. The reverse was true in the wintertime, when a small fire inside the tent kept it warm and cozy. The cloth also proved to be weatherproof, because when the rains would fall the weave of the fabric would contract, making it watertight.

ON THE MOVE

When Abraham left Ur and took on a nomadic form of life, he turned his wealth into flocks and herds so that his wealth could travel with him (Gen. 12:5). The Bedouin followed his flocks from pasture to pasture, water to water. Bedouin's were constantly traveling to new places throughout the year. They would herd their flocks into the depths of the desert during the rainy winter season. During the dry summer months, the Bedouin moved back towards the cultivated lands along the edges of the desert. While near these settlements of farmers, tensions and conflicts often arose.

HELPING THEMSELVES

Not all Bedouin were God-fearing men of integrity, like Abraham. In fact, local farmers had a healthy fear of their desert neighbors. Although they disappeared into the desert for many months at a time, the Bedouin would come back to the edges of the desert where the farmers lived in small towns. Often, they swept upon defenseless villages, especially during the harvests, and stole all that they could. And what better way to fatten up your herds than to let them graze in a nice field of barley? Hatred grew between the Bedouin and the farmers, and feuds continued from one generation to the next.

BEDOUIN HOSPITALITY

The Bedouin were famous for their hospitality, and their generosity was not a myth. When entertaining a stranger, the Bedouin host wouldn't dream of asking the names of his guests, just in case their families were involved in a blood feud. This could cause tension, and the host might be forced to be discourteous. This Bedouin hospitality had religious significance. To show kindness to a guest was to honor one's god, and in turn, one's god would show kindness to him. Abraham displayed Bedouin hospitality when he encouraged the three strange men to sit and rest while he ran to tell Sarah to prepare a meal (Gen. 18:2–8).

FELLAHIN

The Fellahin were the blue-collar workers of the Bible world. Simple folk: farmers and shepherds mostly, who lived out their lives in small towns. The Fellahin were once Bedouins, but embraced farming. They lived a more settled life on the edge of the desert.

CITIES WITHOUT WALLS

Wherever the soil could be tilled and crops could be grown, little agricultural communities sprouted up. These were the towns of the Fellahin. Mud huts provided a home for whole families. Aunts and uncles, cousins and grandparents, children and grandchildren were housed together. It may have been a bit crowded, but there was safety in numbers. You see, the Fellahin towns were small and unprotected. There were no walls to keep out scavenging animals or raiding nomads. The Fellahin were vulnerable, especially during harvest time. The farmers had to be on guard against the attacks of Bedouin, who would sweep through a village and carry off fresh produce, stored grain, animals, and even people. Abraham had to form a posse and head out after a group of such raiders who had captured Lot and his whole family (Gen. 14:14–16).

A GOOD FELLAH

Jesus was a member of the Fellahin. Although a carpenter was considered a craftsman, Jesus left this work when beginning his public ministry. He lived in Capernaum and similar villages, which were communities without walls. He avoided city life, and found his closest friends among the Fellahin class—country folk.

NABOTH

And the Family Farm

In 2 Samuel we find the story of a Fellahin named Naboth, who stands up to his wealthy adversary and refuses to sell the family farm. Naboth owned a lovely little bit of hill country, with slopes covered by carefully tended grapevines. The vineyard had been in the family for generations, and they took great pride in the quality of their fruit and in the wines that they bottled. Although a small operation, it was a nice little business. Naboth was proud of what his family had established and thankful to God for blessing their efforts.

Then, the man who owned the adjacent property decided to do some renovations. King Ahab, who owned extensive lands, was making plans to expand his own gardens. He started to cast a longing eye over the fenceline towards Naboth's rich farmland. Why, it would be the perfect spot for an herb garden. He could see it now: carefully manicured sections and perhaps a birdbath or two. But Naboth refused to sell his little farm (1Kin 21:3). Why should he? He didn't need or want this greedy king's money. No sum could replace the years of toil and sweat that had caused this property to thrive. Besides, the farm was home to his whole family: wife and kids, mother-in-law, his younger brother, a few nieces and nephews. Where would they all go?

Unfortunately, King Ahab did not take no for an answer (1Kin 21:14–16), and Naboth's family lost the vineyard to their greedy ruler.

THE BELLADEEN

The Belladeen were a people of prosperity. These city-folk of Bible times lived in the safety of walled cities. Large gates that closed every evening and opened every morning regulated the comings and goings of strangers. The Belladeen of New Testament times were the merchants, traders, craftsmen, scribes, and booth-keepers that filled the streets of large cities.

DENOUNCED BY THE PROPHETS

During the Old Testament times, Belladeen were few and far between. In fact, these men of wealth were found almost exclusively in the courts of kings. These were courtiers, who held positions of importance within the king's service and lived in the lap of luxury. Haman, in the service of King Ahasuerus, was such a man (Est. 3:1). The prophet Amos even denounced them for their extravagant living (Amos 3:15).

SECTS

The Jews served one God, but they didn't always agree on how to do it. Disagreements on interpretation of the Law led to divisions. Not unlike the variety of denominations we find in Christianity today, there were sects within the Jewish faith during the days of the Bible.

PHARISEES

When we read about the Pharisees in the Gospels, we picture a tight little group of men who followed Jesus at a distance. Their hands are piously clasped together, and disapproving glares are cast Jesus' way as they whisper intently amongst themselves. We know from Jesus' rebukes that these are the "bad guys" (Mt. 23), but who are they really? The Pharisees were a religious sect. In today's terminology, these would be the radical right-wing fundamental conservatives of the New Testament times. Pharisees were concerned with living a holy life before God, so they didn't smoke, didn't drink, didn't chew, and didn't go with girls that do! Religion was the supreme passion of a Pharisee's life. It affected their education, their reading, their culture, their speech, and their day-to-day living. Pharisees ate, drank, and slept holy living.

NOT ALL BAD

During the New Testament times, there were thousands of Pharisees, and not every one of them was bad. Pharisees were faithful Jews, who were awaiting the fulfillment of the promised Messiah. In fact, Pharisees were widely admired by people because of their holy lifestyles. Among these faithful were people like Simeon and Anna, who blessed Jesus in the Temple (Lk. 2:25; 2:36–38). Nicodemus was also a Pharisee, who served on the ruling council (Jn. 3:1). These were sincere servants of God, who hoped for the Messiah to come. Still, the majority of Pharisees were blind to anything but the keeping of their rules. These people were filled with a spiritual pride that made them incapable of seeing that they might be wrong. It never would occur to them that anything else was worthwhile.

"TRADITION"

In their desire to be a perfect nation, the Pharisees took steps to ensure that the Law would never be broken. They added rules and regulations to their religion, which were called the "Tradition." Later, these rules were collected into a complete book, called the Mishnah. These extra rules were intended to ensure that the people would not break the Laws handed down from God by Moses. Unfortunately, all these little laws were petty and difficult to recall. Some rules were downright ridiculous. Not only that, they were almost impossible to carry out. This "Tradition" made everyday life a burden too heavy to bear (Mt. 23:4).

RELIGIOUS SNOBBERY

While Pharisees were admired, if somewhat grudgingly, for their pious lifestyle and religious knowledge, they did not return the favor. Ordinary people were treated with contempt and dislike by the strict Pharisees. Pharisees believed that by keeping every one of their rules, they were living a life pleasing to God. Since the ordinary people of the day fell so far short, they were considered slackers.

LOT

Loving City Living

Abraham's nephew, Lot had taken a risk by following his uncle into the unknown, but it paid off. While God blessed Abraham, Lot became prosperous as well. Having chosen the finer pastureland when they parted company (Gen. 13:12), Lot was even able to shake the desert sands from his feet and move onto plains that were green and well-watered. Wealthy beyond his dreams, and ready to spend some of his hard-earned cash, Lot began shopping in the local marketplaces. There were several cities close at hand, and before long, Lot's family decided to leave the Bedouin life behind them and move into a grand new home inside the city walls. Sodom was a gated community. It offered all the comforts a family could ask for — security from would-be thieves, water from a well, markets that sold exotic foods, and fine clothing. Lot had a three-camel garage. Mrs. Lot had a double oven. The girls each had their own bedroom. What luxury! What convenience!

Mrs. Lot was thrilled not to be constantly washing the smell of sheep out of her husband's robes. Instead, she bought new clothes for him. Soft fabric replaced the coarse goat-hair cloak. Flowing robes were striped in bright colors. A length of real silk from Arabia for a belt. Such finery. Even though they were "new money," they fit right in with their new Belladeen friends.

HAMAN

Courtier to a King

In Old Testament times, the Belladeen were found in the courts of kings. Haman is a good example of such a man. He served in the palace of King Ahasuerus (Est. 3:1). As a man of great wealth who basked in the opulence of the Persian court, Haman wanted for nothing. He strode across marble floors. He ate at the king's table. He was privy to the king's conversations. He expected the respect of the common man (Est. 3:2). Haman could afford to hire men to do menial tasks for him, such as the building of a large gallows (Est. 5:14). He could order the death of any man who displeased him, as he had hoped to execute Mordecai (Est. 6:4–12). Haman was a man of great influence, and was even able to manipulate the king himself in order to pass the law which threatened to exterminate the Jews. Although it was hardly a power-suit, Haman did have a taste for fine clothing, even coveting King Ahasuerus' own robes (Est. 6:8–9). The Belladeen were accustomed to fine clothes, wearing colorful garments sewn from fine material. A flowing robe of light fabric, beautifully striped, would be held in place by a full five yards of Arabian silk, which was wound around the body as a girdle. Sometimes pantaloons were worn under this robe, and these would be tied at the ankles. It was about men like this that God spoke "I will destroy the beautiful homes of the wealthy—their winter mansions and their summer houses, too—all their palaces filled with ivory" (Amos 3:15, NLT).

SABBATH TRADITIONS

The Fourth Commandment says to "remember the Sabbath and keep it holy." The Jews found a day of rest and reflection in this. However, this was not specific enough for the Pharisees. What entailed keeping the Sabbath, and more importantly, what activities broke the Sabbath? If a man carried a needle in his cloak on the Sabbath, he was sewing. If he dragged a chair through a sanded floor, he was plowing. If he picked some grain and rubbed it between his hands—he was reaping and threshing. And in doing all these things, he was breaking the Law.

SADDUCEES

The Sadducees were another religious sect among the Jews. They are known for having a high view of the Law, and only believed in the actual words of the Law. In fact, if something wasn't mentioned in the Law, they doubted its existence. They did not believe in any kind of afterlife—heaven or hell—because neither is mentioned in the Law. They also did not believe in angels or in demons for the same reason. This was the basis of the trick question which they posed to Jesus (Mt. 22:23–30).

> **DID YOU KNOW?**
>
> • It was wrong to eat an egg laid on a Sabbath because the hen had been working.
>
> • Sadducees were priests with pedigrees. Many were in the line of the High Priest, and their families were wealthy.
>
> • The "official" Sabbath burden allowed was the weight of one dried fig.

PHARISEES VS. SADDUCEES

The Pharisees and Sadducees had something of a feud going. While the Pharisees held the Law and "Tradition" in high esteem, the Sadducees refused to live by the traditions of men. If it wasn't in the actual Law, it just wasn't so. Pharisees hated the Gentiles, and longed for the Messiah to come and wrest control of Israel from their hands. Sadducees preferred peace at any cost, and so they were pro-Roman. These two sects were at odds, and neither intended to give any ground to the other. In fact, there was only one matter on which they held common ground: both sects despised Jesus, and they plotted together to have him killed (Mt. 26:3–4).

ROMAN SYMPATHIZERS

Many of the Jews were disgusted with the Sadducees because they had taken sides with the oppressors. Rome was in control of the Holy Land, and the Sadducees wished to avoid anything that would stir up trouble with their masters. The reasoning behind this was rather obvious. The Sadducees wished to keep themselves in power. The Sanhedrin, a council of seventy-one members, held sway over all the Jewish people. The group, largely made up of Sadducees, made the civil and religious decisions. The leader of the Sanhedrin was the High Priest. So long as the Jews were peaceful, and law and order were maintained, Rome was content to leave the High Priest in his position of authority.

SCRIBES AND RABBIS

Scribes first showed up in the Old Testament while the Jews were in captivity. They were men who helped the priests write down the records of the Jewish nation, along with their stories and laws. But as time passed, these scribes became better known as teachers. Since their jobs as copyists made them so familiar with the words of the Law, they became interpreters of difficult passages. Soon, they became the rabbis. Rabbis were the authorized teachers of Jewish religion, and Pharisaical rabbis also taught the "Tradition." Rabbis could solve any puzzling questions about the Law, and their word was final. Scribes and rabbis were influential, and wherever they went they were both feared and respected.

DISCUSSION GROUPS AND DEBATE TEAMS

Rabbis reveled in the finer points of the Law and Tradition. They knew things that the common Jew had never even heard. A wise and respected rabbi was able to establish his own schools, and spent his days teaching his own interpretation of the problems he uncovered in the Scriptures. Eager, young students of the Law would flock to these institutions to listen, learn, and discuss. Naturally, these rabbis were fond of arguments and debates, often just for the sake of argument. These heated discussions gave them a platform to talk about their views of the Law. In the New Testament, we meet one of these "experts in the law," who tried to start an argument with Jesus (Lk. 10:25–28).

ZEALOTS

The Zealots were freedom fighters, who spent most of their time plotting to overthrow the Roman government. The Romans were viewed as oppressors, and Zealots hated them. The hope of this group was that a great leader would come and lead them in a great uprising against Rome. This man would be their Messiah. One of Jesus' disciples was called Simon the Zealot (Mt. 10:4). The rebellion of the Zealots eventually led to the wars which leveled the Temple at Jerusalem, just as Jesus had foretold (Lk. 21:20–24).

THE ESSENES

The Essenes were the monks of the New Testament world. They separated themselves from society and found lonely places to live in the hills that surrounded Jerusalem. Believing that cleanliness was indeed next to godliness, the Essenes bathed frequently and dressed in white garments. They were a quiet, bookish bunch. Many of the Essenes were believed to have acted as scribes, making copies of the Scriptures. The Dead Sea Scrolls, which were found in 1947 in a cave near the northern shores of the Dead Sea, were written or collected by the Essenes. They

wrote on scrolls of leather, wrapped them in linen, and placed them in earthenware pots. Thanks to their carefully maintained library, manuscripts survived for centuries. These scrolls are the oldest manuscripts of the Old Testament in existence.

Neighboring Nations

If good fences make good neighbors, then the Israelites
*should have built more fences. The Jews were constantly embroiled
in conflict with the nations adjacent to their own. Ever since the
Tower of Babel incident in Genesis 11, there have been many
peoples scattered across the face of the earth; each with a unique
language and culture. In the course of Bible history, many nations
came and went. Small cities were built, only to be destroyed. Super
powers swept across the land, then ebbed away; each leaving their
mark in Scripture.*

The Sumerians

In Mesopotamia, where civilization began, the Sumerians hold the distinction of being the earliest identifiable group of people. The Old
Testament refers to them as, "the people of the plain of Shinar." The
Sumerians had several large cities, one of which was Ur. The Bible calls
this city "Ur of the Chaldeans" (Gen. 11:28), and this was the birthplace
of Abram. Years of sediment deposits from the rivers have placed the site
of Ur miles inland; but in the days of Abram, it was a large city with a
bustling sea port on the Persian Gulf.

Sumerian Temples

The Sumerian people had a highly organized city government. They had
factories and schools for their children. They also built temples for worship that were feats of architecture and engineering; some of them massive,
even by today's standards. As a rule, temples were constructed to bring
you closer to your god. That meant that temples went up, and the higher
up the better! The design of these structures was called a ziggurat, and
they resembled a massive, rectangular wedding cake with stairs running
up the eastern side. It is very likely that the Tower of Babel (Gen. 11:1–4)
was a giant ziggurat, reaching higher and higher into the sky with each
layer that was added.

NICODEMUS

The Pharisee

Nicodemus had been a Pharisee from his youth. His parents sent him to the best Hebrew school that money could afford, and he was raised as a "son of the Law." He continued his studies, memorizing much of the Mishnah and learning how to faithfully keep its rules. He knew all the ins and outs, and even a few loopholes. His parents were so proud of him. Even Nicodemus' peers among the Pharisees respected him. He reached the pinnacle of his career when he was elected to serve on the governing council. As a member of the Sanhedrin, he participated daily in debates over the finer points of keeping the Law. Nicodemus maintained a faultless front, and was careful to meet the standards that were expected of him. After all, on his shoulders lay the responsibility of guiding the entire nation of Israel down the path of righteous living. He kept the Sabbath and wore his phylactery for morning and evening prayers. The tassels on his robe were brilliantly blue, and long enough to sweep the floor. Nicodemus was obviously a good man and many admired him as a respected leader of the community. Yet, something was lacking.

Nicodemus had heard some of the teachings of Jesus. Who hadn't? His lessons were the talk of the town. Yet, the Sanhedrin grumbled against his words, and feared the rumors that were beginning to circulate. Nicodemus needed to hear for himself what this Man had to say, so he arranged a meeting with him. Under cover of darkness, to avoid the scandal, he spoke to Jesus (Jn. 3:1–21). Nicodemus' life was changed forever.

AMMONITES AND MOABITES

The daughters of Lot were not exactly "good girls." Concerned that they would not be able to secure husbands, they got their father drunk and slept with him. Each became pregnant and each bore a son, Moab and Ben-Ammi (Gen. 19:30–38). Traditionally Moab's name meant "from father," and Ben-Ammi's name meant "son of my kin." These boys became the founders of the Moabite and Ammonite peoples. Since they were not direct descendants of Abraham, they had no claim on the land west of the Jordan.

MARRY A MOABITESS?

The Moabites were distant relatives of the Jews, being descended from Abraham's nephew, Lot. But this didn't mean they met for family picnics. The Moabites caused nothing but trouble for the Jews. When the children of Israel first entered the land, they intermarried with the Moabites. In this way, they lured the Jews into idolatry (Num. 25:1–2). God was displeased. Executions were ordered. This started all kinds of ill will. The Jews and the Moabites became sworn enemies, and wars were fought between them for hundreds of years. It is no wonder then that the people of Bethlehem were shocked when Naomi came home with a Moabite daughter-in-law in tow (Ruth 1:22). It is also no wonder that a close relative passed on the chance to buy Naomi's land, since it included marrying a Moabitess (Ruth 4:5).

SEASICK SAILORS

The Jews did not take to the sea very well. Accustomed to a land where water was rare and precious, the children of Israel tended to turn rather green when they found themselves afloat. This frustrated King Solomon's dreams for a great navy. He had built an entire fleet to sail the Red Sea (1Kin. 9:26–27), but his men had no experience navigating the sea. This is where Solomon's alliance with King Hiram of Phoenicia became vital. The Phoenicians were one of the "people of the sea." Their sailors were skilled, and Hiram was willing to loan them out to Solomon's royal fleet.

EGYPT

Egypt was far from the Promised Land. It was on a different continent, separated by miles of rocky plains and by reedy quagmires. It was a land of a different race and a different culture. Then come the unexpected twists in history that brought the two nations face to face. The Old Testament refers to the nation of Egypt more than five hundred and fifty times.

LIVING IMAGES

Some animals were sacred in Egypt. A god was often depicted wearing the head of a sacred animal to make the god easier to recognize. Anubis, the god of embalming, is often pictured in hieroglyphics with the head of his sacred animal, a jackal. Falcons were sacred to Horus, as were bulls to Ptah. These animals could not be poorly treated or killed by any Egyptian, or they would suffer the wrath of the god to which the animal was sacred. This could lead to inconveniences. For instance, the temple to the goddess Bastet was overrun with cats.

FITTING IN

Egyptians were of a different race than the Hebrews, so Moses would have stuck out like a sore thumb in the family portraits throughout the palace. While the Hebrews had light olive complexions and black hair, the Egyptians were brown-skinned with stiff brown hair. Even in the hieroglyphics, which depict the Egyptian overseers whipping the cowering Hebrew slaves, there is a definite distinction made between the two peoples. Although Moses was given an Egyptian name, raised in the Egyptian palace, spoken to in the Egyptian tongue, and taught by Egyptian tutors, he could not have failed to notice that he was somehow different in appearance.

AN EGYPTIAN WIFE

When King Solomon was ruling over Israel in all his great wisdom, he actually had an Egyptian wife. She was a daughter of the Pharaoh of Egypt, sent to marry this Hebrew king in a diplomatic effort to ensure

ESTHER

In the Persian Court

Esther probably never had dreams of being carried off by Prince Charming and living happily ever after in a grand castle. But that's just what happened. Kings could do just as they pleased with the people that they conquered, so when the order went out that all the pretty girls were to report to the castle, there was nothing anyone could do. Girls who were the apples of their daddy's eye and their mother's best helpers were suddenly whisked away. Of course, these young women couldn't be expected to appear before the king right off the street. They needed to be polished up a bit—a good bath, a fine-toothed comb, a new dress, and a whole year of beauty treatments. Each young woman brought into the palace was given a place in the king's harem, and for a year they were given mud packs and hot oil treatments. The eunuch in charge of the king's harem took a liking to Esther, and he wanted this girl to win the beauty contest that was coming up. So, he offered to take her under his wing and teach her everything he knew about palace-life. This eunuch had been overseer of the harem for quite a while, and he heard all the wives' and concubines' gossip. He probably gave her inside information on the king's favorite color, his favorite foods and wine, and maybe even where he was ticklish! When it was Esther's turn to go into the king's chamber, Ahasuerus was swept off his feet. This was just the girl for him, and he crowned Esther Queen of Persia (Est. 2:17).

Israel's friendship. Although Egypt was no longer a powerful nation, it was still a famous country with a noble reputation. Solomon had indeed gained international prestige for Pharaoh to think it worthwhile to give him this girl as a bride. She was given her own palace in Jerusalem (1Kin. 7:8; 9:16).

THE MIDIANITES

The Midianites lived in the deep south. They were traders and raiders who lived in the desert. Their land was south of Edom, along the coast of the Red Sea. The Midianites were relatives of the Jewish people, though they had intermarried with the peoples of the south. Midian had been a son of Abraham by his second wife, Keturah (Gen. 25:1–2). The Bible records that Moses met these people in the Sinai Desert and later married Zipporah, a Midianite woman (Ex. 2:21).

THE CANAANITES

When the children of Israel returned to the Promised Land after years of wandering in the wilderness, they did not find immediate rest. Instead, they found a number of foreign peoples occupying the land. These were the Canaanites, and the challenge of driving them out was daunting to the Israelites. Canaanite cities were surrounded by defensive walls of brick and stone, just as we see in the story of Joshua and the Battle of Jericho (Josh. 6:1–2).

THE LAND OF THE PURPLE DYE

The word canaan is similar to a Hebrew word which means "subdued, humbled, lowly." This recalls the words of Genesis 9:25, "May there be a curse on Canaan! May he be the lowest slave to his brothers." However, most scholars link the term canaan with a cuneiform word which means "reddish purple." On the shores of the land of Canaan, there is a snail which secretes a purple dye. This dye was one of the chief products of Canaan, and so it came to be known as the "Land of the Purple Dye."

RAMPANT IMMORALITY

Some scholars think that the Bible is prejudiced in its depiction of the Canaanite people. The Bible states that their lifestyle was immoral. Their great sin was the reason God commanded the Israelites to drive them out of the Promised Land. God tells His people not to commit the abominations for which the Canaanites are so well-known. He says "the land has become unclean, and I punished it for its sins, so the land is throwing out those people who live there" (Lev. 18:25). God is not prone to exaggeration. In their own literature, Canaanites reveal that they were a people who reveled in wanton slaughter, adultery, bestiality, homosexuality, drunkenness, and idolatry. This is why God commanded that the Israelites separate themselves from them. He did not want the Israelites to be influenced by the sinful Canaanite lifestyles.

> **DID YOU KNOW?**
>
> • Egyptians often wore amulets, or lucky charms. The scarab-beetle, the symbol for renewal, was popular.
>
> • The Egyptians referred to themselves as "the people."

PROBLEMS WITH PHILISTINES

The Philistines caused King Saul no end of trouble. His entire reign over the nation of Israel was marred by constant skirmishes with their armies. They fought for control of the land, and the tension was constant. The Philistine problem may have been the very thing that pushed the Israelites to ask for a king in the first place. Some of the Israelite tribes were already under the Philistine's thumb, and were prevented from owning weapons. The Philistines even charged that the Israelites inflated prices for having their farm implements sharpened (1Sa. 13:19–22). The Israelites had no desire to face an uprising of angry farmers with sharp pitchforks!

PHILISTINE SOLDIERS

Egyptian carvings depict Philistine soldiers with spears, long swords, round shields, and triangular daggers. Their bronze armor glittered

DANIEL

In the Babylonian Court

Daniel was just a boy when the Babylonian troops started to comb the city for the best and the brightest. Taken from his home and family, he was given a new name and placed in a Babylonian school for boys. Over the next few years, Daniel was given instruction in the Chaldean language, and taught how to write in the wedge-shaped cuneiform script. He was taught how to count, how to dress, how to bow, and how to behave himself in the court of the king. Then Daniel would have received special training in the Babylonian arts of war, hunting, and leisure. Daniel must have shown an interest in the stars, because he also had classes in astrology and magic. Scholars, sorcerers, and magicians alike were attracted to the night skies filled with brilliant stars. Babylonians had gained considerable knowledge of the stars and planets, and some of their contributions to the science of astronomy have been handed down to us even today. As a student of the skies, Daniel was expected to be able to interpret the movements of the stars. When the King called for Daniel to interpret his dreams, Daniel made it clear that his interpretations were from God (Dan. 2:27–28). His superiors recognized Daniel's integrity, and he became a mainstay of the royal court. Daniel served as a trusted advisor in the courts of Babylonian kings for more than forty years, and in the court of a conquering Persian king after that.

impressively in the sun. Their headdresses swayed with crimson feathers, and when they charged their enemies in battle, it looked like the flow of so much blood rushing across the battlefield. Goliath was by far the most famous Philistine in the Bible, and he was impressive. He was trained as a warrior from the time he was a boy (Gen. 17:33). His skills had been honed by battle, and all of his challengers had fallen to his attacks. He was undefeated, and his reputation as a great man is recorded forever in the pages of Scripture. However, the record also gives him the dubious honor of being felled by a mere boy with no battle experience (Gen. 17:50). How embarrassing for him!

THE QUEEN OF SHEBA

Ceremonial visits between royal houses, accompanied by the exchange of rich presents, were a regular feature of the ancient Near Eastern political scene. They liked to visit with people from their own social class, and check out each other's stuff. The Queen of Sheba had heard of Solomon's renowned wisdom and went to test him with hard questions (1Kin. 10:1–13). The Queen was amazed by King Solomon's wisdom. (She was impressed by his stuff, too!) The queen's state was in southern Arabia, in the area of present-day Yemen. The countries in this region had a virtual monopoly on the immensely valuable spice trade in myrrh and frankincense, a vast quantity of which the Queen of Sheba presented to Solomon. They may have been discussing trade relations, since an agreement would benefit both parties.

THE ASSYRIANS

Carvings show the Assyrian people wearing elaborate fringed robes. Their long hair was curly, and sometimes it was braided. Even their beards are shown with braids or ringlets, trimmed with a square edge. Assyrians were known for their fine clothing, for they were a wealthy people who enjoyed the spoils of many victorious battles. Their homeland was a prosperous nation, with the Tigris River providing an ample water supply. Grapes, olives, apricots, and cherries flourished on their hillsides. Wheat and barley were harvested in abundance from their plains. Although their homes were beautiful and their clothing tasteful, archeological records show that the Assyrians were a ruthless and savage people.

THE BLOODTHIRSTY ASSYRIANS

The Assyrians were a cruel people who seemed to enjoy making war. These fierce warriors showed no mercy on the battlefield. When a city was taken, no one was spared, and all they left in their wake was smoking ashes. Stories of their viciousness were legendary, and everyone was afraid of them (Nah. 2:3). People sent tributes to Assyria in the hopes that they wouldn't be attacked. Even while the Assyrians were at peace, they entertained themselves in dangerous sports. The Assyrians kept wild animals like lions, bulls, and boars, which were used in hunts. One carving from this time shows a savage lion hunt in which the lions were released into an arena, and a king in his chariot pursued them with bow and arrow. The Assyrians were a bloodthirsty and barbaric people.

> **DID YOU KNOW?**
>
> • The Sumerians are believed to have invented writing. They used a form of writing known as cuneiform.

ASSYRIAN WARRIORS

Warriors had garments shaped to allow easy movement in battle. These tunics were made from scarlet fabric. Their armor and equipment were also painted a bright blood-red. This was a form of psychological warfare. The waves of men flowed like a sea of blood across the battlefield. On a practical note, the color of the cloth and armor would hide any injuries, which might have deceived an enemy and renewed the Assyrian's will to win.

THE BABYLONIANS

A person could easily lose himself in a Babylonian city. As you entered Babylon, you passed through The Processional Way, a series of eight gates which served to protect the city and impress the visitor. One of these eight, the Istar Gate, was decorated with images of bulls, dragons, and mythical beasts. However, once within the confines of the city itself, it was easy to lose your sense of direction. The streets of the cities were

THE ETHIOPIAN EUNUCH

The Curious Accountant with a Question

The Ethiopian eunuch was a long way from home when he came across Philip walking along the road (Acts 8:26–40). The eunuch was an African, and a high official in the courts of Candace, queen of the Ethiopians. This particular gentleman must have been both trustworthy and a whiz at numbers, because he was in charge of the queen's treasury. The Ethiopian was just beginning his journey back home, having spent some time in Jerusalem. He had gone to Jerusalem to worship (Acts 8:27–28), so he was probably either a convert to Judaism, or on the verge of conversion. He would have found worship at the temple impossible, though, for Jewish Law excluded eunuchs, let alone Gentile eunuchs, from entering the Temple and participating in worship. But God had a special promise for these men if they committed their way to the Lord (Is. 56:4–5).

The road between Jerusalem and Gaza was long, dusty, and didn't offer much in the way of scenery, so the man had brought along some reading material. With a scroll lying open across his lap, he was reading from the prophet Isaiah, and having some difficulty understanding the text. Just as he was puzzling over Isaiah 53:7–8 (Acts 8:26–40), his vehicle came alongside Philip. They exchanged the expected pleasantries of the day, then the eunuch blurted out the question at the forefront of his mind. "What's up with this?" Philip hopped on board and explained the passage in the light of Christianity. The eunuch heard the Good News about Jesus, believed, and asked to be baptized.

unpaved and wound back and forth with no rhyme or reason. Closely following the twists and turns of these narrow streets were one- and two-story homes built from mud-brick. In the nicer areas of the city, the well-to-do Babylonian was able to plaster and whitewash this home, giving it a much cleaner appearance. The Babylonians were considerable engineers. Although they did not put a lot of thought into laying out their back-roads, they maintained an impressive system of canals and reservoirs. They were also map-makers and mathematicians.

BABYLONIAN ASTROLOGERS

Clear night skies made star-gazing easy, and astrology became the full-time occupation of some Babylonian men. Most kings employed at least a few. Every star was linked to a god or goddess, so it was possible to deduce all manner of things about the will of the gods. Following the movements of the celestial sphere, astrologers would work out the omens and portents that were revealed. Some of their arts were adopted by the Greeks, and so ended up in modern astrology. The zodiac is one legacy of the Babylonian astrologers, as are the three hundred and sixty-degree circle and the sixty-minute hour.

> **DID YOU KNOW?**
>
> • Assyrians buried their dead in the fetal position, with their knees drawn up to their chins.

THE PERSIANS

The Persians conquered Babylon while the Jews were in exile there. Two years later, the Persian king, Cyrus, granted these exiles permission to return to their homeland. The Old Testament Book of Esther is set in the splendor of palace life in Persia. The Persian Empire was one of great wealth, and Persian kings prided themselves on their beautiful palaces. They encouraged craftsmanship of all kinds, and brought men from every part of their empires to further decorate their palaces. Large quantities of gold plate and jewelry have been discovered, revealing the Persians' highly developed skills in making luxury goods.

PERSIA'S NATIONAL HOBBY

The wealthy men and women of Persia had it all: ornate homes, gourmet foods, extravagant jewelry, and an expensive hobby. Yes, people actually had hobbies back in the days of Old Testament antiquity. The Persians weren't pedigree poodle breeders, beachcombers, or knitters. They were collectors, with a passion for only one thing: drinking vessels. This was something more than owning more coffee mugs than is sensible. Whether it was a chalice, a goblet, or a drinking horn, the Persian's collection of drinking vessels were all made of solid gold. And more than just that, each one was different from the other. Persians prided themselves on their number of drinking vessels, and they loved to show them off. In the Book of Esther, King Ahasuerus throws a magnificent feast, and though the guest list was extensive, no two were served with a drinking vessel that was the same as any other (Est. 1:7). When the Greeks destroyed the Persian Empire, history tells us that a part of their booty was a collection of golden drinking horns and cups.

BY INVITATION ONLY

When visiting the palaces of Persian royalty, one did not just tap on the door of the throne room and walk in. Visitors pretty much had to have an engraved invitation in their hands. Only a person summoned by the king could visit him without suffering a harsh penalty. The custom had a practical basis. It gave dignity to the monarch and protected him from assassination. Esther feared going to King Ahasuerus without being called because the punishment for such a visit was death (Est. 4:11). Fortunately for the young queen, Ahasuerus was glad to see her, and bid her to come forward with a dip of his scepter.

THE PERSIAN PONY EXPRESS

When you pay close attention to the details in the Book of Esther, bits of information can be discovered about the Persians. For one thing, the Persian Empire boasted a highly organized postal system. This was a kind of pony express, and letters sent by couriers were forwarded with amazing speed (Est. 3:13). Swift horses or other animals were used to make the dispatch travel even faster (Est. 8:10). As in other areas of the ancient Near East, these letters were "signed" with the imprint of one's seal of a signet ring on the document.

PHILOSOPHY

In Hellenistic culture, philosophy was like a religion. For many people, it offered a clear moral direction—and that was enough for them. Although there were different schools of philosophy, and each had their own practices, the focus was on ethics and how to live. The goals were high ideals: self-sufficiency, freedom, and happiness. Men would sit for hours discussing the finer points of life. In fact, the men of Athens spent so much time chewing the fat, they got little else done. To prevent social collapse, the women of the city had to take practical matters into their own hands. The women of Greece handled the cooking, the cleaning, the finances, and even some of the government. Because women had so much power and influence, they were able to financially assist in the ministry of Jesus (Lk. 8:1–3).

SPEAK GREEK!

During the years just before Jesus was born, Greek became an international language for the eastern Mediterranean and beyond. It was the language of trade, and of education and writing, even for people who still usually spoke their own languages. In this way, the entire known world was united. Even the Jews, who had clung to their own ways for so long, were influenced by it. Like most Jews, Jesus was bilingual, speaking both Aramaic and Greek. Paul, a strict Jew, wrote in Greek and understood Greek ways of thinking. Most of his work was in Greek-style cities, especially in Asia Minor, which at that time contained some of the largest and richest Greek towns, such as Ephesus. The New Testament was written in Greek.

SPORTS ENTHUSIASTS

Sports were an important aspect of the Hellenistic life. Physical exercise had a religious significance in Greek culture, and was dedicated to the gods. When the Greeks came into a new town, one of the first things that was built was a coliseum, where sporting events could take place. Young athletes competed to prove their strength and endurance. These competitions would draw large crowds, even from among the Jewish population. Rabbis complained because the young men in their Hebrew classes would rush through their work in order to get to the coliseum in time to watch the races. The orthodox Jews protested because of the dedication of these games to gods like Zeus, along with the fact that the athletes usually competed naked.

GREEK GODS

The Greeks were a very religious people, and they had many gods. Being logical, the Greeks attempted to build entire family histories for these gods. They resembled the soap operas of today. Although divine, these gods behaved like human beings—often jealous, vengeful, and adulterous. Long after people stopped believing in the Greek gods, their names have been remembered. Some of them have been immortalized as the names of our planets:

- **Zeus,** the ruler over the other gods *(a.k.a. Jupiter)*
- **Ares,** the god of war *(a.k.a. Mars)*
- **Hermes,** the messenger of the gods *(a.k.a. Mercury)*
- **Poseidon,** the god of the sea *(a.k.a. Neptune)*
- **Hades,** the god of the dead *(a.k.a. Pluto)*
- **Aphrodite,** the goddess of love *(a.k.a. Venus)*

THE ROMANS

The Romans were good organizers, but creativity was not a Roman strongpoint. Although not very original, they were practical, loyal to the state, hard-working, and disciplined. They were very different in character from the Greeks who had come just before them. By conquering Greece, Rome became a world power. However, the Greeks had a remarkable influence over their conquerors. The Romans studied Greek language and thought. They copied Greek styles of art and writing, and spoke Greek. They even adopted all of the Greek gods, giving them new Roman names.

LIFE IN ROME

Rome was filled with tall buildings, which lined the narrow, congested streets. The crowded city never slept, for the constant noise of carts continued through the night. Free men and slaves from every known country in the world walked the streets. While the nobles and emperors lived in great mansions, the common people lived in fear of fire. The crowded homes were built almost on top of each other, and they knew that one spark could spell disaster. The emperors tried to buy peace by providing the commoners with entertainment. They organized gory spectacles, which were held in the coliseums. Gladiators, prisoners, slaves, and wild animals were pitted against each other in death matches.

MYSTERY RELIGIONS

Mystery religions were popular in the Roman Empire. A man could choose a religion, but he was never quite sure just what would be required of him. Worshippers were admitted step-by-step into the secret inner spiritual knowledge of the faith. One long-standing mystery religion that survived for years involved the Persian god, Mithras. He was the soldier's god. Men advanced from rank to rank in this god's service, fighting against evil. For a time, Mithraism was one of the most serious rivals to Christianity.

FREEDOM OF RELIGION...AT FIRST

It was the Romans' custom to tolerate different beliefs. Other religions were allowed to flourish throughout the empire, as long as the citizens remained loyal to the state. By keeping their subjects happy in this area, the Romans were able to maintain peace. Judaism was allowed and, at first, Christianity also, because it seemed to be a kind of Judaism. However, as time passed, the Romans began to use emperor-worship as a test of loyalty. Some emperors required people to worship him as "lord and god." This meant that the Christians, who would not agree to this, had to be ready to suffer for their faith. Persecution soon followed.

TOLERANT DICTATORS

Rome's aim was to make good Romans out of its new subjects. This was quite a challenge, because the conquered peoples burned with hatred towards Rome. Still, wherever the Romans went, they tried to win the favor of subdued peoples. The Romans may have been in charge, but they tried not to rub the people's noses in it. Instead, they made improvements. Wherever the Romans went, they built good roads and aqueducts. They set up organized city governments, and brought in garrisons of soldiers and colonies of Roman citizens—in the name of peaceful co-existence. The Roman Senate decided to allow Palestine as much self-rule as prudence permitted, so the Jews were still allowed to manage their own affairs.

ROMAN CITIZENSHIP

Roman citizenship offered many benefits: the right to vote being one of them. Citizenship also protected a person from certain indignities: he could not be bound, scourged, or imprisoned without a trial. If a Roman citizen felt he was being unjustly treated in a court of law, he could appeal to Rome. Rome used citizenship as a means of further endearing itself to the nations under its control. The empire would sometimes grant Roman citizenship to non-Romans. It was like winning the lottery, and an otherwise unimportant person could hold the same rights as a Roman senator. This citizenship was jealously guarded and highly prized. No wonder the Roman authorities in Philippi panicked when they realized that Paul and Silas were not just a couple of trouble-making Jews. The Philippians had unwittingly bound, beaten, and imprisoned a couple of Roman citizens (Acts 16:35–40).

STAR-GAZERS

The Magi, or wisemen, from the East were astrologers who spent their nights studying the portents of the stars. They brought gold, frankincense, and myrrh—wealth, worship, and healing. The gold probably came from Africa; the frankincense was a gum obtained from the bark of a resinous tree in Central India and had a fragrant smell when burned; the myrrh was a healing medicinal gum that relieved pain—it was obtained from a shrub growing in Arabia.

THE CUSHITES

The land of Cush lies south of Egypt in what is now Sudan, Africa. Cushites often served in the Egyptian armies as mercenary soldiers. Cush, which means "black," was the traditional homeland of the descendants of Ham (Gen. 10:6–8). Egyptian artwork shows these dark-skinned soldiers armed with spears and with the bow and arrow. In this nation, a queen, referred to as "the Candace" ruled over her people. The Ethiopian eunuch in Acts 8:26–40 is described as a high official of Candace, in charge of the royal treasury.

SAMARITANS

When the Persian king, Cyrus, allowed a small group of Jews to return to their homeland, he encouraged them in rebuilding their temple. He gave them gifts of all kinds to help furnish it (Ezr. 6:1–5; 5:8). Once they arrived back home, these Jews didn't get to work right away. The prophets Zechariah and Haggai had to scold the Jews for building "paneled houses" for their own comfort before the Temple was begun. With the urging of the prophets and a lot of hard work, the foundation was finally laid. Seeing the efforts of the Jews, a bunch of people from Bethel offered to help. They were the descendants of the Israelites who had intermarried with the people of other nations; distant cousins who were willing to roll up their sleeves and help raise the walls. They even worshiped Yahweh alongside the gods of other nations. How neighborly! But Haggai spoke bluntly to them and said they were unclean. He refused their offer of help, and they resented it bitterly. So began a "family feud" that would last for centuries. These people were later called the Samaritans, and they never forgot Haggai's snub. This explains the many jibes and bitter references to the Samaritans during New Testament times, for the Jews had no dealings with them.

CHAPTER FIVE

THEIR LANGUAGE

t's all Greek to me! The people of the Bible were faced with foreign languages all the time. **Many men knew more than one language**—one which they spoke at home, and one that was used in business and trade. Jesus himself was bilingual, able to speak Greek and Aramaic.

BABEL

Students struggle to conjugate verbs as they fulfill their college language requirements. Couples stare in confusion at the menu of a fine restaurant. Seminarians walk around with Greek and Hebrew vocabulary flash cards in their pockets. And it all goes back to Babel. The people of the earth pulled together and constructed the architectural monstrosity that eventually pulled them apart. The Tower of Babel was built in an act of rebellion. For their arrogance and disobedience, the human race was divinely confused. With brick and mortar lying forgotten at their feet, people struggled to understand what was happening. Foreign languages were created, and the peoples were divided.

DID YOU KNOW?

- Sumerians were list-makers. Archeologists have found inventories of Sumerian words that cover multiple tablets. These were early dictionaries.

- Hebrew has all of the common characteristics of the Semitic languages—especially the guttural quality of strong consonants, which are occasionally heard in modern German and Russian.

LET'S CALL IT SUMERIAN!

When hunting through the dusty libraries of ancient cultures, archeologists decided that several of the oldest languages must have borrowed from an even older writing system. They just didn't know what that language was. Then, tablets with a language unlike any other were discovered in the ancient city of Sumer. They dubbed the language, Sumerian. This writing contained picture-symbols, and words were distinguished by the tone of voice in which they were said.

SUMERIAN DICTIONARIES

Many Sumerian words depended on the way in which they were said. This was more than just the proper enunciation of "The rain in Spain falls mainly on the plain." The same sounds, pronounced in the wrong tone of voice, meant different things entirely! Precision was essential. So to keep things straight, the Sumerians kept dictionaries. Tablets have been found with long inventories of all the items that were found in a typical Sumerian's life. They carefully listed all the names of plants, animals, and fish. They kept records of proper grammatical constructions. They even had multilingual dictionaries, which listed terms in Sumerian with their translation into the languages of neighboring countries.

UGARITIC WORDS

"Ug"-aritic is not named because its speakers grunted and said "ugh" a lot. It is an ancient "Western Semitic" language, which was first discovered on tablets in a city called Ugarit. This was the language spoken by the Canaanites, who lived in the Promised Land while the Israelites were still wandering in the wilderness. When the Israelites were led by Joshua in driving the Canaanites out of the land, they did an incomplete job. Many Canaanites remained, and their influence is seen even in the Scriptures. Many Ugaritic words, and even some whole expressions, are found in the first few books of the Bible.

CAN I BUY A VOWEL?

Hebrew bears absolutely no resemblance to any European language. Any seminary student can tell you that. Hebrew is written in all consonants. There are twenty-two letters, and not one of them is a vowel. In many of the ancient texts, all these consonants are strung together with no spaces between the words. And to make it more confusing, Hebrew is read from right to left. Still, it has been around longer than any other language in the world—more than 3,500 years!

PLAY ON WORDS

Most Hebrew words had just three consonants. They were then marked for different pronunciations by adding vowel sounds before, between, and behind those three consonants. Because of this, a three-letter root could be tweaked into several different words. These words then sounded very similar. It would be quite proper in Hebrew to say "The smiter smote the smitten." This may seem redundant to us, but the Jews loved their peculiar phraseology. Hebrew was a poetic language, and it depended on this natural redundancy for effect. In fact, it also led to many common expressions, which were essentially a play on words. Unfortunately, they become lost in the translation process.

TRANSLATION FRUSTRATIONS

Some words in the Old Testament are untranslatable. The Hebrew language has changed over the centuries and their exact meaning has been lost. An example is found in the narrative of Joseph. The Hebrew states: Ketoneth passiym. The first word is definitely coat; no problem. But the second word appears nowhere else in the Old Testament. Translators have had to guess at its meaning. It has been interpreted as a coat "of many colors," a coat "with long sleeves," a coat "with much embroidery," and even as a coat of "choice wool." The simple fact is that no one knows what the precise meaning is, and there is no way we can find out.

SCRIBES

Without printing presses and copy machines, the writers of the Old Testament had to depend on good old pen and paper to get their letters out to the public. This meant going to the scribes. A scribe patiently copied a document whenever extras were needed or the original was getting a bit ragged. Accuracy was paramount, and scribes took great pains to ensure that exact copies were made. By the time Jesus was born, the most recent Old Testament book, Malachi, had been copied and recopied by scribes for more than four hundred years. The books that Moses had written had also been copied and recopied for over a thousand years. All that while, the scribes had guarded the text of the Old Testament, carefully reproducing it line by line and letter by letter.

"THE COUNTERS"

Scribes took pride in their work, and they liked to be thorough. Any mistakes in their copying would have been disastrous. In a world without spell-check, men had to be meticulous. In their quest for copy-perfect scrolls, the scribes earned the title "the counters," because they actually counted every letter of every book of the Scriptures to make sure they hadn't left anything out! As a way of double-checking, they figured out which letter appeared in the middle of each book. Their great pains in preserving the original wording of the Scriptures is why the Old Testament has been handed down intact to us today!

EGYPTIANS AND HIEROGLYPHICS

When Egyptians wrote, they used pictures and signs on papyrus with a pen that had been dipped in charcoal. The picture of an eagle stood for an "a," a lion stood for the letter "l," and an owl represented the "m." A page of Egyptian writing looks like a long series of birds and animals and people. These are the hieroglyphics. Later, the hieroglyphics were abbreviated somewhat to save time, and only a part of the picture was drawn to express a letter or a sound. Pharaohs often covered their palace walls, statues, temples, and obelisks with picture stories of their great deeds. It is because the Pharaohs were fond of pub-licizing themselves in this way that we know so much about them.

ARAMAIC

The Jews spoke Hebrew. They had since they could remember. They spoke Hebrew on the ark. They spoke Hebrew in their nomadic tents. They spoke Hebrew while in Egypt. They spoke Hebrew when they entered the Promised Land. They spoke Hebrew when they were captured by the Babylonians. They spoke Hebrew while they were in captivity under the Persians. Then something changed. Hebrew dropped out of everyday use, and was only used in worship services. The ordinary people adopted a dialect of their own called Aramaic.

ARAMAIC IN THE OLD TESTAMENT

Whole passages of the Old Testament were written in Aramaic (Dan. 2–7; Ezr. 4–7; Jer. 10:11). Aramaic was the chief Semitic language of the Persian Empire, and it became the common language of the Jews after the Exile. From that time, they began translating the Old Testament into Aramaic. Scribes even adopted an Aramaic-style when writing their Hebrew letters. Jewish scholars hold Aramaic in higher esteem than Hebrew because it is the language of the Talmud, and other works of the Jewish tradition.

ARAMAIC AT HOME

By New Testament times, Aramaic was the language that all Jewish boys and girls spoke at home. Although Greek was common throughout the known world, and many spoke both languages, it was Aramaic that they were taught from the cradle. It was the language of Jesus and his disciples. In fact, even though the New Testament is written in Greek, we find a number of Aramaic expressions translated into Greek. Jesus' commonly used phrase "Verily, verily" is an Aramaic expression (Jn. 5:24, 6:47; 8:51). Others are Talitha qumi— "Maiden arise" (Mk. 5:41); Ephphatha— "Be opened" (Mk. 7:34); and the cry from the cross, Eli, Eli, lema sebaqtani— "My God, my God, why have you forsaken me?" (Mk. 15:34; Mt. 27:46). In the New Testament epistles, we find the Aramaic Abba—"Daddy!" (Rom. 8:15; Gal. 4:6) and Maranatha—"Lord, come!" (1Cor. 16:22).

THE DEAD SEA SCROLLS

A shepherd boy out in the wild with his flocks, entertains himself by throwing rocks up and into the various caves that dot the hillsides around him. His steady aim and strong arm led to the discovery of the century. One rock after another thudded onto the soft dirt floors of the caves, but the last rock made a crashing sound. Investigating the noise, the shepherd discovered that his rock had shattered an earthen pot, which was filled with old scrolls. These jars were stacked in the cave. It was an entire library of ancient scrolls, the oldest copies of the Old Testament known to exist.

READY FOR A TREASURE HUNT?

When archeologists unearthed the Dead Sea Scrolls, they also discovered what amounts to a mystery worthy of the talents of Indiana Jones! Along with the many carefully preserved scrolls containing the Old Testament Scriptures, were two very unique scrolls. These scrolls were in Hebrew, written on thinly beaten sheets of copper. The copper scrolls describe a vast treasure—twenty-six tons of gold and sixty-five tons of silver—hidden in sixty-four locations throughout Israel. Most scholars believe the treasure is a hoax or a myth. Others think that the treasure was indeed taken from the Temple and hidden before the Roman legions arrived in AD 70.

GREEK WAS GREAT!

The Greeks were the first to have a complete alphabetic system. It was easy to learn and it greatly enhanced the spread of Greek as a trade and commercial language. In fact, many cultures that could write their languages only with great difficulty, adopted Greek for their written communication. Greek was also easy to read, and became the vehicle for some of the greatest literary works of Western civilization. Among these were the poetry of Homer, the history of Herodotus, the medicine of Hippocrates, the mathematics of Archimedes, the drama of Sophocles and Aeschylus, and the philosophy of Plato and Aristotle.

THE SEPTUAGINT

Jews who were forced out of Israel during the Dispersion eventually forgot their native Hebrew and also their every-day Aramaic. Like most everyone else in the world, they spoke Greek. It became glaringly obvious that if they were going to be good Jews, they needed their Law to be written in Greek. In 250 BC, in the city of Alexandria, seventy scribes were invited to come and translate the five books of the Law into the Greek language. Legends say that the seventy men worked in solitude, finished their translations, and discovered that each of the seventy Greek translations were identical. This resulting work is called the Septuagint—written LXX for short. The Septuagint allowed Gentiles to read about the God of the Jews for the first time, and many became members of synagogues if they believed in him.

DID YOU KNOW?

- Aramaic was the common language for diplomats and traders all over the Near East from 750 BC until Alexander the Great brought Greek to the region.

- Modern Greek is very different from New Testament Greek. One who speaks modern Greek fluently will be stumped trying to make sense of the ancient text.

A VAST VOCABULARY

Koine Greek was the language of absolutely everyone in New Testament times. Since the Greeks loved their discussion, philosophy, and poetry, Greek became elaborate in its vocabulary and precise in its grammar. There was just the right word for any situation. The poetry of the famous Greeks like Homer and Sappho is virtually impossible to translate into English. A single word in the Greek language may require a sentence to explain all the nuances that it carries over into the English language. The language of the New Testament is expressive, and its shades of meaning yield insights into the Scriptures. A good example of this is found in Galatians 6:2, 5. These verses seem to contradict one another, for verse 2 says "Bear ye one another's burdens" while verse 5 says, "every man shall bear his own burden." The English versions have translated two different Greek words as burden. The word in verse 2 is *baros*, which Greek philosophers used to denote the burden of temptation. The word in verse 5 is *phortion*, which denoted the responsibility imposed by the Law (Mt. 23:4; Lk. 11:46). So in effect verse 2 means, "Support one another in carrying the weight of temptation," while verse 5 means, "Assume the duty that the Law places upon you." Hundreds of passages in the Greek New Testament can be given their full meaning only by referring to the Greek text.

CHAPTER SIX

THEIR STYLE

Whenever it is time for the annual Christmas pageant at church, we all know what to expect. A sign goes up on the bulletin board asking us to lend our old bathrobes. Instinctively, we know that a towel should go on every little child's head, tied into place with strips of fabric. Mary should be in blue. Joseph should have sandals on. The shepherds should carry staffs. **Why do we know this?** Wealthy sheikhs and humble shepherds fill the pages of our Scriptures, and their style of dress is uniquely different from our own. Their robes and flowing headdresses are unmistakable trademarks of desert-dwellers even today.

EVERYDAY CLOTHES

Clothing was quite expensive in Bible times. Woven cloth was hard to come by, and fine linens and silks were a luxury. These fabrics were made into simple garments, and basic styles were the same for all people, rich or poor. Most people only owned the clothes they wore every day. There weren't even pajamas. At bedtime, you simply loosened your belt, took off your shoes, and lay down on your mat to sleep.

The Men

The men of Israel paid little attention to the passing fads and fashions of surrounding nations, so their clothing styles remained unchanged from generation to generation. The basics for the Jewish man were simple: an inner garment, an outer garment, a girdle and sandals. Any variation in this outfit was in the quality of the fabrics, detailing in the cut of the cloth, or in the colors used. Quite practically, these clothes were the best for the hot climate in which the Jews lived.

THE BASIC TUNIC

Every man, woman, and child wore a tunic, or inner garment. This simple undergarment, a kind of close-fitting, long undershirt, was made from cotton or wool, and was usually left its natural color. Paul uses the tunic, held in at the waist by a girdle, as a metaphor for the lifestyle of God's chosen people (Col. 3:12), and everyone understood that he was talking about basics.

NEW OR USED?

The tunic was really just a sack with openings cut in it for the head and arms to pass through. In the marketplace, a brand new tunic was normally sold without the neck opening cut so that the seller could prove that the tunic was unused.

UNDERWEAR?

Boxers or briefs wasn't an issue in Old Testament times. Men simply didn't wear underwear under their robes. The inner garment, or tunic, was apparently considered quite sufficient. In fact, when a man was wearing just his inner garment, he was said to be naked (1Sa. 19:24; Is. 20:2–4). By New Testament times, styles had changed a bit and a kind of undergarment was in use. The loincloth was like a short slip or apron. Peter was probably stripped down to his loincloth while working in the family fishing boat (Jn. 21:7), and Jesus was crucified wearing only his loincloth (Jn. 19:23).

CITY CLOAK, COUNTRY CLOAK

The "outer garment" worn by Bible men was a kind of coat worn over the lighter fabric of the "inner garment." In the countryside, a man's cloak was his only protection from driving winds and cold nights. For warmth, these outer garments were made from a thick, woolen material or goat's hair. At nightfall, the owner wrapped himself in this cloak to sleep (Ex. 22:26–27). In contrast, the cloak found in the homes of the very wealthy was more of a luxury. Instead of the rough cloth used by the shepherd and farmer, the rich man's overcoat resembled a loose dressing gown with wide sleeves. This might have been made of fine linen or silk and served only a decorative purpose.

DID YOU KNOW?

- In the Near East, the number of robes that you owned was a measure of your wealth. Consequently, a closet full of clothes indicated that a person was rich and powerful, and a lack of clothing proved you were poor.

- Since a second suit of clothing was such a status symbol, it was nearly unthinkable for John the Baptizer to tell people to give away their spare coats (Lk. 3:11).

SEAMLESS STYLING

The earliest cloaks were made in two pieces, with a seam that ran horizontally across the waistline. As the cloth was made upon the loom, stripes could be woven into the fabric that would fall in a vertical pattern on the finished robe. One popular pattern involved using camel's hair, which was brown, and goat's hair, which was black. As dyes were introduced, Jewish men favored the color red in their cloaks. The garment that Jesus wore must have been the latest fashion in Galilee because it was woven without the center seam (Jn. 19:23). Looms able to handle the full length of fabric needed for a cloak like this were invented during his lifetime.

JOSEPH'S COAT

The "coat of many colors" that we read of in our Bibles was probably white. This may seem a bit of a letdown for us, but it was enough to inspire jealousy and murder back in Genesis. The Book of Hebrews states that the coat was made of "many pieces," indicating that some fancy tailoring was involved. Joseph's coat may have been a fine linen garment with long, pointed sleeves. Long sleeves prevented the wearer from doing heavy labor, and so Joseph was not expected to do the same work as the other brothers. Such a coat was only worn by two people in the clan: the sheikh himself (Jacob), and his successor. This was the cause of outrage among the ten older brothers. Jacob was making it clear that Joseph was his favorite and the future leader of the clan.

DID YOU KNOW?

- A Jewish man's tunic was usually red, yellow, black, or striped. But at a grand wedding, given by a prosperous family, the host might give his guests special white robes to wear (Mt. 22:11).

- To "gird up the loins" is a picture of readiness to work and willingness to serve (1Pet. 1:13), but to "loose the girdle" is an indication that a person is either resting or lazy (Is. 5:27).

EMBROIDERED ROBES

When a wedding feast was posted on the local social calendars, nothing said "party" like an embroidered robe. Jewish men prized these elaborately decorated garments, which were reserved for such celebrations. A fine set of clothing in the cedar chest back home indicated that the owner was prosperous, for the poor only had the clothes they wore every day. When Samson threw a party to celebrate the finalization of his marriage arrangements, he posed a riddle that would result in thirty fancy robes for his closet if nobody solved it (Judg. 4:12–13). A fresh set of clothing for every day of the month would have made him the talk of the town. It's no wonder he was so upset when he was cheated out of his prize.

FRINGES

The God-fearing Jewish man always wore a blue fringe at the bottom of his cloak. This was not so much a fashion statement as an act of obedience to God, who had commanded their presence in Num. 15:38–39. Jesus wore such a fringe on his cloak, and it was probably this bottom part of the cloak that the woman touched when she was healed of a flow of blood (Mt. 9:20). The Pharisees, who always seemed to think that bigger was better, wore fringes that were long and loud. Their heavily tasseled hemlines were intended to impress others with their obvious obedience to the law. This fancywork was costly, and so was the blue dye used to achieve the desired color. Yet the common man had to comply with God's Law. How was this to be afforded? To prove their devotion, even the poorest of Jews were expected to have a minimum of four blue threads in their tassels.

BELT

The belt worn by men of Bible times is called a girdle. The girdle was often made of a wide band of colorful cloth. Elijah and John the Baptist both wore girdles of leather (Mk. 1:6; 2Kin. 1:8). It was tied about the waist of the inner or outer garment, and greatly improved the appearance of an otherwise shapeless outfit. Some men wore girdles with intricate embroidery stitched into them, but these belts were not purely decorative. It helped to keep the long flowing robes in check while the men worked. It could serve as a kind of tool belt for the workman. The girdle also regulated the length of one's robes, which could be pulled up and shortened when speed was necessary. A fastener attached to the girdle allowed it to be either loosened or tightened.

GIRD UP!

Can you imagine trying to run a race in a formal gown? The fabric gets tangled up between the legs and trips you. What a nuisance! To make quick time, a lady knows she must lift her skirts up above her knees and then hoof it! When working on the seashore with fishing nets, or plowing and hoeing in the fields, the long flowing robes worn by men of Palestine got in the way, too. The solution was to either strip down or gird up. The biblical expression "to gird up the loins" refers to a method of tucking the robe up between the legs and into the belt. This allowed the men to work much more freely.

POCKET OR PURSE?

So where did the man of Bible times keep his house key, wallet, spare change, and the keys to his camel? In his purse, of course! Actually, the purse referred to in Matthew 10:9 and Mk. 6:8 was more of a pocket. A man's girdle was folded and sewn double so that a pocket was formed. It was held secure when wrapped around the body and buckled. Often there was a leather strap to open and close it. Jewish men also used a scrip, which may have been similar to our modern purse. David's scrip was a small bag carried over the shoulder in which he placed the five stones he gathered when facing Goliath (1Sa. 17:40).

FASHIONS FOR FEET

Sandals were the universal footwear. They were a necessary protection from the hot sands underfoot. Sandals were so commonplace throughout the land of Palestine that they represented the most insignificant item of clothing (Gen. 14:23). They were the most inexpensive merchandise in the marketplace, and even the poor wore them. In fact, going without sandals indicated a state of abject poverty (Lk. 15:22). The sole of a sandal was made from carved wood, tough leather, interwoven rushes, or layers of animal hides that were sewn together. This base was strapped to the foot by means of a simple leather thong, which passed over the foot and between the big and second toes. A more elaborate sandal was in use during New Testament times. Long leather thongs were crisscrossed over the top of the foot through a series of loops along the edges of the sole, then wrapped around the calf.

ELIJAH'S MANTLE

The leader of the clan, when he was old and ready to transfer the staff of leadership to his heir, would also give him his cloak. The passing on of the cloak symbolized the transfer of authority from father to son. Elijah and Elisha seemed to have a kind of father/son relationship even though they were not related. Elisha even asked to be named Elijah's rightful successor (2Kin. 2:9). As Elisha watched the chariot of fire whisk away his mentor, he cried out "My father! My father!" and then tore his own robe in two. In its place, he was given Elijah's mantle (2Kin. 2:13) along with authority from God to continue where Elijah had finished.

DID YOU KNOW?

- The Hebrews often ripped the outer garment in times of great distress. Since clothing was so valuable, it was indeed a sign of intense grief to tear it to pieces (Ezr. 9:3, 5; Job 1:20, 2:12).

- The front of a woman's outer garment was long enough for her to tuck it up over the girdle to serve as an apron. The apron might have been used to protect the clothing during work, or to carry things (Ruth 3:15).

A BRAND NEW ROBE

A fine new robe was an expression of respect and courtesy when it was bestowed upon a man. The guest of honor at a celebration might be

ABRAHAM

The Wealthy Sheikh

Abraham probably looked like a splendid old sheikh. Although his home was nothing more than a sprawling tent, he was a wealthy man, as shown by his large encampment and many flocks of sheep and camels. His clothing was rather simple, and similar to those of any other Bedouin man in the area, but Abraham's garments were of the finest quality, as befitting a man of his status. These desert nomads dressed in layers, starting with a white cotton undershirt that reached the knees. This would have been tied at the waist with a brightly colored sash. Sarah may have made this belt herself, weaving it on a loom with brightly dyed threads of red, green, and brown. Such a belt may have even been embellished with bits of precious metal, like gold and silver. Over this inner garment would be worn a cloak made from camel's hair, goat's hair, or wool. Camel's hair was brown and goat's hair was black, so sometimes the two were woven together in a decorative pattern so that they made wide vertical stripes. Wool that was included in such a garment could be dyed in a variety of colors. Red was especially popular, and could be achieved using the bodies of an insect that burrowed in local oak trees. Abraham would have protected his head from the sun with a large flowing scarf of silk, bound around with a rope of camel or goat hair. On his feet were sandals of sturdy leather, to block the heat of the hot sands. In his hand, Abraham carried a staff of leadership, which showed his place as head of his clan. When he retired at night, he would have pushed this staff into the ground outside his tent door, indicating that the leader of the encampment slept within. Bedouins almost never cut their long curling hair, so Abraham's would have been carefully gathered under his headdress, and a long beard would have flowed over his chest.

honored by placing a fine robe on him, as the prodigal son's father did (Lk. 15:22). Also, when a man began a new job—especially if that job was of great importance—he was given a special robe on his first day of work. Joseph was given a robe when he was taken from the prisons and put into leadership over the land of Egypt (Gen. 41:42). This was a robe of honor. In contrast, if an official disgraced his position somehow and was demoted, his robe was taken from him as a sign of his dismissal.

SACKCLOTH AND ASHES

At a funeral, it is not difficult to find the widow. She is easily distinguished by her "widow's weeds"—draped from head to toe in black. The wearing of black is a traditional way of expressing our grief at the death of a loved one. Jewish people also wore black while in sorrow. The black hair of a goat was woven into a rough fabric called sackcloth. Although normally used for feedsacks (Gen. 42:25; Josh. 9:4), this was the traditional material to wear during times of sorrow. When Joseph was sold by his brothers, Jacob put on sackcloth to mourn (Gen. 37:34). Sackcloth was uncomfortable to wear, and when a person's grief was extreme, he would wear this itchy cloth right next to his skin, as Job did (Job 16:15). To further express his despair, a sackcloth-wearer would go sit in an ash heap and throw ashes over his head, as Mordecai did (Est. 4:1–3).

The Women

The everyday clothing of the women of Bible times differed very little from that of their menfolk. However, it was distinctive enough for it to be shameful for a man to wear women's clothing, or for a woman to appear dressed as a man (Deut. 22:5). A woman wore the inner garment, the outer garment, a girdle, veil, and sandals.

LADY IN BLUE

Women wore an outer garment just as the men wore. This was most often a robe made from fabric that was dyed blue with the rind of pomegranates. The lady's robe was longer than that of a man, with a border and fringe that covered the feet (Is. 47:2; Jer. 13:22). The neckline was often embellished by embroidery. In many areas of Palestine, the style of embroidery on a woman's garments identifies the tribe or village to which she belongs. The sleeves of the women's robe are much longer than those of the men, and are often tapered to a decorative point.

NOTHING UP THIS SLEEVE!

So where did a woman of Bible times keep her grocery list, her egg money, and her favorite Sabbath brooch? Up her sleeves, of course! The sleeves on a woman's robe could be made from as much as three yards of woven material. These long, wide sleeves provided a hiding place for personal possessions, that could be carefully tied or pinned inside and effectively hidden. When there were dishes to wash or bread to knead and the sleeves became a nuisance, women tied them up behind their necks to free up their hands for work.

VEILS

Women of Old Testament times wore a veil most of the time. This was simply a square of material used to give protection from the sun. The fabric around the face was folded in such a way as to provide a kind of brim, and the rest of it was allowed to fall in folds behind to shield the neck and shoulders. A braided cord held the veil in place. A veil of lightweight material was sometimes worn over the face so that only a woman's eyes could be seen. This ensured modesty in public places, for only a husband could look upon his wife's face. This is why Rebekah hid her face from Isaac before they were married (Gen. 24:65).

> **DID YOU KNOW?**
>
> • A man selling property took off his sandal and gave it to the buyer as a token that he gave up his right to the property (Ruth 4:7–8).

VEILS FOR VIRGINS

In New Testament times, a Hebrew woman no longer wore a veil over her face at all times. The veil over the head was in use for protection from the sun and as a covering for prayer (1Cor. 11:6). In fact, any respectable woman would not think of going out without some kind of covering over her head. Only prostitutes showed off their hair, in hopes of attracting the attentions of men. The veil over the face during these times was more often an act of modesty on the part of young virgins who were old enough to be married. It was at the marriage ceremony that the veil was lifted from the bride's face. Then it was laid on the shoulder of her bridegroom while it was pronounced, "the government will be upon his shoulders" (Is. 9:6, KJV).

TRACKING IN THE SAND

Hebrew children learned very young to take off their sandals before coming into the tent after playing outside. Mom was probably right there with her hands on her hips overseeing the process. Jews did not wear shoes indoors. The simple sandals worn by peasant women were designed to be slipped off easily at the entrances to their tents so that their tasks were not interrupted by having to stoop to unlace their footwear. In fact, once they removed their sandals, they washed their feet. This kept that pesky sand from getting into their beds (they slept on the floor, after all!) and cooled their weary feet after the outdoor work was done.

ACCESSORIZE! ACCESSORIZE! ACCESSORIZE!

The Men

Jewish men had a fondness for improving their personal appearance, and they often used jewelry to do this. They wore bracelets, rings, chains, and necklaces of various kinds. This kind of ornamentation lent a man dignity and respectability.

STAFF OF LEADERSHIP

No well-dressed sheikh would be dressed for success without a few distinctive accessories. As a token of his leadership, he would carry a staff.

This was usually carved from the wood of an almond tree. Aaron, as leader of the Levite clan, carried such a staff. When this staff miraculously budded, it brought forth almonds, indicating God's choice of the house of Levi as his priestly tribe (Num. 17:1–9).

BRACELETS

The wealthy men of Bible times sported bracelets. More appropriately, these could be called "armlets" or arm bands, and they were most often worn by people of nobility. Egyptian pharaohs are often shown in hieroglyphics wearing bands of gold on their upper arms. These were commonly worn by Persian kings, like Ahasuerus in the Book of Esther. These bracelets were elaborately formed from rare metals and encrusted with precious jewels. Saul's armlet was probably a sign of his royalty (2Sa. 1:10).

TOP HAT AND TAILS

When the occasion demanded something a bit more formal, wealthy Jewish men could really put on the ritz. A richly ornamented headdress was worn for special occasions and on holidays. The headdresses worn by royalty were especially elaborate in some cultures. The Scriptures also mention the wearing of a headdress at times of mourning (2Sa. 15:30). The priests of the temple wore a headdress much like a turban as a normal part of their clothing (Ex. 28:40).

CHAINS OF OFFICE

Government officials of the Near East had chains of gold placed on them as symbols of their sovereign authority. We see Joseph and Daniel were both honored in this way (Gen. 41:42; Dan. 5:29).

> **DID YOU KNOW?**
>
> • Jewelry made from gold and silver was used as money before the introduction of minted coins (Job 28:15–18). Both Hebrew women and men wore bracelets (Gen. 24:30).
>
> • Moses was told to remove his shoes when God spoke to him from the burning bush (Ex. 3:5) because he was standing on holy ground. For the same reason, priests in the temple at Jerusalem went about all their tasks barefoot.

JOSEPH

The Egyptian Governor

Uprooted by the treachery of his brothers and sold into slavery in a foreign land, Joseph was immediately introduced to a new definition of style. Egyptians shaved their heads and bodies to keep cool and clean, so once Joseph was given a government position, shaving and bathing became a part of his daily routine. Strangely enough, considering the strict hair-cutting policy, he was expected to wear a wig on important occasions. These wigs of thick black hair had a straight bang across the eyebrows and were curled into many ringlets that fell down the back. There were also false beards.

Egypt was famous for fine linen, and most of it was not dyed. The cool white fabric was starched heavily so that the robes stood out stiffly from the body. Sleeveless clothes allowed fancy armbands and bracelets to be displayed. Joseph was a chief official, so although he wore a short kilt of white linen, which was common to all Egyptians, his cloak was a piece of finery. A sign of his position, this loose-fitting cloak with long, flowing sleeves was probably made of lightweight fabric, like silk. As Pharaoh's chosen governor, a single band of color would have been allowed near the base of Joseph's robe, again showing his high office. A girdle about Joseph's waist would have been embroidered richly with golden threads, and from it, tassels would hang down to his knees. About his neck was placed a chain of office, made from heavy gold and bearing a scarab—a gem cut into the shape of a beetle. The Pharaoh gave Joseph a signet ring with which he would stamp all of his decrees and orders. For shoes, there were sandals woven from papyrus: the same rushes from which paper was made. Most Egyptian men wore a conical hat. At the least, a square of white linen was folded and tied over the head as protection from the sun.

AMULETS

The peoples of the Near East were a superstitious lot, and so it is not surprising that they created magical charms to protect themselves from evil spirits. The amulets referred to in the Bible were earrings worn by women (Gen. 35:4; Judg. 8:24), or pendants hung from chains around the necks of the men. Such amulets had sacred words or pictures of gods engraved on them. Another kind of amulet consisted of words written on a piece of paper that was rolled up and sewn into a small linen sack. The Jewish practice of wearing phylacteries may have been in opposition of this superstitious practice.

PHYLACTERIES

God commanded the Jews to make reminders of his faithfulness and of his laws. Over the years, they came up with some unique ones—this one was as plain as the nose on your face. A phylactery was a small box-like bundle that was tied right onto the forehead. Hebrew men wore them during their prayers. Some wore them for morning and evening prayers, others just at the morning prayer time. There were actually two types: the second type was tied onto the upper left arm near the elbow. A phylactery had four compartments inside, each containing a piece of parchment on which a Scripture was written. These four verses were: Exodus 13:1–10, Exodus 13:22–26, Deuteronomy 6:4–9, and Deuteronomy 11:13–21. These admonitions to remember and obey God's law were folded in animal skins to make a square pack. The frontlet was then tied to the forehead with a leather thong or ribbon. The phylactery that was worn on the arm was tied near the elbow. Then the thong was wound around the arm, crisscrossing until it reached the top of the middle finger. Jesus condemned the Pharisees, who wore ridiculously large phylacteries to call attention to their piety (Mt. 23:5).

SIGNED, SEALED, AND DELIVERED!

One accessory that the important man of Palestine never did business without was his signet ring. This could be worn on the finger or on a chain around the neck. Whether made from clay or wrought out of metal, a signet ring was carved with a special seal that was unique to its owner. Rather than being a decorative object, a man's signet ring served the practical use of sealing official correspondence. Because each man's seal was unique unto itself, it guaranteed the authenticity of a document. King Ahasuerus allowed his seal to be used to sign into law the proclamation that endangered Queen Esther and the rest of the Jews. King Darius' seal was placed on the law that landed Daniel in the Lion's Den, and then was used again to seal Daniel inside (Dan. 6:17).

The Women

The prophet Ezekiel said that the nation of Israel was like a young woman who bathed and anointed herself (Eze. 16:10–13). But the ladies of Bible times had few choices when it was time to dress. There was little variety in the wardrobe of those early days. Most often, a woman had one outfit, and it looked just like everyone else's. Same old blue robe; same old heavy veil. What's a girl to do? Accessorize! Even though her clothes were simple, her jewelry, make-up, and hair treatments could transform her into a royal bride, and set her apart from the rest of the crowd. In fact, personal ornamentation was so important to women that Peter needed to warn them to keep their priorities straight. "It is not fancy hair, gold jewelry or fine clothes that should make you beautiful. No, your beauty should come from within you—the beauty of a gentle and quiet spirit that will never be destroyed and is very precious to God" (1Pet. 3:3–4).

Despite his warning, women used various ornaments to adorn themselves from head to foot—delicately carved frontlets, moon-shaped crescents, drop pendants on twisted golden neck-lace cords, arm bands, nose rings, and tinkling anklets. Ezekiel's analogy of Israel and the young woman, along with a passage in Isaiah, give us a vivid picture of the kinds of adornments that women used in Bible times (Is. 3:18–23).

ANKLETS

Ankle bracelets were worn quite commonly by the women of ancient times. Depending upon the taste and status of the wearer, an anklet might be made of gold, silver, or iron. These adornments flattered the feet, but more importantly they made noise while a woman walked. Several anklets could be worn together, so that they jangled at every step. Another kind of anklet was fashioned with tiny bells, to produce a musical tinkling sound. Women of high rank wore hollow anklets that were filled with pebbles, so that a rattling sound could be heard as they passed through the markets. "And it was so, when Ahijah heard the sound of her feet" (1Kin. 14:6).

DID YOU KNOW?

• In ancient Bible times, women wore dark eye shadow around their eyes. At first, this was to protect their eyes against the strong sunshine, but it soon became a matter of fashion.

BODY PIERCING IS BIBLICAL!?

Actually, in Old Testament times and beyond, it was very customary for young women to have pierced ears and pierced noses. A jeweled nose ring was a highly prized adornment. A hole was bored through the nostril so that the jewel in the nose ring would lie against the cheek (Eze. 16:12). Because of their costliness, a new nose ring would make the young woman the envy of all of her friends. Sometimes they were bestowed upon a girl by a prosperous suitor as a part of his bride-price. When Abraham sent his old servant, Eliezer, to find a wife for Isaac, he found Rebekah and gave her gifts—a ring and two bracelets of gold.

Rebekah would have immediately recognized their presentation as part of a marriage proposal—and a good one at that (Gen. 24:22).

GOLD EARRINGS

After enduring the ten plagues, Pharaoh finally dismissed the Hebrew slaves. Their Egyptian neighbors were so glad to be rid of them that they presented them with their earrings as a parting gift (Ex. 12:35–36). Maybe they were trying to bribe them to never come back! These earrings were probably large hoops of solid gold. Such earrings often served as amulets, or good luck charms, that were supposed to keep evil spirits at bay. Later, Aaron was badgered into melting them down and creating the golden calf (Ex. 32:2).

MONOGRAMMED HANKIES?

The word that is translated "handkerchief" in the New Testament is better translated "napkin" or "towel." These were colorful cloths, often embellished with beautiful needlework. A lady always had her hankie tucked up her sleeve. Such cloths were used for wrapping things that were being carried (Lk. 19:20) or for wiping one's brow during the heat of the day. A cloth like this was also used to cover the face of the dead. John 20:7 tells us that the napkin that was covering the face of Jesus was found rolled up and lying separately from the linen grave clothes.

BRACELETS

The common women of Bible times wore bangle bracelets or chains about their wrists (Eze. 16:11), in much the same way that women wear them today. However, if a woman was of royal birth or high social status, her bracelet was a gold band which she wore above her elbow. Such a bracelet is a status symbol in Near Eastern countries today, just as it was during King David's time (2Sa. 1:10).

HIGHBROW HEADDRESSES

Jewish women copied the styles of neighboring countries by weaving gold and jewels into their hair as ornamentation (1Pet. 3:3). These were worked into carefully arranged braids and shining coils of oiled hair. Elaborate headdresses were worn by wealthy women in many of the Near Eastern countries. Costly concoctions of fine fabrics and feathers were worn only by the social elite. In contrast, Christian women were encouraged to keep their apparel modest (1Ti. 2:8–9). The veils that Jewish women wore would hardly be considered headdresses.

PERSONAL GROOMING

Imagine living in a world where there were no hot showers, no mouthwash, and no nail clippers. How well would we manage without antibacterial soap, a toothbrush, and lip balm; let alone deodorant, shaving cream, and a curling iron? In our eyes, the people of Bible times suffered in a primitive world without the most basic of necessities for personal cleanliness. Yet, Rachel's beauty moved Isaac to tears, and Sarah attracted the attentions of kings. Just how did Prince Absalom manage that heavy head of curls? What were Queen Esther's beauty secrets?

The Men

Jewish men from Bible times may not have followed the same standards of cleanliness that appeal to women nowadays, but that doesn't mean they didn't have a certain flair when keeping up appearances. True, baths were difficult to come by, and shaving was unheard of. Still, men kept their beards neatly trimmed, and worked to achieve a lustrous shine to their hair.

OILY HAIR

Although we might blanch at the thought of pouring olive oil into our hair today, this was definitely the custom during Bible times. Looking your best included well-oiled tresses, and the glossy curls that resulted were admired. Men often achieved this fashionable shine by pouring perfumed oil over their hair, especially for celebrations (Ps. 23:5). This fragrant dousing also helped mask any undesirable body odor the heat of the day may have produced. At a fancy dinner party, guests who arrived were anointed with oil as a part of the welcome. Jesus mentions this custom in Luke 7:45 when he rebukes Simon the Pharisee for neglecting to wash his feet and anoint his head with oil.

HAIR STYLE

Hebrew men gave their thick wavy hair a lot of attention, for they considered it to be an ornament in itself. Hair had to be styled in accordance with God's guidelines. The Jewish men were not to shave their hair off, because this was seen as an imitation of the heathens. They were also not supposed to resemble the Nazarites, who never cut their hair (Eze. 44:20). Long hair was considered to be unnatural on a man (1Cor. 11:14). So the Jews were content to keep their hair carefully trimmed in styles that were not too long and not too short.

BEARDS

All Jewish men had a beard. They kept their beards carefully trimmed to keep them tidy and maintain their shape. To shave off a beard or to let it become

DID YOU KNOW?

- The Assyrians, whose many conquests provided them with a life of luxury, were known for their expensive clothing (Eze. 23:12). To say that a man wore "Assyrian" garments was to say that he was dressed in the best that money could buy. Today we might say he was wearing an Armani suit.

- Egyptian women, who are seen in hieroglyphics with heavily painted eyes, also tattooed their hands, feet, and faces. Red iron oxide was used by the ladies of Old Testament times as rouge.

DAVID

The Shepherd Boy

As the youngest son in a family with eight boys, David was put to work watching the sheep. This was a humble task, and his clothes for the job were both rough and simple. David probably wore a short goatskin jacket over a torn, knee-length cotton shirt. He probably went barefoot. Daily, he drove his flocks through the rough desert plains and hills, looking for grass, water, and shade in the midst of stunted shrubs and scrub. Each morning, he would leave his bed early and call to his father's flock of sheep and goats. David knew each of them by name, and they recognized his voice.

The shepherd's accessories were necessities for the job before him. Slung over his shoulder was his shepherd's scrip, which was a small bag filled with his food for the day ahead. It was in such a scrip that he placed the five stones gathered before facing the giant, Goliath (1Sa. 17:40). The hill country was filled with wolves, jackals, and lions, which were a danger to the sheep in David's flock. In his belt was tucked his "rod," a heavy oaken club studded with nails to drive away these predators (1Sa. 17:35). In his hand was his staff, which he used as a walking stick, and occasionally to help guide the sheep. David's sling was always close at hand as well, and the many hours spent alone on the hillsides provided ample time to practice his aim. The sling could also be used in herding because a well-placed stone in front of a sheep's nose could turn a wandering sheep back towards the rest of the flock. Simple music was also a companion for a shepherd in the fields. Sometimes he made a reed pipe by binding together two hollow reeds and cutting holes in them. David seems to have also carried a small lap harp, upon which he composed music that was lovely enough to sooth King Saul in his distress (1Sa. 16:23).

overgrown would have been a sign of mourning and great distress. Looking at the paintings archeologists have uncovered, we see the Judeans are depicted with curls all over their head and short, curled beards that were rounded at the corners. In contrast, the Assyrians had long square cut beards, the Egyptians sported a false pointed goatee, and Romans preferred to be clean-shaven.

TAKING HOLD OF HIS BEARD

Although a handshake is enough to show respect in our country, saying "hi" in Palestine involved kissing the cheeks of your acquaintances. When greeting a good friend, it was not uncommon to take hold of his beard to pull him in close for that little peck on the cheek. We can see from this tradition just how treacherous David's general, Joab, was when he murdered Amasa (2Sa. 20:9–10). Joab took hold of Amasa's beard, as if to kiss him in a friendly greeting, and while holding him there, thrust a dagger into his belly.

The Women

Yesterday's scented oils and elaborate braiding may have been replaced today by cold creams and permanent waves, but the motivation was the same then as it is now. Women were trying to look their best. Even Bible-time babes, with their exotic olive complexions and flashing dark eyes, looked for ways to enhance their natural beauty. Look at the lovely Esther, who was selected to compete in King Ahasuerus' beauty contest: she underwent a year-long beauty treatment in his harem before ever being brought before him (Est. 2:12)!

BATHING BEAUTIES

Women of Bible times never knew the pleasure of a good soak in a warm bubble bath. Still, people did need to wash, and a kind of bathtub was used. A shallow earthenware bowl with a ridge in the middle on which to place the feet was used. A woman could sit on a stool next to the bowl, placing her feet on the ridge, and manage a fairly good sponge bath. If Bathsheba was typical, this took place in the evening (2Sa. 11:2). For a full bath, where one was able to duck down into the water and really feel clean, they had to find a large, outdoor source of water. Even Pharaoh's own daughter had to bathe in the river (Ex. 2:5).

COSMETICS

For the most part, respectable Jewish women did not "paint their faces" by using today's equivalent of lipstick, eyeshadow, and blusher. In fact, Jezebel, the Bible's primary example of a heavy make-up user, was not really Jewish. She was the daughter of a Phoenician king, and her use of cosmetics may have been a Phoenician style. Hebrew women did use something like modern mascara, however. Women who used paint to enlarge their eyes are mentioned by two of the Old Testament prophets (Jer. 4:30 and Eze. 23:40). This may reflect the fact that this was becoming a widespread practice among the women of Palestine.

> **DID YOU KNOW?**
>
> • When the Bible says that Leah had "tender eyes" it may not have been a bad thing. This could have meant that while Rachel had a lovely figure (Gen. 29:17), Leah had very beautiful eyes.

NAIL POLISH

Modern nail polish comes in an amazing array of colors—each in a tiny bottle, with a clever little brush inside the cap for easy application. It may surprise you to learn that women have been painting their nails for centuries. Apparently it was even in vogue during Old Testament times, when women used oils and the crushed leaves of the henna plant to color their fingernails and toenails. There was not much variety in color choices, but they looked great in their open-toed sandals!

PERFUME

Perfumes were a mainstay of the woman's daily beauty regime. In the days before antiperspirants and deodorants, strong perfume was the only defense one had against body odor. Pleasing scents could be achieved in different ways. Some women simply wore a pouch around their neck filled with aromatic grasses or spices. Scented oils could be rubbed into the hair and skin. True perfumes could be purchased in the marketplace. These costly wares came from far away lands: frankincense and myrrh from Arabia and Africa, aloes and nard from India, and cinnamon from Ceylon.

PATENTED PERFUME

Women enjoyed the use of perfume throughout Old Testament times, but one particular fragrance was so special that no woman was allowed to use it. God had given the priests and Levites a formula for the perfume that they used in their tabernacle rituals. The ingredients included myrrh and cinnamon. It must have been made up of God's favorite scents, and that heavenly aroma was off-limits to everyone else. The Law forbade anyone from copying the scent for personal use (Ex. 30:4–38).

MIRROR, MIRROR ON THE WALL!

No woman could manage to keep her eyeliner straight or her hair artfully arranged without the help of a mirror. Very early in history, vanity dictated the invention of mirrors. Mirrors in Palestine were made of highly polished metal They came in sizes that ranged from small handheld mirrors to full-length mirrors that hung on the walls of palaces. Mirrors that were brought by the Hebrews out of Egypt were primarily made of copper. By New Testament times, the Romans had learned how to make mirrors out of glass. Much to the lady's dismay, however, these mirrors often gave a cloudy and distorted reflection (1Cor. 13:12).

THEM THERE EYES

In the cultures of the Near East, where many of the women had the lower half of their faces veiled, sparkling and lively eyes were considered a thing of true beauty. Because of this, while the Jewish women avoided much of the elaborate face-painting techniques of their neighbors, they did give some attention to making-up their eyes. The equivalent of today's eyeliner was made from a mixture of powdered kohl (green copper carbonate) or galena (black lead sulphide) and oil or vinegar (Eze. 23:40). Women used small applicators to carefully apply these compounds to their eyelashes and eyelids to make their eyes more noticeable (Jer. 4:30).

HAIRDRESSING

In Old Testament times especially, the hair was an important feature. It was rarely cut. Paul the apostle said that hair was a natural veil, or covering, for the woman; he indicates that, in his day, it was shameful for a Christian woman to cut her hair (1Cor. 11:15). Women braided or curled their hair. It was often kept in place by beautiful ivory combs. In Roman times, the hair was piled on top of the head and kept in place by a net. The wealthy had nets of gold thread.

PRIESTLY GARMENTS

Beginning with Aaron and his sons, the entire tribe of Levi was set apart as servants for the Tabernacle, and later for the Temple. God gave specific instructions for the clothing that they should wear. The clothing of the priests differed greatly from that of the common Jew. Furthermore, the high priest's clothing was very different from that of the common priest.

Common Priests

When considering the scope of the Scriptures, we find that we are not completely unfamiliar with priests. In the Old Testament story of Samuel, we find a lad who served in the Temple and wore a linen shirt, which his mother made for him (1Sa. 2:18–19). In the New Testament we find Zechariah, whose turn to serve in the Temple found him speechless before an angel, who informed him that he would soon become the father of John the Baptizer (Lk. 1:6–10). These men wore the clothing of the common priest.

PHARISEE

Dressed to Impress

Pharisees were admired in their day for their strict keeping of the Law. Unfortunately, this admiration seems to have started an ugly trend on the part of these respectable men. Instead of keeping the Law as an act of obedience to God, it became a means to maintaining their good reputation. The Pharisees set themselves to outdo any other man in obedience to the Law. In their minds, bigger was better. For example, God had commanded that the Jewish men wear a fringe of tassels on their cloaks to remind them of the constant presence of the Lord's commandments. The Pharisees wore such long and heavy fringes that their tassels dragged upon the ground. Jesus condemned the Pharisees for this practice (Mt. 23:5). Another example involves the phylacteries that Jewish men wore on their foreheads during prayers. These looked like small boxes that were bound in place by leather thongs. The Pharisees' phylacteries were ridiculously large, once again to call attention to their righteous lifestyle.

BREECHES

There was one exception to the Old Testament's no-underwear policy. The priests who served in the temple were given short linen breeches to wear under their robes. God, in his great wisdom and foresight, ordained the use of these undergarments for his servants. This prevented considerable embarrassment. You see, the altar upon which sacrifices were offered was up a short flight of steps (Ex. 28:43). If the priest's robe happened to catch a gust of wind, the worshippers below would have been given a glimpse of things decency did not allow.

WHITE ROBES

While on duty in the Temple, the priests all wore pure white linen robes. These were specially made by expert weavers. Priestly robes were designed in a fashion that could only be worn by the temple servants. The white linen was made into a seamless garment, with a diamond or checkered pattern woven right into the fabric. Very accomplished weavers could even work letters and words into the very fabric of these robes. The garment that Jesus wore was also a seamless robe, which was appropriate considering his priesthood (Jn. 19:23; Heb. 4:14–15).

FOOTLOOSE

While sandals were certainly considered appropriate attire during their off-hours, the priests were to be barefoot during their duty shifts. When reporting for duty at the Temple, they were to wash their hands and feet before entering (Ex. 40:30–31), and leave their shoes behind. This may seem a risky practice, since the daily tasks would put tender feet in close proximity of wood splinters, hot coals, and the hooves of various animals being brought to sacrifice. However, the reason behind this practice is simple. The area on which the priests served was holy ground. Just as God commanded Moses to remove his sandals (Ex. 3:5), so the Temple priests removed theirs.

The High Priest

The high priest was set apart as the only man who could go into the presence of God. Once a year, he entered the Holy of Holies to make atonement for the children of God. Just as his position and duties were unique from those of the other priests who served in the Tabernacle and Temple, so was his clothing unique. The high priest's garments consisted of seven parts—the ephod, the robe of the ephod, the breastplate, the headdress, the embroidered coat, the girdle, and the breeches (Ex. 28:42). One of the distinctions that separated the high priest from the common priest was the sprinkling of his garments with anointing oil (Ex. 28:41; 29:21).

THE EPHOD

The ephod worn by the high priest was a beautifully embroidered linen garment. It was worn over the breeches and under the breastplate and robe, and was embroidered in gold, blue, purple, and scarlet. This garment was fastened at the shoulder by a large onyx stone.

THE GIRDLE

The girdle, or belt, which the high priest used over his ephod was made of blue, purple, and scarlet fabrics interwoven with gold thread (Ex. 28:8). The girdle of the high priest's garment was wound around the body several times from the breast downward. The ends of the girdle hung down to the ankles (Ex. 29:5).

ROBE OF THE EPHOD

The robe which the high priest wore was less extravagant than the embroidered ephod which it covered. This linen robe was dyed blue (Ex. 39:22),

DID YOU KNOW?

• A priest was not allowed to shave his head or rip his clothes, even to mourn his mother or father's death (Lev. 21:10–11).

• Every man born into the Levite clan did not necessarily serve in the Temple. In Leviticus 21:5, we see that baldness disqualified a man from the priesthood.

and was longer than the ephod. It had no sleeves, but simply contained slits in each side through which the arms would pass. The bottom of this garment had a long fringe, on which were embroidered blue, purple, and scarlet pomegranates. Between each pomegranate hung a bell, which allowed the other priests to keep track of his movements as the high priest came and went from the holy place (Ex. 28:32–35).

WITH BELLS ON

The high priest's job seemed one of great privilege. Here was a man who had the snazziest clothes in the whole temple, carried the sacred lots, wore jewels on his chest, had seen inside the ark of the covenant, and had walked into the Holy of Holies. But even the high priest had something to keep him humble: bells on his robe.

The fringe of the high priest's robe was lined with little golden bells, which tinkled together whenever he moved. Their purpose was something more than decorative, though. The high priest served in the inner rooms of the temple, where no other priest dared peek. When it was time for the annual trip into the Holy of Holies, the other priests would tie a rope around the high priest's ankle and send him in. The other priests waited, holding their breath and listening to the sound of tiny bells as they moved back and forth in the room beyond the veil (Ex. 28:32–35). They all knew that if the high priest had done anything to displease God while in his presence, he would be struck dead. If the bells suddenly stopped, that was their cue to haul on the rope and pull out the body of the priest.

DID YOU KNOW?

- The high priest's garments were made of plain linen, as were all the clothes of the priests (1Sa. 2:18; 2Sa. 6:14). The high priests clothing were passed on to his successor after his death.

- The breastplate worn by the high priest was called the "breastplate of judgment" (Ex. 28:15), possibly because it contained the Urim and Thummim, the sacred lots, that showed God's judgments upon men (Num. 26:55; Josh. 7:14, 14:2; 1Sa. 14:42).

BREASTPLATE

The breastplate and ephod were called a memorial (Ex. 28:12, 29) because they reminded the high priest of his relationship to the twelve tribes of Israel. Exodus 28:15–30 describes the high priest's breastplate. This was a carefully embroidered piece of cloth about ten inches square which had been doubled over to make a pouch. Twelve precious stones, each bearing the name of one of the twelve tribes of Israel, were affixed upon it. The upper corners of the breastplate were attached to the ephod, and the bottom two corners were attached to the girdle. The fastenings that held the breastplate in place were made of gold or rich lace. The pouch created by the folding of the fabric was where the sacred lots, the Urim and Thummim, were kept.

TURBAN

A turban, also called the miter, was the official headdress of the high priest (Ex. 28:39). A fine linen cloth, about eight yards in length, was wound and folded about the head. Pinned onto the front was a gold plate upon which were written the Hebrew words for "Holiness to the Lord" (Ex. 28:36; 39:28–30).

EMBROIDERED COAT

This particular coat was long-skirted, made of linen, and embroidered with a pattern as if stones were set into it (Ex. 28:4). The common priests also wore this garment.

CHAPTER SEVEN

THEIR HOMES

B e it ever so humble, **there's no place like home.**
The people of Israel were not known for their
awe-inspiring architecture. While the Canaanites
and Assyrians were building cities, the Hebrews still lived
in tents. It was not until their conquest of the Promised
Land that they chose more permanent homes by moving
into the houses abandoned by the Canaanites. Compared
to the startling edifices of Egypt and the extravagant decor
of Persia, they were nothing. In fact, the Greeks and the
Romans considered Palestine pitifully backwards. The Jews
were a "project" that needed renovating, updating, and civi-
lizing. Their influence on the cities of Palestine is one of
the main reasons why we see such a difference between the
homes in Old Testament times compared to the world we
find in the New Testament.

THE NEIGHBORHOOD

Location, location, location! In Bible times, life was greatly influenced by location. The neighborhoods that built up around a sea port like Ephesus were vastly different from those that were carved into the caves of Petra in Edom. Some towns were merely a cluster of humble abodes surrounded by fields of grain, while others were improved by occupying forces with sewer systems, roadways, and theaters.

CAVES

Although by Bible times people had moved out of the original cave dwellings that were abundant in the ancient Middle East, there were always people who lived in caves. Lot lived in a cave after his escape from Sodom (Gen. 19:30), and the Edomites made and enlarged caves in the rock face at Petra for living and for public affairs. There were caves under the homes in Nazareth that were contemporary with Jesus, and traditionally Jesus was born in a shepherd's cave. Caves were always used for escape (Josh. 10:16, 1Sa. 22:1; 1Kin. 18:4), and the Philistines taunted the Israelites for using holes in the ground to hide themselves (1Sa. 14:11).

DID YOU KNOW?

• It is hard to realize that in Bible times, the country was heavily wooded and remained so until the ravages of the Romans and later, the Turks.

ENCAMPMENTS

When a nomadic family had grown over the course of a few generations, many tents were needed to accommodate all of the extended family. The sheikh's tent was located in the center of the encampment, facing the direction from which visitors were likely to approach. The tents of his relatives fanned out from his in ranks. There was an order to the tents, and during the wanderings of the Israelites, we find that there was a strict order for the pitching of tents (Num. 2). Within these large encampments, some kind of sign marked the leader's tent. The Bedouin custom was to put an upright spear by the tent door of the sheikh (1Sa. 26:7).

HOUSES OF HAIR

The name that the Bedouin used for his home is literally translated "house of hair." The long, rectangular Bedouin tents were made from cloth that was woven from the hair of goats. The long black hair of the goats they raised was shorn in the spring, and the women wove the cloth themselves. The roof, the walls, and the dividing walls inside the tents were all made from this fabric. In the heat of the summer sun, the outsides of these tents were hot to the touch, but the inside remained blissfully cool. The reverse was true in the wintertime, when a small fire inside the tent kept it warm and cozy. The cloth also proved to be weatherproof, because when the rains would fall, the weave of the fabric would contract, making it watertight.

TENT-DWELLING ETIQUETTE

The tents of the nomads were carefully divided into two sections. One was for the "boys" and one was for the "girls." The women's portion of the tent was separated by a curtain from the men's half, and it was strictly off limits. Only the head of the family was allowed to cross into this private area of the home. A male stranger who entered a woman's quarters could be punished with death. Sisera hid in Jael's tent, but paid for it with his life (Judg. 4:18–21). The women's section of the tent held all the household supplies, cookware, and clothing. This is where the children played and napped. The men's part of the tent was open, with an awning offering shelter from the sun. Here, men would welcome their guests and entertain them. Although the men could not see the activities going on behind the curtains, that did not mean that the women were not keeping an eye on them. Many holes were concealed in the woven fabric, and the women were able to peep out at the men and eavesdrop on their conversations. Sarah was caught listening in like this (Gen. 18:9–10).

VILLAGES

There was one big difference between a town and a village in ancient times. It had very little to do with population and it had nothing to do with how many stories the local buildings could boast. It didn't matter if there was a certain fast food restaurant or coffee shop chain established in their area. The difference between a town and a village depended upon its defenses. A village did not have a wall. In Old Testament times, these villages were mostly farming settlements, which built up around a dependable water supply. Villagers needed to be on constant guard against the attacks of raiding nomads and wild animals.

TOWNS

Since the village life left people vulnerable to attack, many would pull together to build walls around their settlements. Once a group of people had raised their walls, they were upgraded to town-status. Towns in early Israel were pretty small, having only about two hundred homes and a population of about 1,000 people. Towns were crowded and dirty, but they offered safety. In the earliest days, people lived in outlying villages for most of the year. During peacetime, they tended their fields and their animals for eight months of the year. During the winter months, or when invasion threatened, they would gather into the safety of the towns.

CROWDED CONDITIONS

In the winter months, towns offered cramped conditions to cooped-up people. Things could get pretty messy. The houses were little more than shanties, and they were joined together house-to-house. Where the streets sloped with the hillsides, houses were built right on top of each other. No organized streets led through the settlement. The unpaved paths between houses were so choked with mud and rubbish that they often rose higher than the floors of the houses along them. When the rains came, the whole mess turned into a filthy swamp. Town life stank, and people were glad to return to their fields in the spring.

> **DID YOU KNOW?**
>
> • The oldest aqueduct in history is located in Ninevah, the royal city of the Assyrians. It was part of a canal that brought water from the mountains thirty-five miles away.

GATEWAY TRAFFIC

As time passed and cities grew, they became more organized. The fortified gateway became the hub of life in the town. With the opening of the gates each morning came the bustle and noise of a new day. Merchants arrived and set up shop. People came to buy and sell. Elders sat in council meetings. Beggars, peddlers, workers, scribes, visitors, and a variety of animals

would also flock to the city gate. In large towns, there was a market square for traders to set up their booths. Farmers brought in their produce for sale, and called out the advantages of their offerings to passers-by. Sometimes, each trade had its own area, but there were no shops as we think of them today. This was a time of open-air markets, and goods were set out by the sides of the streets. Each night, the traders packed away their wares and the gate was closed and barred for the night.

WATER FROM THE WELLS

The Israelites tried to ensure a ready supply of water by maintaining wells. Shepherds and herdsmen would provide a well for their flocks, often at great expense (2Chr. 26:10). The well was community property. The opening was covered by a stone (Gen. 29:2), and a low wall surrounded the well to protect it from blowing sand. This also guarded against trouble from clumsy people who might fall in. A drinking trough would stand nearby for thirsty animals. The water was brought up from the well in leather buckets or water skins. Fetching water was a woman's work. When Rebekah offered to draw water for Eliezer and his camels, he accepted this courtesy. It never dawned on him to offer assistance, because this was a woman's job. To be a male water-carrier was to hold a lowly and despised occupation. This also explains why the disciples had no trouble following Jesus' directions in finding a room in which to hold their Passover meal. They were to go to the town square and watch for a man to come for water. To see a man carrying water from the well was unusual, and the disciples would be able to spot him quickly (Mk. 14:13).

ALL FOR A DRINK OF WATER!

Getting the next day's water supply could be very difficult depending on where your hometown's water source was located. Sometimes the well was located in the center of town. A few Old Testament cities were built above underground springs. Hazor was one of these cities. In Hazor, a woman would walk through the streets to a deep shaft. There she descended two man-made slopes for thirty feet and five flights of stairs to the water tunnel. Once there, she followed even more stairs to the

water level to fill her large water jug. She needed considerable strength to climb back out of the watershaft with a heavy water jug. But it wasn't all bad. The trip for water gave her a chance to talk with the other women of the village.

AT THE WATER COOLER

In the cool of the evening, the women came from all directions, some from long distances, to fetch water from the local well. Carrying water was a never-ending task that was hard work, but it was a chore that every woman looked forward to at the end of her day. This was their chance to get out of the house and steal a few minutes visiting with her friends and neighbors. All the tidbits of local gossip were passed around. Whose daughter was betrothed? Who had a new baby? Who was wearing a new robe? Whose son was having his bar mitzvah? The well was the gathering place that drew the community together. Once all the water jars had been filled, then the women would move away, carrying their heavy pitchers on their heads and shoulders with grace and ease.

Bringing "Civilization" to the Hebrews

The Greeks and the Romans must have found the cities of the Hebrews very uncivilized, for whenever they came to a town, they would renovate it. Gradually the towns of Palestine became better organized, with a layout that had been carefully planned. The cities of New Testament times were very different than the fortress towns of early Israel. Tall buildings sprouted up along the narrow streets, some of them several stories high. The Greeks tried to bring in beauty, and built theaters and gymnasiums. The Romans tried to bring in order and efficiency, and so built aqueducts, sewer systems, and public baths. Shops were built along a main street, side streets intersected roads at right angles, and houses were built in blocks of four.

Roman Roads

All roads may lead to Rome, but that's only because Romans built them! Wherever the Roman legions marched, they left a neatly-laid trail of stones behind them. Over the course of five centuries, they completed a complex road system that extended to the farthest corners of their domain. Normally, these roads were surfaced with gravel, but they upgraded their workmanship when nearing a large city. Cart and chariot drivers appreciated a smooth ride, so the Romans paved their city streets with large, carefully fitted stones. When building an important road, Roman engineers like to do things correctly. First, they would dig a trench the full width of the road—that was four or five feet deep. Then, they would build up layers of large and small stones, sometimes even a layer of concrete. These road builders took pride in their work, and built them to last. Some of the largest Roman roads are still usable today!

Aqueducts

These huge feats of Roman architecture were a familiar sight to city-dwellers throughout the New Testament world. Aqueducts were a kind of bridge-wall used to carry water into Roman cities from nearby mountain ranges. An aqueduct could span large distances. For instance, the water system used by the ancient royal city of Ninevah brought water from a mountain range that was thirty-five miles away. These systems provided the irrigation that became a necessity in the rainless months from March to October. Often, these waterways were built in such a way that the upper level carried the water, but a lower level provided a roadway for travelers. The city of Laodicea had such an aqueduct system, and the water transported across it would have been warmed by the sun until it became lukewarm.

OWNING LAND

When the Israelites first entered Canaan, each of the twelve tribes was given a plot of land. Each person's land was considered a gift from God, and so was not bought and sold casually. In fact, every fiftieth year was a year of Jubilee for the Jews. Any land which had been mortgaged to another person during the previous forty-nine years had to be returned to the family during the year of Jubilee. This ensured that each of God's people kept their inheritance in the land. This old equality began to break down under the rule of kings. Starting in the days of David and Solomon, a wealthy class of rulers and officials developed. They bought up land from the poor, and big estates began to take the place of small family farms. People who lost their land were forced to hire themselves out as laborers. These poor were often oppressed and suffered great hardships.

THE YARD

Much of the character of the front yard and its contents was determined by the family business. The family of a potter would have a pit of clay and a potter's wheel in its courtyard. The dyer's front yard might have steaming vats of colorful dyes and skeins of colored yarn drying on a clothesline. The front yard of a fisherman might have a group of people mending fishnets. Still, many aspects of the yard of a Jewish family were fairly consistent: a cookfire, a garden, a passel of bright-eyed children, and a handful of animals.

JOHN ON PATMOS
Home is an Island

John, the beloved disciple and author of one of the four gospels, was considered a troublemaker. Although he had grown quite old, watching each of his fellow disciples martyred one by one, he continued with his ministry. The Romans couldn't get him to stop teaching about Jesus, so they decided to put him somewhere out of the way. Hoping to limit his circle of influence, John was forced to call Patmos home. The island of Patmos was off the coast of Greece, in the Aegean Sea. Just ten miles long and six miles wide, the small, hilly island, had once boasted luxuriant palm groves and a thriving population. By New Testament times, though, the land had become desolate and people had abandoned it. Since the landscape was so uninviting, the Romans used this bit of wasteland as a prison, and sent criminals and political exiles there. Patmos was a mining colony, and the prisoners were obliged to break rocks all day long under the hot sun. These were salt mines, and the rock salt they scrabbled for went to pay the many legions of Roman soldiers.

Accustomed as he was to the forested hillside and green valleys of Palestine, John was faced with a gloomy landscape and wild seas. Instead of the Temple at Jerusalem, an ancient temple to the goddess Diana dominated the view. John was truly isolated here. Too old to be much use with a pick and shovel, John was often left alone. Among the cliffs under the pagan temple, he found a cleft in the rocks—a small cave. Here he would go to pray and to remember. As he formulated his thoughts, he found himself composing a history of his time with the Master—the Gospel of John. It was also in this little grotto that John received the visions that were put down as our Book of Revelation. In the midst of severity and loneliness, John found that God was still very near.

WHAT A DIFFERENCE A WALL MAKES!

A courtyard made all the difference in the world in ancient times. Owning a home with a courtyard was proof that you were making ends meet. The most basic model was a small enclosure added onto the house. Even a tiny econo-courtyard changed a family's entire day-to-day routine. For one thing, the animals could be kept outside. This did wonders for the smell inside the home, not to mention the condition of the floors. Also, cooking could be done over an outside fire, allowing the household to breath easier, in a smoke-free environment, while Mom was making dinner. Security was also improved. The front door and the stairs to the roof were both situated in the courtyard area, keeping strangers from wandering through. It also became safer to throw open the windows, which let in more light and fresh air to a home. Luxuries like a personal cistern were now a possibility as well.

CISTERNS—A MODERN CONVENIENCE

The Israelites wandered in a desert wilderness for a very long time. All the while, they saw nothing but hot, shimmering sand. They were always shaking sand out of their sandals, blinking sand out of their eyes, and swatting at sand fleas. It is no wonder that they began to daydream about the homes they would have once Joshua led them into the Promised Land. And just what did the hopeful homemakers want to have in their dream homes? A two-car garage and central air? Of course not! But they did dream big. After years of trudging through a dry and barren land, they wanted water. More specifically, they wanted a cistern in their front yard (Deut. 8:6–18). Cisterns were a modern convenience of the day, and it was something of a status symbol to have one of your own. In fact, years later when Sennacherib was trying to convince the Israelites to surrender to his forces, he promised to provide cisterns for everyone if they would cooperate (2Kin. 18:31). The farmers of Palestine depended upon the water collected in their cisterns. Cisterns also supplied water to the housewives of a city or village. From ground level, a cistern often looked like a hole in the ground about three feet across.

Actually cisterns were made with bottle-shaped openings, so that the lower chamber widened to some twenty feet in diameter and depth. The deeper the cistern was dug, the cooler the water would be that was stored there. Joseph was thrown into a dry cistern such as this by his brothers (Gen. 37:24). Escape would have been impossible without someone lowering a rope. The floor, walls, and ceilings of this "room" were coated with plaster to make it waterproof. Better yet, a cistern was carved out of solid rock, which held the moisture even better than a clay-lined cistern. To prevent evaporation, a cover was made to fit over the top.

How Does Your Garden Grow?

In the courtyard of a villager's home, there would have been a garden plot. These were carefully watered and tended to supplement the family's menu. In season, the homeowners could enjoy radishes, cucumbers, onions, leeks, and garlic. There were herbs, like caraway, cumin, mint, mustard, parsley, sage, and thyme. In the warmer climates, a garden could include melons, grapes, apricots, figs, and pomegranates. Many gardeners take advantage of every inch of soil in their plots by planting two crops together. Pumpkins can be planted in a cornfield, where they

ramble between the stalks. Pole beans can be planted with sunflowers so that they climb together in the summer's heat. But the Israelites didn't believe in blending crops. Seed symbolized the Israelites themselves—the "seed" of Abraham—and just as God forbade the Israelites to marry pagan peoples, he forbade them to mix their garden seed (Lev. 19:19; Deut. 22:9). This law constantly reminded the people that they must remain a separate race.

A PET

What parent hasn't been tempted to place an irresistible, wriggling puppy under the Christmas tree to surprise and delight a young boy? In the days that follow, the boy slips food off his plate to the puppy waiting under the table, and the pup spends his nights at the foot of his new master's bed. A boy and his dog—they are inseparable. In the Jewish home of Old Testament times, there was a similar desire to provide young children with a pet. This pet would also be inseparable from its master, eating from the same dishes and sleeping in the same bed. Only it wasn't a Christmas puppy, it was a Passover lamb! Even the poorest families in Palestine hoped to save enough money each year to buy a pair of lambs at Passover. One lamb was killed and eaten, and the other became a playmate for the children.

DID YOU KNOW?

- By New Testament times, Jewish families began keeping a small flock of chickens in their courtyards.

- The droppings of the animals were always carefully collected and dried in the sun; these were then used in the brazier as fuel for cooking and heat in the winter when sticks could not be found.

THE HOUSE

Four walls and a roof over their heads—along with a door, a few windows, and a floor. In some cases, home was even less—only a tent offering shelter from sun, wind, and rain. Whatever the struc-

ture, the house was called "home" by a family. Dad pruned the fig tree and built a cistern for his wife. Mom baked bread, swept, and kept the oil lamps filled. Little children ran up and down the stairs and slept with the family lamb curled at their feet. Teenaged daughters watched out the window for potential suitors to walk past while they took a turn grinding more barley into flour. Sons on the verge of manhood studied their Hebrew by lamplight after working all day beside their fathers. The home may have been humble, but the family that lived within its walls was bursting with life.

HOMES OF THE REGULAR FOLK

The majority of people in Bible times lived very simple lives. They worked to put food on the table, and they raised a family. The homes were just as simple. In Old Testament times, tents were used for centuries. It wasn't until the Jews moved into the abandoned homes of the Canaanites that they experienced living with walls and windows. Still, these houses were very crude by today's standards. Crowded together, these mud-brick homes were dark inside, had no glass in the windows and often sported a leaky roof. But as it says in Proverbs, "It is better to have little with fear for the Lord than to have great treasure with turmoil" (Prov. 15:16, NLT). The same went for the house.

AHAB IN SAMARIA
Home is a Palace

Ahab does not receive high marks in the Bible. He was an ungodly king, ruled more by whim and emotion than by integrity. He married poorly, uniting with Jezebel, princess of Phoenicia and daughter of a Baal priest. She brought her false gods with her into her new home, and fully expected to woo the whole nation of Israel into worshipping them. Jezebel's influence led Ahab straight down the path of idolatry. In the face of God's Commandments, they practiced the unthinkable. God's prophets were slaughtered, little children were sacrificed, and God's children were led astray.

Despite all this, Ahab was an undeniably good soldier. He led his troops into victory, and increased both his boundaries and his wealth. Ahab built several fortresses and palaces, but the prettiest by far was his home in Samaria. Samaria became Ahab's capital city during his reign, and there he built his Ivory Palace. Ahab's palace was set on the summit of a hill and surrounded by high walls. The main gateway had a columned courtyard, and a sparkling pool of water lay in the midst of the larger palace courtyard. Windows with balconies let air and light into the upper stories. The dining halls were massive, with tables enough to seat all eight hundred and fifty prophets of Baal and Asherah. Most impressive was the richness with which Ahab had furnished his home. Ivory had been imported from every possible distributor, and it was used to ornament every room in the house. Intricate inlays of precious ivory were set into the chairs, tables, and even the bedsteads. Personal effects, like combs and makeup boxes were made of ivory. Ahab's receiving room, was paneled in ivory from wall to wall. Each section was like a plaque, ornately carved with Egyptian-style designs. Guests would crane their necks in astonishment to see the luster of wealth that surrounded King Ahab.

MUD BRICKS

Many of the common Jews who lived in the towns and villages of the Bible had homes that were built from mud bricks. These bricks were made from the clay soil, which was mixed with chopped straw, put into molds, and left to dry in the sun. Clay was plentiful in Palestine, and the Hebrews molded clay bricks by the thousands. The Egyptians put their slaves to work making bricks (Ex. 1:14; 5:7–8), and there are hieroglyphics showing Hebrews at this task under the watchful eye of their Egyptian taskmasters. To make the clay bricks more durable, kings and wealthy householders hardened them in charcoal-fired kilns (Nah. 3:14). The Tower of Babel would have been made from baked bricks.

SEASONAL INCONVENIENCES

Each season had its inconveniences when you lived in a house made from mud-bricks. People already shared their living space with a variety of animals, both wanted and un-wanted. While the goats and chickens might be part of the family, the mice and snakes that found their way into cracks in the walls were definitely pests! During hot weather, the house was alive with insects. The smells from the animals and from the refuse that clogged the streets were constant, and worse after a good rain. Speaking of rain, inclement weather brought dripping water into a home, making a muddy mess everywhere. Roofs would leak and walls seeped with the moisture. In the winter, temperatures dropped and even more rain fell. The fire around which the family warmed themselves filled the house with smoke.

KEEPING OUT THE WEATHER

Having a roof over your head in Bible times did not necessarily mean that you stayed dry. The roof was constructed by laying brushwood across rough sycamore beams and binding it all together with mud. A heavy roller was kept on the roof to compact the material after rain. Roofs were not watertight and therefore had two characteristics—leaks and a green color. The period of November to March (the rainy season) was a cold and miserable time. Proverbs 19:13 refers to the continual drip of water. The roofs were green because the seeds in the mud sprouted (2Kin. 19:26; Ps. 129:6; Is. 37:27).

PRACTICAL USES OF THE ROOF

Having a flat roof did have a few advantages in the days of the Bible. It made an excellent vantage point (Is. 22:1; Mt. 10:27), it was a cool place to sleep on a hot summer's night, and it provided a place to dry out crops for storage (Josh. 2:6). If the house was built into a steep hillside, the roof was sometimes used as a threshing floor. Trellises were sometimes put on the roof and vines trained over them, adding to the available gardening space for a family. The rooftop became a place to get away from the noise of the house below and find a place for meditation and worship (Zeph. 1:5; Acts 10:9). The roof provided a platform for shouting out news to one's neighbors. So busy were these rooftops, that the law required that a railing should be built around them to prevent people from falling (Deut. 22:8).

> **DID YOU KNOW?**
>
> • The mud walls of a simple home were reinforced with reeds and rushes, or with stakes plastered with clay. These walls were very insecure, and often became breeding places for serpents and vermin (Amos 5:19).
>
> • The Israelites used their roofs as a place of retreat and meditation (Neh. 8:16; 2Sa. 11:2; Is. 15:3; 22:1; Jer. 48:38).

PLATFORM LIVING

Many of the one-room homes in the ancient world were built with a raised platform in the back half of the house. The family lived on a raised platform, farthest away from the door. The platform served as the bedroom, the dining room, and the pantry. The rest of the house looked like a scene from Dr. Doolittle, with any combination of cattle, donkeys, goats, sheep, chickens, and dogs. This indoor stable had its practicalities, as a family benefited from the warmth of their animals in the winter months. The droppings were also collected and dried to use in the cookfires when wood became scarce. The children of the house had ready playmates, and many children coaxed to share their food and their beds with a pet lamb or a puppy.

THE FLOORS

In the tents of the Bedouin, the floor was the cool sands under the shade of the tents. Mats, mattresses, and cushions could be laid across the floors for sitting and sleeping. In the one-room brick homes of the common folk, the front part of the home was simply stamped-down earth. This was the domain of the animals, so people had to watch their step in the foyer! The back portion of the home was a raised platform made of stone. This is where the family lived, and where the mattresses were brought out at bedtime. By New Testament times, tiles were being laid on many floors, and beautiful mosaic patterns were being created. The homes of the wealthy featured highly polished stone floors, which were cool underfoot in the heat of the day. On these marble floors, beautiful rugs were scattered for comfort and decoration.

A ROOM WITH A VIEW

In ancient houses, a window was nothing more than a hole in the wall. It was generally rectangular, and placed high up on the wall to let in light

and air. Often, it was covered with a lattice, to keep out intruders and animals. In larger homes, the windows opened into the central courtyard and the outside street, allowing cross breezes to stir through the house. Glass was too expensive, so insects buzzed freely in and out unless a cloth was tacked over the window opening. In the winter months when cold rains fell, a heavy woolen cloth was draped over the window to keep out the weather. Mansions were sometimes equipped with large windows that opened onto a balcony in the front of the house. These would overhang the street below, and were used mostly during festivals and other special occasions. Jezebel was probably standing at such an outer window when she was seized and thrown to her death (2Kin. 9:30–33).

DOORS

The doors of ancient houses were not hung on hinges. Instead, the door rotated on a circular shaft, which fit into sockets carved into the top of the doorframe and in the floor of the threshold (1Kin. 26:14; Prov. 26:14). In the villages, the peasants made the doors of their homes very low and a person had to stoop to enter them. This kept out wild beasts and enemies. Some say it was a means of preventing the roving bands of Arabs from riding into the houses. Doors were equipped with a lock and key. These keys were made of wood or metal, and some were quite large. This made them conspicuous to carry around in public (Is. 22:22). Treasurers or other civic officers carried these huge keys as a symbol of their high office.

COURTYARDS

If a family was doing well in life, then they had a courtyard. It was sort of like having a picket fence. The front yard was surrounded by a low wall to keep out stray dogs and strangers. This little enclosure was a sign that the occupants of a house were living above the poverty line. Inside the courtyard would be a small garden, a fig tree, a few chickens, and maybe even a well and cistern. The wealthy in Bible times would have large courtyards, and their entire house would be built to surround it. These elegant courtyards were surrounded by shady trees, paved with a mosaic of tile, and graced by fountains of cool water.

HOMES OF THE WEALTHY

During their captivity under the control of the Persian Empire, the Jews picked up a taste for the finer things in life. The Persians were renowned for their extravagant lifestyles, and the kings spent vast fortunes in creating elaborately decorated palaces for themselves. When the Persian king, Cyrus, sent the Israelites back to their homeland, they were anxious to set up housekeeping for themselves again. The Bible tells us that the Israelites built large and costly houses in Judea (Jer. 22:14; Amos 3:15; Hag. 1:4). These were the homes of the wealthy, who had put their own comfort ahead of their promise to rebuild the Temple. This small segment of society lived in luxury and their homes were furnished with the best that money could buy.

DID YOU KNOW?

- The people used their rooftops for private conferences (1Sa. 9:25). They also went there for private worship (Jer. 19:3; 2Kin. 23:12; Zeph. 1:5; Acts 10:9) and to shout public announcements or bewail the loss of loved ones (Jer. 48:38; Lk. 12:3).

- With neighbors all enjoying their rooftop patios in the cool of the evening, it was easy for news to be shared. When something exciting had happened, the home-owners could literally "shout it from the rooftops."

ONLY THE FINEST BUILDING MATERIALS

The materials for building were abundant in Palestine. It wasn't exactly a trip to the local Home Depot, but well-to-do homeowners could easily obtain stone, brick, and the best timber for ornamental work in their houses. They often used hewn stone (Amos 5:11) and highly polished marble (1Chr. 29:2; Est. 1:6). They also used large quantities of cedar for their wall paneling and ceilings, often with moldings of gold, silver, and ivory (Jer. 22:14; Hag. 1:4). Perhaps their fondness for ivory accounts for the Bible's references to "houses of ivory" and "ivory palaces" (1Kin. 22:39; Ps. 35:8; Amos 3:15).

PALATIAL ESTATES

The greatest luxury of all was to be found in the temples and royal palaces. King Solomon, for example, built his palace using well-cut stone, and he lined his walls with cedar. King Ahab's palace at Samaria boasted beautiful carved ivory inlays and expensive furniture. Herod the Great had two palaces: a summer palace with lovely gardens at Jerusalem, and a winter palace at Jericho.

THE SUMMER COTTAGE

The truly elite of ancient days owned more than one home. The wealthy could build "summer houses" and "winter houses" for their comfort during those seasons (Amos 3:15). Summer houses might be located near the water, to take advantage of the breezes. Winter homes might be built on high ground, to avoid the muddy plains left behind by the winter rains. Summer homes were built partially underground, then paved with marble. This allowed the stone floors underfoot to remain cool, no matter the temperatures outside. These summer houses generally had fountains in the central courtyards, which added the comforts of cool water and fresh air. Every aspect of these homes was designed to bring people refreshment in the torrid heat of summer.

THE FLOORPLANS

Realtors would have trouble enticing a sale by listing ancient homes in the local paper: "Cozy home available. Bedroom platform doubles as the eat-in kitchen. Sunken family room doubles as a stable. One window/no glass, all-wood door, stone threshold, stairs to roof. Estate includes pomegranate tree. Three goats negotiable." Once you crossed the threshold of a typical Old Testament home, the basic floorplan was as simple as they come—one room! By New Testament times, some homes had grown, consisting of a few rooms surrounding a courtyard. The wealthy enjoyed such perks as a second story on their house and a separate stable for their animals.

HEROD IN CAESAREA

Home is a Sea Port

Herod, appointed governor over Judea, was given a present for his loyalty to the Roman Emperor, Augustus. The small Phoenician port city wasn't much, but it was his. Herod made plans to make his city a showplace, and began to build the city that would become Caesarea. He hired engineers and architects to construct a completely artificial harbor. For years, men dropped massive rocks into the sea to slow the waves and create a safe harbor. Once finished, it was the biggest harbor in the ancient world. The two outstretched arms of the piers were set with huge statues, welcoming boats to Herod's great new city. Caesarea rivaled the other major port cities and quickly lured in business. Traders from the Far East, Rome, and Greece sailed into his capital city, bringing their riches with them.

To please the people, an entertainment complex of sorts was built. An amphitheater was constructed, where horse races and sports events would take place. There was also a theater, whose backdrop was the blue harbor waters. Herod's own palace was built on a promontory which jutted out into the sea. His home was set in this conspicuous spot, in plain sight of both the theater and the amphitheater. The people were continually reminded that these wonderful shows were the provision of Herod. He wished to remind his subjects of the gratitude that was due.

Herod also wished to impress Rome by naming his new city, after Caesar. Imitation is the best form of flattery, so he purposely used Roman designs in laying out his city. There were baths and swimming pools, an aqueduct, and theater. Herod even erected

a temple to Caesar. Everything was constructed from white stone, which was quarried in the nearby hills. Sailors coming in to harbor would see the city off in the distance, sparkling like a diamond in the sunlight.

Ringing the Doorbell

In a nice neighborhood in a Bible-time city, the streets were lined with locked doors. Behind each gate and peephole sat a servant, who guarded the wealthy homeowners from pesky visitors. Vacuum cleaner salesmen and Girl Scouts could be politely turned away, while honored guests could be admitted with style. The servant was the household porter, whose responsibility it was to greet guests and take messages. Rhoda was the porter at the door of a home where early Christians had gathered when Peter came knocking (Acts 12:13). Once the porter greeted a guest, he was led into a porch, which was furnished with benches. From there, a short flight of stairs led into the open courtyard.

DID YOU KNOW?

- The Bible may refer to the alliyah when it mentions the "little chamber" of Elisha (2Kin. 4:10), the "summer chamber" of Eglon (Judg. 3:20–23), the "chamber over the gate" (2Sa. 18:33), the "upper chamber" of Ahaz (2Kin. 23:12), and the "inner chamber" where Ben-Hadad hid himself (1Kin. 20:30).

- Some homes in the cities of the Bible were constructed on a slope. Instead of putting in a walk-out basement, builders would fit a stable around back in the hillside under the house.

The Central Court

The courtyard stood at the center of a home. All of the doors and windows in the home opened into this central court. It was designed to admit light and air into the surrounding rooms. The floor was paved with rock or tile, to help shed the rain. Sometimes the home was built around a well, and the courtyard would surround a fountain or cistern (2Sa. 17–18). Crowds would gather in a host's courtyard on festive occasions (Est. 1:5). Jesus probably sat in the central courtyard of a home, teaching, when a group of men lowered a paralytic man into the midst of the crowd to reach him (Lk. 5:19). The early Christian church would gather in these large homes, sitting around the courtyard on mats and chairs provided by the host. A simple stairway of stone or wood led from the court to the rooms above, and to the roof. Larger houses might have more than one set of stairs.

Show Him to the Master's Quarters!

Upon entering a house, a guest would be shown to the master's quarters. The door to this room would face the front gate from across the courtyard. Whether discussing business dealings or welcoming visiting family members, the man of the house would receive his guests in this room. The master's quarters would be furnished handsomely, with couches along the walls and a raised platform at the back. In a smaller home, the raised platform would do double duty as a couch during the day and a bed by night. Guests entering this room would remove their sandals before stepping onto the raised portion of the room.

The Rooms for the Ladies

In the homes of long ago, the rooms in which the women lived were kept separate from those that the men used. In the tents of the Bedouin, the women's quarters were curtained off from the front of the tent, and only the man of the house could cross its threshold. In the palaces of Old Testament times, the women's rooms would be set apart as the king's harem, guarded by eunuchs. In the homes built in New Testament times, the rooms assigned to the wife and daughters were usually upstairs. Again, only the master of the house could enter these apartments. The homeowner bestowed the greatest expense on these rooms, making them beautiful for their wives and family. Because of this, they were sometimes called the "palaces of the house" (1Kin. 16:18; 2Kin. 15:25) or "the house of the women" (Est. 2:3).

The Upper Room

Just up a flight of stairs from the courtyard was the upper room. This was the banquet hall of the home, furnished in elegance. The rooms below were just for everyday use. The upper room was built to overhang the lower part of the building, so that the upper windows opened like balconies to the streets below. The ceilings were high, and the room was spacious, light, and airy. The Last Supper was celebrated in such a room (Mk. 14:15), and Paul was preaching in an upper room when Eutychus fell from the rafters (Acts 20:9–12).

THE BEDROOM

During Bible times, parents did not have the luxury of a separate bedroom. In fact, they did not have the luxury of a bed! In a recess in the wall of a mud-brick home would be stacked several animal skins and some mattresses stuffed with straw or feathers. These could be spread out on the raised platform in the back of the home for bedtime, then re-folded and stored away again during the day. Bedtime preparations were simple. Everybody took off their sandals and their belts, and Mom checked to make sure the lamp was full of oil. That's it. Everyone laid down—Dad and Mom each took an edge, and the children were in the middle. In cool weather, an extra animal skin might be thrown over the top, but in the poorest of homes people only had their own clothing to keep themselves warm.

THE KITCHEN

In the homes of most Bible-time women, the kitchen was not an elaborate affair. In many cases, the cooking was done in the corner of a one-room house or outside in the family's courtyard. A few essentials were included in every woman's kitchen setup: a water jar, an oil jar, a bin for storing grain, a means for grinding grain into flour, and some kind of oven for making bread. There were bowls and spoons, a skin bottle for making butter, and a handful of precious spices.

THE BATHROOM

In the span of time between the Old and New Testaments, homes for the wealthy were being designed with a separate room to be used as a bathroom. These special rooms had tubs set into the floor. What luxury. Seventy years before Christ, one man is even said to have invented a centrally heated bathroom, with a hot water supply.

THE ALLIYAH

The alliyah was a kind of "bonus room" that the Jews sometimes built over the porch or gateway of their house. It was usually just one or two rooms, and it was used for a variety of purposes. Some householders used it for entertainment, some for storage, some as a quiet place to rest and meditate. Jesus probably referred to the alliyah when he spoke of going into the "closet" to pray (Mt. 6:6). The alliyah was much more private than the main roof of the house, where the whole family gathered and the neighbors looked on. This extra room had steps leading directly down to the street, and another flight of stairs connecting it with the central court of the home. This made it a perfect apartment, like the one occupied by Elisha in the Shunammite's house (2Kin. 4:10).

THE FURNISHINGS

A glance around the inside of an ancient home would *have had to be a quick one, because it wouldn't have taken long. The typical homes of Bible men and women were simple, containing only the necessities of life. Even the homes of the wealthy in Palestine would have seemed empty to modern eyes.*

HAVE A SEAT!

There was no such thing as Dad's recliner, Grandma's rocker, and Mother's favorite chair. If anything, there was only the chair. The luxury of a piece of furniture was just that—a luxury. When furnishings were few, many folks found themselves sitting on the ground. Mats and cushions might be provided to make the floor more comfortable. Those who were handy with a knife might whittle away at some sticks and create a low stool on legs. Mary probably had it made, being married to a carpenter (Mt. 13:55). One way that people found to get around the whole furniture dilemma was to create built-in seating. During construction, a family would leave a ledge about a foot tall around the entire edge of a room. Although low, the ledge provided a place to sit and rest.

DINING ROOM TABLE

As with everything else in the ancient home, dining room tables progressed from the most basic form to something more elaborate as time passed and wealth increased. In "the olden days" when people lived in nomadic tents, the only table to speak of was a mat on the floor. Made

Peter in Galilee
Home is a Fishing Village

Peter's family had been in the fishing business since anyone could remember. The house he had grown up in was spacious enough for a big family, with little tiles pressed into the floor to keep the dirt out. He and his brother had slept all summer in a lean-to they had built up on the roof. Peter and Andrew still spent a lot of time together. He and his brother put in long hours on the boats, fishing through the night hours, working the nets under the stars. Although he and his wife kept a house of their own in Capernaum, Peter still spent most of his time in the outdoors. He had been casting lines and mending nets since his fingers could manage the knots his father taught him to tie. He had gained strength enough to throw a large net by the time he passed his bar mitzvah, giving it that flick of the wrist that sent it spinning out over the water. Their village was a busy little place, centered around two things—the synagogue and the Sea of Galilee. He was familiar with the waves, and could manage the sail. He knew just how he liked the anchor line coiled, and was fussy about his nets. He and Andrew often spent their hours with the Zebedee boys, James and John. Their father had the largest fishing operation in town, with servants assisting with the work. John had told them that their dried fish were actually sold in the Temple at Jerusalem, right near the Fish Gate. Peter's aspirations did not run into such a grand scale. Looking about him at the blue-green water, the overhanging trees, the waving flowers on the hillsides, he was content. Andrew was more prone to wander, going to listen to teachers and preachers—like John the Baptizer near the Jordan. He was a fisherman, and that's all he knew. His father had fished, as had his father before him. At that moment, he could not imagine anything else he would rather do.

from an animal skin or leather, it was laid out on the floor for mealtimes, then the "table" could be hung from the tent poles once the meal was finished. As time passed and homes got bigger, so did the dining room table. Elaborate feasts are described in the Old Testament, where the tables were laid out with gold and silver serving dishes (Est. 1:6–7). At these big bashes, the tables were much more table-ish—wide, sturdy, elevated. However, they were still fairly low to the ground. Around these tables would be set an array of pillows or lounge chairs, so that the guests could recline while enjoying a slow-paced meal. The disciples are described as reclining at the Last Supper (Jn. 13:23).

BED

The women of Bible times did not look forward every year to shopping the January white sales at the local department stores. Their beds and bedding were spare, often consisting of a mat, which was brought out of its cubby-hole at the end of the day and spread out on the floor. Proper beds were not unheard of, though. Og, King of Bashan, boasted a bedstead that was thirteen and a half feet long (Deut. 3:11)—now that's king size! By New Testament times, beds on frames had become more popular and commonplace.

THE BRAZIER

Heating in the home was accomplished by building a fire. During the wet winter months, the fire was kept lit as long as there was fuel for it. The task of gathering the fuel was given to children. Sticks and dried grass (Mt. 6:30) as well as thorn bushes (Is. 10:17) were common enough. If a family had a few animals under its roof, like sheep or goats, then their droppings had been carefully collected and dried for the purpose of fire-building. One of the most important fuels was the wood of the white broom plant. Its embers stay hot for a long time and even the seemingly cold ashes can be easily fanned into a blaze. The fire could be made in the open, in a shallow hole dug in the floor, or else in a brazier (Jer. 36:22–23). There were no chimneys in the Jewish homes, so while these fires warmed the home and its family, they created a choking haze of smoke as well.

CHARCOAL FIRES

Charcoal is familiar to those who spend their summers grilling on the patio. It has a distinctive smell, and the smoke from a charcoal fire lends its aromatic flavor to meat and vegetables on the grill. Most of the Jews gathered stubble and sticks or dried animal dung for their fires. Charcoal burned hotter and cleaner than any of these, and only the wealthy could boast of a fire that was fueled by charcoal. Only twice in the Bible is charcoal mentioned. The first was when Peter crouched at a fire in the courtyard and denied Jesus three times (Jn. 18:18). The second occurrence was on the shores of Galilee, when Jesus kindled a fire and prepared a meal for his disciples (Jn. 21:9). The sight and smell of that charcoal fire must have cut Peter to the quick.

LAMPSTANDS

No room was complete without a lampstand. Whether rich or poor, light was provided in a home. It was the most important item in any household. Early on, an oil lamp was just a little clay saucer of olive oil with a pinched area on the lip to hold the wick in place. These lamps would stay lit for two or three hours before needing to be refilled. Later, closed containers were developed with two holes—one for the wick and one in which to refill the oil supply. These lamps were safer and more efficient. Later, larger glazed and decorated lamps were made with handles and multiple wicks to provide additional light. In the homes of the wealthy, lamps could be made from metal, and fashioned into elaborate candelabras. The higher the lamp, the better the light, so a lampstand was a

DID YOU KNOW?

- Archeologists discovered an extensive complex of stables, capable of housing as many as four hundred eighty horses, at Megiddo. They date from the time of King Ahab.

- Furniture was not elaborate. The rich Shunammite woman furnished the room of Elisha with only a bed (perhaps merely a mattress), a table, a stool, and a candlestick (2Kin. 4:10–13).

necessity. Lamps were sometimes perched on a projection from the wall or hung from the ceiling. The simplest lampstands were made from tree-branches pushed into the earthen floor. If nothing else was available, the lamp was put on an upturned bowl or even on the floor.

NIGHTLIGHTS

Nobody in Palestine would dream of sleeping without a nightlight! Even in the humblest of homes, a lamp was kept burning throughout the night. The light indicated to anyone passing by that there were sleepers present. To sleep without the comforting glow of an oil lamp was a sign of utter poverty. It was so important to keep this lamp burning, that even the poorest of families would spend their money buying lamp oil before considering their need for food. A dark house was a deserted house. So when Job predicts the ruin of wicked people, he says "the lamp is dark in his tent" (Job 18:5–6). Isaiah describes a Messiah who will trim the wick and replenish the oil in a lamp that is guttering and on the verge of going out. This was a comforting picture of God's care for his struggling people. Proverbs praises a prudent wife by saying "her lamp does not go out at night" (Prov. 31:18).

> ### DID YOU KNOW?
>
> • When the oil in a lamp began to run low, the wick would smolder. This meant that the lamp would need to be refilled from a container or it would go out (Mt. 25:8).
>
> • The lamp symbolized a family's existence and its dignity (Job 21:17; Jer. 25:10).

BASKETS

Baskets in today's households are usually decorative, but in Bible times they were practical, versatile, and completely essential. Most of the biblical baskets we see were for humble purposes, like carrying figs (2Kin. 10:17) or serving as a kneading bowl (Deut. 28:5, 17). Baskets were also woven by men who sought to build a better bird trap (Jer. 5:27; Amos 8:1). The baker who came to Joseph with troublesome dreams spoke of carrying baskets of bread upon his head (Gen. 40:16). However, some baskets have achieved startling notoriety. Moses' little boat of bulrushes was woven from papyrus by his mother's own hands (Ex. 2:3), and Paul was forced to make his escape from enemies by going over the wall in a basket (Acts 9:25).

BOTTLES

The nomadic Israelites kept their milk, wine, and water in bottles. A plastic two-liter bottle or a glass pop bottle might be the images that come to mind, but this is hardly the sort they used; although theirs did have an equally distinctive shape. Their bottles were made from animal skins, and looked rather like headless goats. These were hung up in tents where they were constantly exposed to the smoke from cook fires. After long exposure to the smoke, they became black, hard, and shriveled. Psalm 119:83 declares, "for I have become like a wineskin in smoke." Jesus also spoke of the uselessness of trying to mend old wineskins and filling them with new wine again, for "the new wine will burst the wineskins and be spilled" (Lk. 5:37–39). Industrious housewives used these skin bottles as butter churns as well. A bottle was suspended by ropes from a tripod, filled with milk, then pushed like a small swing.

STORING AWAY THE FOOD

Every house had storage bins made from either clay or stone. These were used for keeping grain, meal, and flour (1Kin. 18:33). Sometimes these storage containers were buried into the floor of the house, where the food stayed fresher. The surrounding earth helped to keep the contents cool. A well-stocked pantry might also include smaller jars containing dried figs or

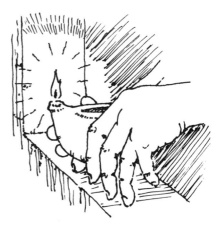

ELISHA IN SHUNEM
Home is a Spare Room

The life of an itinerant prophet was not easy. Elisha hardly sat still long enough to call a place home. He had no wife to make a little haven for him, and traveled many miles in a year. One day he was invited by a wealthy elderly woman and her husband to stay in their home. "Please, come back and stay with us whenever you're in the area," they invited. And so Elisha did. It was good to know that he was always welcome there. In fact, he stopped by whenever he had a chance. Soon, it occurred to the Shunammite woman that she and her husband could do a bit more for this man of God. One evening, when they were ready to retire, she nudged her husband and said, "Wouldn't it be nice if we could build Elisha a room of his own, up on the rooftop?" He would have his own little apartment, and all the peace and quiet that he required. They quickly set to work, hoping to finish before Elisha made his way through town again. When it was finished, she placed a bed, a table, a chair, and a lamp within. This ancient room was luxurious by the day's standards. When Elisha and his servant came through town again, he was pleased by the gift. He offered to put a good word in for her with the king, but she declined. She was well cared for. Sitting at the table in his new room, he mused aloud, "What can we do to thank them?" Elisha asked his servant what he thought. The servant sat thoughtfully, then stated the obvious. "They have no children, sir." Calling the kindhearted woman into the room that she had made for him, Elisha told her that for her gift of love, she and her husband would have a baby boy, in the coming year. "Please, don't tease!" She trembled at the chance to hold her own babe, but her husband was very old. A year later she held her infant son in her arms (2Kin. 4:8-17)!

raisins. If the family lived near the water, there would also be dried fish, or fish packed in salt. Olives were a staple of the Palestinian diet, and special jars were made for storing olive oil. These jars were glazed to prevent the oil from oozing out of them. By New Testament times, glass bottles were being made, but they were very expensive. Large earthenware pots were used for carrying water from the local well and storing it in the home. A filled waterpot might weigh as much as fifty pounds.

CHAPTER EIGHT

THEIR FOOD

Food was not just a matter of survival in Bible times. For the nomads especially, **it was an opportunity to show hospitality.** An old proverb from the area says that the measure of a guest's regard for his host is seen in the amount of food that he eats. Literally, "the food equals the affection." So, it was customary for the host to serve the best that he had, in generous portions.

BREAD

Bread was the all-important staple food of the ancient Near East. Bread was so basic a food that it became synonymous with life itself. "Breaking bread" was the equivalent phrase for "having a meal."

WHEAT

Wheat was a primary grain crop in portions of Palestine, but it was touchy in the heat. The best areas for wheat production were in the coastal plains and near the Jordan valley, where water was more plentiful. Wheat was the staple of the Hebrew diet, for wheat flour was the main ingredient in the bread they ate every day. When the children of Israel were wandering in the wilderness, Moses spoke to them of God's Promised Land, where there would be fields of wheat (Deut. 8:8).

BARLEY

Barley was a staple crop in Palestine because it wasn't as fussy as wheat or oats. Barley was hardier, and could be grown on poorer soil than wheat. It also had a shorter growing season, but it was less valued than wheat (Ps. 81:16). Its durability in the summer heat made it a dependable crop. The Hebrews harvested abundant barley crops, because it was too warm for oats or rye so near the desert. Naomi and Ruth arrived in Bethlehem during the barley harvest, so that is what Ruth was gleaning in the fields of Boaz. Barley was considered to be the food of the poor. The bread made from it was coarse and dark in color (Judg. 7:13). Most people favored the lighter loaves made from wheat. Jesus didn't turn up his nose at dark bread though, for he used barley loaves to feed the five thousand (Jn. 6:9–11). Barley was even used regularly in offerings at the Temple (Num. 5:15). But, for the most part, the barley crops were planted as animal feed (1Kin. 4:28).

BAKING BREAD

The women of Bible times baked bread every day. In fact, most women started the whole process from scratch every day, beginning with the grinding of the grain. Usually, the dough was made from wheat or barley flour. The baker added water, seasoned with salt, then dropped in some leavening. The leaven was a little ball of fermented dough that had been saved back from yesterday's batch of bread. After kneading the dough and allowing it to rise, it was formed into small disks for baking.

UNLEAVENED BREAD

Unleavened bread was made from the same ingredients as leavened bread—flour, oil, and water—but lacked the yeasty stuff to make it rise. It was a sort of quick bread, which could be whipped up and baked without waiting for the dough to rise. Unleavened bread was kneaded in a bowl, then rolled into disks and pricked all over with a sharp tool. Once it was baked, the bread was flat and could be rolled up around other foods. It was also folded and used as a scoop in the place of forks and spoons. When the children of Israel made their way out of captivity and into the wilderness, the women hastily packed up their bread bowls. They had been observing the first Passover, and there hadn't been a speck of yeast in any household for a whole week. When it was time to leave, there was no time to prepare a fresh batch of leavening (Ex. 12:39). So they ate unleavened bread during their first days of freedom.

DID YOU KNOW?

- Rice was available in Israel during New Testament times, and enough farmers planted the stuff that it was exported to other countries as a cash crop.

- For most of the year, cooking was done outside, but in the winter an indoor oven was used.

- When the seven-year famine hit, there was still bread in Egypt, meaning that they had grain as well as all kinds of other stored foodstuffs to eat (Gen. 41:54).

BREAD OVENS

The simplest method for baking bread was to scoop out a hole in the ground, make a fire in it, then remove the ash from this hot pit. The bread dough was then pressed onto the sides of the hole, where they would cook

PASSOVER

At Mark's House

Mark walked towards the town square, shoulders hunched. He hoped nobody would see him fetching water for his mother. She was in a hurry making preparations for the evening meal, and she needed the water. Since all the servants were busy in other areas of the house, he had been given the task. This was women's work! Thankfully, all was quiet at the well.

Just then, a small group of men came into view, making their way towards the well. Mark kept his eyes down, pulled the last of his water up from the well and hurried towards home. As he rounded the corner of his street, he glanced over his shoulder. The men who had come to the well seemed to be headed in the same direction. Mark was suspicious. They were coming after him with intent eyes. They were following him (Mk. 14:13)! Ducking through the gateway of his family's courtyard and into the kitchen, he dropped the water jar onto the counter. The kitchen smelled of sweet spices, charoseth—a mixture of apples, raisins, and cinnamon, and wine for the Passover supper that night. Then came the knock at the door. The men were there, and they politely stated "The Teacher says, 'Where is the guest room in which I may eat the Passover with my disciples.'" Without batting an eye, the men were shown to the upper room. "You must tell your Master that he is welcome here tonight. We will make everything ready for him."

Tables, low chairs, and cushions were brought into the upper room. Wine was poured and an extra chair was left for Elijah, as tradition dictated. Soon it was dusk, and time to serve the meal. Mark helped his mother and the others carry the meal to the

upper room. His mother proudly placed the folded napkin containing unleavened bread in the center of the table. The bitter greens, roasted eggs, a bowl of salt water, and the sweet, charoseth found their way onto the table. With the arrival of Jesus and his disciples, Mark's family experienced the most memorable Passover ever.

through. Another method involved placing stones in the fire. When they were quite hot, the stones were removed from the flames and set on the hearth. Then the disks of rolled dough were placed on them. Some women used a large earthenware bowl, which they placed upside down over a fire. The outside of the bowl became hot as a griddle, and bread baked up quickly on its surface. In wealthy homes, true ovens made of pottery were installed. These were dome-shaped, with an opening at the top to let smoke escape. A fire was lit inside, and the baker would stick dough to the walls inside of the dome near the top. During New Testament times, ovens were invented that were divided, so that a cooking area was self-contained and kept separate from the fire.

FUEL FOR THE FIRE

Bread was often cooked over a fire made from animal dung, which did little to enhance the bread's flavor. During the summer months, sticks and stubble were gathered and burned in the family fire, but families had to plan ahead. The droppings of animals were collected and dried throughout the summer months. Then, when the winter rains fell and not a dry twig was to be found outdoors, the dung was burned. Despite the smell, the dung gave off a steady supply of heat. Jeremiah protested when God asked him to cook his bread over human dung. Doing so would have been a defilement for the prophet (Eze. 4:15). God relented, and allowed him to continue using animal dung instead.

BREAD OF HEAVEN

There had been nothing like manna before, and there has been nothing like it since (Deut. 8:3). This was the bread of heaven (Ps. 78:24) that came down every morning with the dew (Num. 11:9). The children of Israel woke up one day and there it was. "What is it?" they asked each other. That's "manna" in Hebrew, and the name kind of stuck (Ex. 16:31). The stuff was hard to describe. The color was like that of bdellium (Num. 11:7). The taste was like wafers made with honey (Ex. 16:31), or like coriander seed (Num. 11:7). They were to gather the manna in the morning, before the sun got too hot. Every day the Israelites were to gather enough to last their family the day with no leftovers. Those who tried to hoard the manna found they had a pot of worms by morning (Ex. 16:20). This quickly deterred housewives from trying to squirrel away a little extra. The only exception was on the day before the Sabbath, when the women were to gather two day's worth of food. For some reason, that manna stayed fresh throughout the next day (Ex. 16:24). Miraculous though this bread of heaven was, the Israelites grew sick of it and complained over the lack of variety in their diet (Num. 11:6).

PARCHED GRAIN

It was customary in Palestine to roast wheat that was nearly ripe. When the heads of grain were fully developed, they were gathered early, stalks and all. Holding a bunch of the wheat at the base, the wheat heads were held over a fire—kind of like toasting marshmallows. Once the sheaths had blackened, the kernels of wheat were toasted. This was the "parched grain" that Boaz offered to Ruth (Ruth 2:14). The husks of the blackened wheat heads were rubbed between the hands to get rid of the chaff, and the parched grain was ready to eat. Another simple way to toast the wheat was to place it in an iron pan over a fire and stir the grains constantly until they had browned evenly. It was something of a delicacy,

DID YOU KNOW?

- Bread was always pulled apart with the hands, and not cut with a knife. This is where the phrase "to break bread" comes from in reference to the communion service (Acts 20:7).

- Melchizedek, the king of Salem, brought out bread and wine to welcome Abraham and his caravan to his kingdom (Gen. 14:18).

and is sold even today in the markets of Palestine. Parched grain was eaten in place of bread sometimes (Lev. 23:14; Josh. 5:11; Ruth 2:14), and it was perfect trail mix for armies on the move (1Sa. 17:17).

THE SHOWBREAD

Once a week, bread was baked in the Temple. This was the showbread, which was placed hot from the oven on a special table in the Holy Place of the Temple. The table was spread with a beautiful blue cloth (Num. 4:7). Once, when David and his men arrived in Nob, they were hungry enough to eat a horse. Unfortunately, there was nothing available for them to eat but the week-old showbread that had just been removed from the sanctuary (1Sa. 21:6). The priest allowed the men to take it to eat, and David and his men ate it with no condemnation (Mk. 2:26).

FRUITS

Fruits were an important food in Bible times. They were seasonal additions to an otherwise ordinary menu. What couldn't be eaten was usually dehydrated and stored away for use during the long winter months ahead.

GRAPES AND RAISINS

The land of Palestine provided a perfect climate for growing grapes. When the children of Israel prepared to enter the Promised Land, the spies brought back grapes that were the size of plums (Num. 13:23). The vines were planted throughout the hillsides, and the walls and watchtowers that surrounded the vineyards were a familiar sight in Judah (Is. 5:2). Grapes were eaten fresh at harvest time, though most ended up in the wine presses. Bunches of grapes were also set out to dry in the sun. This created raisins, which were kept in clusters (1Sa. 25:18) or pressed into cakes. Raisins were easy to transport, so Abigail sent one hundred clusters of raisins to David's army (1Sa. 25:18). They were also fit for royal festivities. When David was made King of Israel, one of the foods brought in for the feasting was "cakes of raisins" (1Chr. 12:40)!

GRAPE GLEANING

Not everybody had a vineyard, and many people were too poor to buy fresh grapes in the market. However, God made provision for the poor in every community. At the time of the harvest, the grape pickers were to go through the vineyards, harvesting the crop. However, they were not allowed to go back over the vines that they had already picked (Lev. 19:10). That meant that any missed fruit, as well as fruit that hadn't quite been ripe were left hanging in the vineyard. The poor were then allowed to search through the orchard and take whatever remained. These were the grape gleaners. The fruit they took was dried and stashed away, and would help to see them through the winter days ahead.

FIGS

Fig trees were abundant in the land of Canaan. Every person in the congregation of Israel dreamed of the day when they could settle in the Promised Land, where every home would have its fig tree and its vine (1Kin. 4:25). The coarse, large-lobed leaves of the fig tree were full-size by summertime, when the homeowner needed shade from the hot summer sun. Nathaniel was found resting under a fig tree (Jn. 1:48–50). Figs were a soft-fleshed fruit. They were extremely perishable, so whatever wasn't eaten in the first few

DID YOU KNOW?

- Adam and Eve used leaves from a fig tree to make coverings for themselves once they realized that they were naked (Gen. 3:7).

- Sometimes dried figs were mixed to create a poultice for medicinal purposes. Isaiah applied a fig poultice to King Hezekiah's boil (2Kin. 20:7; Is. 38:21).

days after harvest had to be dried. The first ripe fig of the season was a mouth-watering treat. "It will be greedily snapped up, as an early fig is hungrily picked and eaten" (Is. 28:4, NLT). Many Bible cities borrowed their names from the fig tree. The city of Bethphage's name means "house of the unripe fig" (Mt. 21:1). Bethany is "house of figs" (Mt. 26:6), Almon-Diblathaaim means "Almon of dried figs" (Num. 33:46), and Taanath Shiloh means "the fig of Shiloh" (Josh. 16:6).

DRIED FIGS

Dried figs were a wonderful addition to the meager winter diet. They were also invaluable to a city under siege. Large fortified cities would squirrel away huge amounts of dried fruit, just in case of an attack. The best figs from the harvest were dried individually. Second-best fruits were strung together on strings to dry in long festoons. The humblest of figs were simply pressed together into large cakes. These cakes of fig were kept on hand in most pantries. Abigail had enough of them in her larder to send two hundred cakes of figs to David and his army (1Sa. 25:18).

POMEGRANATES

The Jews found beauty in the pomegranates, for pomegranate fruits and blossoms were used to adorn the temple and the garments of the High Priest (Ex. 28:33; 1Kin. 7:18). The Song of Songs also speaks of orchards of the trees, filled with their bright red blossoms (Song 4:13; 6:11). Pomegranates are about the size of an orange, and they have a thin, leathery skin that ranges from bright red to a red-blushed yellow. Once cut open, pomegranates reveal a heart filled with hundreds of glistening rubies. These are the seeds, each surrounded by a translucent, brilliant red pulp. The seeds are edible, and have a sparkling, sweet-tart flavor.

CITRUS FRUITS

Nothing helps beat the heat like a tall, cool glass of lemonade. Something about the tart flavor and fresh smell of a lemon is just plain refreshing! Now young Jesus was definitely not setting up a lemonade stand on his corner every summer. Citrus fruits were just becoming available in New Testament times. The slopes leading onto the coastal plain were becoming lined with young orange, lemon, and lime trees. They were a new-fangled luxury for the Jews. However, in

Old Testament times, citrus fruit was not yet being cultivated. What the Israelites did have, however, was the citron. The citron has less actual fruit and less juice than an orange or lemon. The peeling can be over an inch thick, leaving little room for the tart fruit at its center. The Jews used the citron as part of their harvest festival (Lev. 23:40; Neh. 8:14–15). In fact, when the Jews were dispersed after the destruction of the Temple, they took little baby citron trees with them to ensure a supply of fruit for their festivals in the future.

OLIVES

Olives were the most important crop in all of Israel. The tree itself looks like an apple tree, and when it is in bloom, the clusters of flowers are reminiscent of lilacs. The olives look rather like plums hanging on the tree. They are green first, and then turn a pale color before changing to black when they are fully ripened. Olives were eaten fresh during the harvest in October. Some were pickled in salt water. However, the lion's share was pressed for their precious oil.

DID YOU KNOW?

• Men who had taken the Nazarite vow could not eat or drink anything that was "produced by the grapevine, from seed to skin"—that included grapes, grape juice, wine, raisins, and the molasses-like sweetener that was made by boiling down grape juice (Num. 6:3–4).

OLIVE OIL

The Israelites used olive oil for absolutely everything—including cooking. Green olives yielded the oil. They were gathered in baskets and thrown into pits. The best olive oil was actually stomped or beaten from the green fruit (Ex. 27:20; Mic. 6:15). This first oil was clearer and lighter than later pressings. Lower grades of oil were produced by crushing the olives, pits and all, with big stones. These presses were designed so that one large stone was turned on top of another stone. There was a large olive press located on the Mount of Olives in Jerusalem, for Gethsemane (Mt. 26:36) means "Garden of the Olive Press." The resulting oil was cloudier, with a stronger flavor. It was used as lamp oil by the Israelites.

DATES

Dates are not mentioned by name in the Bible, but they were certainly grown. The date palm was a bountiful plant, providing anywhere from two hundred to one thousand dates each year. A cluster of dates weighs about twenty-five pounds, so a single tree could yield six hundred pounds of fruit each year. Dates were eaten fresh or dried. Date juice was sweet and thick, and it could be boiled down to create date honey. They were also used in a special sauce called "charoseth," made from dates, figs, raisins, and vinegar, in which everyone dipped their bread at the Passover meal.

VEGETABLES

Vegetables were not a dreaded part of the supper hour for children. Indeed, for many children they were the only food available! After a long winter of eating dried bean soups, the coming of spring and summer brought a welcome variety of fresh produce to the table.

EAT YOUR BEANS

The beans mentioned in the Bible were not your usual snap bean or yellow wax variety that grow on compact little bushes in neat garden rows. The Bible bean was a feisty climber that grew to be three feet high. The beans were left on the plants to dry, and the pods yielded large, coarse seeds. These dried beans were often crushed and mixed with other grains to make coarse bread. Though not particularly appetizing, they were good roughage. Generally speaking, these beans were only eaten by poor people. Ezekiel was told to use beans in his bread recipe (Eze. 4:9). Fava beans were probably grown. These bright green

DID YOU KNOW?

• The children of Israel, wandering in the wilderness, longed for the melons that they had grown in their gardens in Egypt (Num. 11:5).

• Peas were grown in the gardens of Palestine during Bible times, and they were dried and stored in jars for winter use.

beans were shelled like lima beans and eaten fresh or dried for storage. Garbanzo beans were found in most gardens in Palestine during Bible times as well. This is the main ingredient in hummus, a seasoned paste made from the mashed beans. Garbanzos were often toasted over a fire to make a crunchy snack.

CUCUMBERS

Cool, fresh cucumbers fill the dreams of the avid gardener, and the prospect of the first few cukes of the summer can make the mouth water. The Israelites' minds were fixed on cucumbers all the while they gathered the manna in the wilderness. They missed the fresh vegetables of spring and summer. There were two varieties of cucumbers that were grown. One was long, dark and slender. The other was smaller, whitish, and smooth-skinned. The Hebrews used to build towers in their large gardens. These were like lifeguard towers with a shaded hut on top, and a guard sat there during the harvest time to make sure that no thieves were helping themselves to the ripening vegetables. At the end of the harvest, they stood empty. In Is. 1:8 it says that Zion was abandoned "as a hut in a garden of cucumbers."

GARLIC AND ONIONS

These two vegetables grew very well in the hot climates of Palestine. They were used to flavor vegetable stews and savory meat dishes. Even more prominently, garlic and onions were staples of the Egyptian kitchen. While the family of Jacob lived in Egypt, they became very familiar with the regional cooking of that area. In fact, a typical breakfast in Egypt consisted of mashed fava beans

with garlic, hard-boiled eggs, and a side of pickles and onions. These were the very foods the Israelites missed most after they left there (Num. 11:5)!

POTTAGE

While vegetables were in season, they were eaten every evening for supper. Beans, lentils, and peas were dried and stored in earthenware jars. The most common way of serving the veggies was in a vegetable stew, or pottage. In 2 Kings 4:38–41, we find some men gathering wild gourds to make a stew. Most famous is the pottage for which Esau traded his birthright. Jacob must have learned a thing or two about the culinary arts from hanging around the tents with his mom. His stew was made from lentils, seasoned with olive oil and garlic. Lentils were similar to garden peas, and in Palestine the red ones are favored. Jacob's thick red soup was enough to make Esau's stomach rumble!

SALAD GREENS

Many different fresh greens were gathered and added to the soup pot or the salad bowl in ancient times. Turnip and beet greens, lettuces, endive, parsley, watercress, chicory, sorrel, and dandelion were all seasonal favorites. Dressed with a little olive oil and garlic, they were a wonderful change from the dried foods eaten all winter long. Many of these greens were combined with the eye-watering horseradish to make the bitter herb dish called for at the Passover table (Ex. 12:8).

MEATS

Most ancient people ate meat sparingly. Beans and fresh veggies comprised most everyday meals, but when company was coming or there was something to really celebrate, it was time to kill the fatted calf!

BOILED DINNER

For the most part, meat for mealtimes was either boiled or stewed with vegetables. Even the meat that was brought to the Temple for the priests and Levites to eat was boiled in a large pot. Each priest would come to the pot and fish out a chunk of meat with his fork (1Sa. 2:13–14). That was his family's portion for the day. The main exception to this rule was at Passover, when a lamb was roasted over the fire (Ex. 12:8–9). This preparation was so favored by some young priests that they were willing to disobey God in order to get it. Eli's sons would corner the priest in charge of boiling the meat and snag some of it raw (1Sa. 2:15). That way they could grill it up themselves.

MUTTON

Ordinary folks did eat mutton, but usually only for special occasions. Lamb was plentiful in the spring, and roasted lamb was the annual dish of the Passover festival (Ex. 12:8). However, there were some perks to letting the animals reach maturity. The variety of sheep that was kept in ancient times was the broad-tailed sheep. This animal's tail was pure fat and kept on growing as the sheep aged. Some shepherds constructed little wheeled carts for the sheep that helped them carry their own tails! The fat from a single tail could weigh as much as fifteen pounds. This was considered to be the best part of the sheep and a real delicacy. It didn't seem to matter to folks that God had made claim on all fat (Lev. 3:16).

DID YOU KNOW?

• Lamb was a part of the Passover meal, and would have been included in Jesus' Last Supper.

• The pure fat from an animal was sacrificed to God, since it was considered the richest or best part (Lev. 3:16).

KID

A young goat was commonly dressed for mealtimes. There were plenty of kids in the spring, and even the poor could afford to bring one or two to the dinner table during the year. A kid was also used in sacrificial offerings (Ex. 12:3; Num. 15:11). The prodigal son's big brother was incensed when he heard that his father was brining on the fatted calf to welcome the wanderer home. He whines to his dad, "All these years I have worked

SARAH

Feeds the Angels

Among the scattered tents of the nomads, hospitality was a duty that was taken seriously. Every home stood prepared to welcome in guests on short notice. Sarah's home was no different. Just that morning she had checked her storage jars in the women's section of the tent. She had gone through her appetizer checklist—dried figs, pumpkin seeds, raisin clusters, parched grain, locusts, date cakes, and goat cheese. She was ready for anything. Nomadic wives prided themselves on being good cooks, and at ninety years of age, Sarah's experienced hands had turned out many a tasty dish.

During the hottest part of the day, Abraham walked out to greet some men and invite them in to rest. "…I will get some bread for you so you can regain your strength. Then you may continue your journey" (Gen. 18:5). But a nomad always brought out the best he could afford, and Abraham was a wealthy sheikh. He walked briskly through the camp, giving the various orders that would set the tents into a flurry of activity. He poked his head into Sarah's quarters to let her know that she should start the bread. She had seen the guests take seats under the shade of the terebinth trees, so she knew that they would be staying. Sarah had already assembled most of the appetizers for the meal that would be prepared, and a servant had been dispatched with towels and water so that the travelers could wash the dust from their feet. Abraham's next stop was out in the folds, where a fatted calf was selected and handed over to another servant to dress for dinner. Some of the meat was skewered and set over the flames to roast. As the sizzle and the smell of the meat filled the encampment, Sarah brought out a large bowl, filled with soft loaves of pita bread, still warm

from the fire. With butter and milk, the meal was complete. Sarah watched from behind the curtains of the women's quarters as the men ate. Abraham served them, making sure that they had plenty to eat. Unknown to Sarah, the meal she had organized was food for the angels, and their visit would change her life forever.

hard for you…and in all that time you never gave me even one young goat for a feast with my friends" (Lk. 15:29). The meat prepared from a young goat must have been similar in taste to that of venison. Rachel was able to fool her husband into thinking that the spicy meal she made for Jacob to bring to him was wild game, fresh from the hills (Gen. 27:9).

THE FATTED CALF

There were no butcher shops in ancient times, where a family could go in and order a nice roast or a leg of lamb. If meat was to be eaten at a meal, the family had to do their own butchering. This is why ancient people saved beef for special celebrations. There had to be enough people on one's guest list to warrant bringing on the fatted calf, let alone a full-grown steer. Since there were no refrigerators or freezers, the host wanted to be sure that all the meat was polished off in one evening, so that no leftovers went to waste. The calf was handy, for it was tender and yielded a smaller quantity of meat (Gen. 18:7; 1Sa. 28:24; Amos 6:4). The joyful father called for his servants to kill the fatted calf to help celebrate the return of his prodigal son (Lk. 15:25-32).

FISH

Fish were an acceptable food for the Jewish people so long as there were varieties that sported both fins and scales. While the children of Israel

were in Egypt, they had access to an abundant supply of fish. They were quite easy to catch after the Nile River had been flooding, for the receding water trapped the fish in shallow pools. Once they had left Egypt and were wandering in the desert, they thought back with longing to the meals of delicate meat they had enjoyed (Num. 11:5). Since the sea was far off and the Jews didn't spend much time on the waves, most fish was imported from seafaring nations (Neh. 13:6). This fish had been sun-dried, pickled, or salted. Isaiah 19:8 and Habakkuk 1:15–17 make reference to various types of fishing gear.

FISHING IN GALILEE

In Jesus' time, fish was part of everyday meals along the coast of Galilee. There were twenty-three varieties of fish in the lake. Fishing villages dotted the coastline, and whole families made the fishing business their business (Mt. 4:21). Jesus' first disciples were fishermen who worked on that freshwater lake (Mk. 1:16). Fish were mentioned throughout the Gospels, from the feeding of the five thousand (Mt. 14:19) to the fish with the coin in its mouth (Mt. 17:27). Fish were so abundant in the Sea of Galilee that nets were often weighed down with catches of six hundred pounds. When Jesus called out to the disciples in their boat to throw their nets out over the other side of their boat, they pulled in one hundred fifty three fish (Jn. 21:11). The boat was swamped with the weight of them.

> ### DID YOU KNOW?
>
> • The Romans introduced chickens to Palestine. A rooster played a central role in the story of Peter's denials of Jesus. (Mt. 26:74–75).
>
> • Jesus ate fish at least once after his Resurrection (Lk. 24: 42–43), and perhaps again (Jn. 21: 9–13).

MEAT OFFERED TO IDOLS

In the large cities of New Testament days, there was always a temple or two in town dedicated to the worship of some idol. Just as in the Temple at Jerusalem, sacrifices were brought. Often enough, the idolatrous temples had more animals brought in than the priests could consume. Being enterprising folks, the priests and priestesses went into business. They opened up butcher shops near the temple grounds. When animals were brought to the false gods by worshipers, they were dedicated to the idol, sacrificed, then hustled down the road for sale. Since everybody shopped in these meat markets, new Christians were suddenly confronted with a moral dilemma! Was it okay to eat meat if it had been previously offered in a pagan temple (1 Cor. 8:1)? Could they continue shopping in town, or should they boycott?

POULTRY

The Levitical code allowed the Jews to eat poultry, but they didn't get to cut their teeth on chicken. Early on, people set snares for smaller birds, like quail (Num. 11:31–32) and partridge (1Sa. 26:20). There were a few birds running about in people's barnyards, like ducks and geese (1Kin. 4:23). King Solomon kept peacocks in his gardens, having imported them from exotic ports of call (1Kin. 10:22). One of the most famous poultry feasts occurred in the middle of nowhere. After ages of eating nothing but manna, the children of Israel began to complain. "We want meat!" they griped (Num. 11:18). God looked down on them and gave them just what they asked for, and then some. Flocks of quail were blown in their direction, and when the exhausted birds dropped around the camp, folks were ecstatic. The quail were so thick that they were piled nearly three feet deep, and it took three days for the Israelites to gather all they could. The smell of roasting meat filled the camp that night. However, there was a sur-

> ### DID YOU KNOW?
>
> • Jesus used the mother hen as a metaphor to illustrate his protective feelings toward Jerusalem (Mt. 23:27).
>
> • Sheep and calves were usually slaughtered for the table only when the household was entertaining guests (2Sa. 12:4).

plus. They laid some of the birds in the sun to dry—quail jerky (Num. 11:32). They ate quail for a whole month, "until it comes out of your nostrils" (Num. 11:20). Just as God had said, they couldn't stand the sight of it!

LOCUSTS

Odd as it sounds, it was perfectly all right under Jewish food laws to eat locusts (Lev. 11:22). Yep, those hopping, long-legged, crunch-when-you-step-on-them bugs! The Bible says that John the Baptizer practically lived on these critters (Mt. 3:4). Now, people who are disgusted by the thought of eating insects have suggested that locust beans are the intended food. They say that John just had a sweet tooth, and liked the sticky-sweet carob pods that hung from trees in his neighborhood. Nice try. Face it, he ate bugs. Locusts were captured and dried, then kept in sacks. When anybody got the munchies, it was like bringing out the chips. They were big at parties!

DAIRY PRODUCTS

While meat was eaten sparingly by common folk in ancient Palestine, dairy products were on everybody's table. The source of all these fine dairy products was, of course, milk. However, it was not cow's milk. The dairy herd of ancient times was anchored by the nanny goat. Goats were raised primarily for their milk. This was then turned into butter, cheese, and yogurt and even an alcoholic beverage.

BUTTER

Homemade bread is one thing, but homemade bread with butter! Now that's the ticket! Even in ancient times, people loved to serve a dish of butter at meal times. This was especially true if you had company. Abraham served butter to his angelic visitors (Gen. 18:8). Butter was usually made from goat's milk, though just about every domesticated animal in the herd was milked. Milk was placed in a skin bottle, which was then shaken, squeezed, or swung on a rope until the butter formed. Some women hung a goatskin bottle on ropes from a tripod. Then, they merely had to give the swinging bottle a push to keep the motion going (Prov. 30:33).

CHEESE

Legend has it that cheese was first discovered by a wandering Arab. He was preparing for a journey across the desert, and packed a bottle of milk made from sheep's gut for his road trip. The combination of the trace enzymes in the sheep's stomach, the heat of the day, and the constant sloshing turned the milk into curds and whey. (That's the same stuff that Little Miss Muffet liked to eat!) When the traveler decided to take a break and get a drink, he found that his milk had chunks in it. The Arab was able to drink the watery whey to satisfy his thirst, and the cheese curds satisfied his appetite. Bam! Cheese was born. Cheese is mentioned a few times in Scripture. Jesse sent cheese along for the captain of the army in which his oldest boys were serving (1Sa. 17:18). Cheese and curds were among the provisions made for David and his weary army (2Sa. 17:29). The most colorful mention of cheese comes from the complaint of Job. He accuses God of curdling him like cheese (Job 10:10).

DID YOU KNOW?

• Jael gave Sisera a bowl of camel's milk to drink. Sisera's exhaustion caught up with him, and the warm milk put him right to sleep (Judg. 4:19).

• Bottles made of animal skin were often hung in tents, where they were exposed to smoke from the cook fires. Sometimes, skins of wine were deliberately hung in the smoke to give the wine a peculiar flavor.

BEVERAGES

Water wasn't always the best beverage in Bible times. The stuff that bubbled up out of springs was great, but for a lot of people, water came from a cistern. That often meant drinking rainwater that had been sitting around for months. Juices, coffees, and wines were preferred for mealtime.

WATER

Although water was the basic liquid the Israelites used in cooking, it was not very good for drinking. Water from the local well or spring was generally safe enough, but water from the family cistern was far from safe. Even in Roman times, when water was brought to the towns by aqueduct or pipeline, the water was still not fit to drink. For this reason, other liquids such as goat's milk and wine made better drinks.

WINE

Noah gets credit for being the Bible's first vintner. He planted a vineyard, distilled some wine, drank it, and got drunk (Gen. 9:21; 1Ti. 3:8).

Not an auspicious start for a beverage that was so common in Bible times. Drunkenness was always condemned (Eph. 5:18). Palestine was full of vineyards, and most of the grapes were used for winemaking. Vineyards are mentioned in several of Jesus' parables (Mt. 20:1; 21:33; Mk. 12:1; Lk. 20:19). Solomon described wine as that which "makes glad the heart of men" (Ps. 104:15) and as "a mocker" and "a brawler" (Prov. 20:1). Paul advises Timothy to "use a little wine for your stomach's sake" (1Ti. 5:23). Priests who were on duty in the Temple couldn't partake of any wine (Lev. 10:9), nor could Nazarites, who had taken a vow (Num. 6:3). The grapes were pressed in September, and the occasion was a great excuse for a celebration (Is. 16:9), though things could often get rowdy (Judg. 9:27).

WINE CELLARS

To maintain the quality of aging wine, ancient farmers built wine cellars to store their wine jars. These cellars were dug into the ground, often within the floor plan of a house or barn. Little nooks and crannies were made in these pits to hold a ten-gallon jar. When a large stone was set over the top of the cellar, the temperature inside the cellar would remain unchanged by the weather outside. On large farms, the cellars could hold more than sixty wine jars—that's about 22,000 gallons of wine.

SWEETS

There was nothing like a little something sweet to *brighten one's countenance (1Sa. 14:27). Though sugar was not available in ancient Palestine, folks used fruit, nuts, and honey to concoct sweet treats to eat.*

ALMONDS

A proper wedding would hardly be complete without those little bundles of pastel candy-coated Jordan almonds used as party favors. What makes them so special? Many people think that the almonds grown in Palestine are the best almonds in the world. When Jacob sent his boys to Egypt to buy grain, he sent almonds along as a gift to smooth the way with Pharaoh (Gen. 43:11). Almonds from the East are a delicacy.

PISTACHIOS

Pistachios grew wild in the hills of Palestine. In ancient times, their nuts were eaten right off the tree or else fried in oil and salted to make a savory snack. Pistachios have a greenish kernel inside their tough tan shells, and its delicate sweet flavor made them perfect for desserts. They are the basis for such treats as baklava, nougat, and Turkish delight. In Bible times, pistachios were chopped and added to puddings, stuffings and fruit compotes. They were rolled into doughs, smothered in honey, and served up as a sweet finale for special meals.

HIVES FOR HONEY

There was no cane sugar in Israel, so honey from wild bees was the main sweetener in ancient times (Ex. 3:8; 13:5). Swarms of bees hid their sweet stuff in some strange places, and glad was the boy who found their stash. Samson found honey in an animal carcass (Judg. 14:8-9) and brought home some of it to Dad and Mom. As Winnie the Pooh can attest, bees have always favored old hollow trees (1Sa. 14:25–27). Honey could also be found in a hole in the rocks (Deut. 32:13; Ps. 81:16). John the Baptizer found honey in the wilderness (Mt. 3:4), and Jesus ate a honeycomb shortly after his Resurrection (Lk. 24:41–43).

> **DID YOU KNOW?**
>
> • God's words are sweet like honey (Ps. 19:10), pleasant words are like honey (Prov. 16:24), and wisdom to the soul is like honey (Prov. 24:13-14).

GRAPE SYRUP

The Jews had a fondness for something that they called honey—but it wasn't honey at all. Grape juice was boiled down until it reached the consistency of molasses. Grape syrup is the honey mentioned in Genesis as a part of the gifts Jacob sent to Pharaoh in Egypt (Gen. 43:11). It was also a commodity that the Jews could use in trade with other nations (Eze. 27:17). This grape syrup was used as a sweetener, like jam, or could be diluted to make a beverage. Similarly, thick, sweet syrup was made from the juice of dates. That was called date honey.

HERBS AND SPICES

Spices were useful for making rather common foods more interesting. Heavy seasonings could also cover up the off taste of meat that was beginning to turn. The Israelites used a variety of spices in their cooking, some of them quite exotic.

BITTER HERBS

During the ceremony of the Passover meal, the Hebrews were commanded to eat bitter herbs with the lamb (Ex. 12:8). They were to symbolize the bitterness of their bondage in Egypt. Usually, this dish was prepared using lettuces, endive, coriander seeds, tansy, horseradish, parsley and watercress. It was a salad with some kick to it.

SALT

Salt was found on the southwestern shores of the Dead Sea, where evaporation left deposits of rock salt along the banks. Salt was used for seasoning food, which would otherwise have a flat taste (Job 6:6). Meal offerings at the Temple were to be salted as well (Lev. 2:13; Ezr. 6:9; Eze. 43:24). Salt was vital in food preservation. Meat, fish, and olives were all packed in salt to prolong their usefulness. It had many other uses as well. Newborns were rubbed with salt, because it was thought to toughen the skin (Eze. 16:4). Salt that had lost its saltiness was kept at the Temple in Jerusalem, where the marble floors could become slippery in winter rains. The priests would scatter it on the courtyards to provide traction. This was the salt that was "trampled underfoot" (Mt. 5:13).

"Worth One's Salt"

The idea of a worker being "worth his salt" is a very old one. Salt was a precious commodity in ancient times, for it improved the flavor of just about anything it was sprinkled on. Without the savor of salt, one's meals were flat and uninteresting (Job 6:6). Back in the heyday of the Roman Empire, a portion of a soldier's pay was measured out in salt. A soldier kept his packet of salt safe, for it made his army rations more bearable. This salt payment was called a "salarium." It is from this old Roman term that we get our word "salary." So, if you are worth your salt, your paycheck should show it.

Spiced Dishes

The lands of the Bible were full of strong herbs and spices. What wasn't to be had locally was brought in by merchants from India and Africa. The seasonings helped to give a bit of punch to a rather mundane menu. Caraway, dill, mint, mustard, parsley, sage, and thyme were but a few plants that were used for seasoning food. Isaiah mentions cumin (Is. 28:27). The bay tree appears in the Psalms, where it is called "a native green tree" (Ps. 37:35). Cinnamon is mentioned by Solomon (Prov. 7:17). The children of Israel compared the flavor of manna to the spice coriander (Num. 11:7). Pharisees were such sticklers for obeying the Law that they even tithed ten percent of the spices that were used to season their food, right down to the grains of salt. Jesus says that they measured out a tithe on their mint, anise, and cumin (Mt. 23:23).

Mealtime

Meals were a gathering time for family and friends. The hospitality of a shared meal allowed people to show one another how much they were esteemed. A wife and mother spent the better part of her day in meal preparations. She took pride in providing her family and her guests with tasty dishes from the recipes she had learned to prepare at her mother's side.

BREAKFAST

The morning meal was usually eaten sometime before noon. Since it was one of only two meals a day, breakfast was eaten when it was convenient. It was usually a light meal and consisted of bread, fruits, and cheese. Sometimes the bread had something inside, like olives or dried fruit. Lots of working men ate their breakfast on the fly. They munched on their bread rolls as they walked to work in the morning. Jesus himself prepared the most famous breakfast mentioned in Scripture. The disciples had gone back to fishing on the Sea of Galilee, and had just spent a long night out on the water. Weary and frustrated from catching nothing, the disciples made for the shore. There, beside a fire, was Jesus. He had prepared bread and fish for them to share (Jn. 21:9).

SUPPER

A mid-day meal was practically non-existent in Bible times. It was too hot during the day to feel much like eating. So, the main meal of the day was eaten in the evening. Once the evening breezes began to blow in from the coast and the temperatures began to moderate, appetites perked up again. The evening meal would have included meat, vegetables, bread, butter, and wine.

MEALS FOR THE NOMADS

Nomadic hospitality is legendary. Among these tent-dwellers, travelers were always welcomed. Abraham is a wonderful example of Bedouin generosity. When strangers came near to his resting place, he called to them, welcomed them, and urged them to rest while he went inside to "prepare a mere morsel of bread" (Gen. 18:2–6). Water was brought for the men to wash their feet, then they were settled in a shady spot to rest while Abraham bustled off to make dinner arrangements. With this humble offering, Abraham turned right around and had Sarah prepare a great feast for the men, using the best that the couple had on hand. He popped his head into the tent and told Sarah to make cakes of fine meal. Next, he chose a fatted calf from his herd and ordered one of his servants to get it ready to cook. He also brought out milk and butter to eat with the bread. The mere morsel turned into a regular Bedouin feast (Gen. 18:8). As the writer of Hebrews urged, "Do not forget to entertain strangers" (Heb. 13:2). Like Abraham, you never knew when you might be entertaining heavenly visitors!

Meals for the Poor

The evening meal in a poor home in Palestine depended heavily on the family's garden. Vegetable stew, seasoned with herbs from the yard, was served in a common pot. Everybody dipped in with a sop—a piece of bread used to scoop out a mouthful. The family gathered close around, sitting picnic style on a mat on the floor. If there was company for the meal, Mom usually managed to find some meat to add to the pot. Some condiments were offered to help liven the meal, like olives, pickled onions, or toasted pumpkin seeds.

DID YOU KNOW?

• The nomads welcomed a traveler into their homes as a member of their family, but for a limited period of time. More specifically, a guest was welcome for exactly three days and four hours!

Meals for the Rich

In the homes of the wealthy, cooks were employed to provide elaborate meals for the family. Meat was served in large quantities, and several side dishes were served as well. In Rome, a dinner party was served in several courses. Hors d'oeuvres were followed by wine mixed with honey. Then three main courses were brought out in succession. When the guests had eaten their fill, the scraps were tossed into the fire as a token sacrifice to their gods. As a grand finale, pastries and fruit were served, followed by more drinks and an evening of entertainment.

CHAPTER NINE

THEIR EVERYDAY LIFE

There is no getting around the fact that everyday life for a man was worlds apart from the tasks at hand for a woman in Bible times. While he was busy at work or in the marketplace meeting and greeting, his wife was running the household and caring for young children. This chapter gives a peek into these two distinct versions of day-to-day living.

The Men

Most of a man's day was wrapped up in the job he held. These are described in the chapter called "Their Jobs." So, outside of the office, what were the everyday interests of the Bible-time man? In a land where famines were common, the change of seasons and its accompanying weather patterns were scrutinized. Feasts and holy days rolled around fairly often as well, so a man paid heed to the calendar, and planned his days around them. Another factor that affected a man's life was politics. Then too, men were given the opportunity to enjoy certain leisure-time activities. Sports were a popular pastime, especially in New Testament times.

FARMER'S ALMANAC

A farmer in Bible times always spent his day with one eye on the sky. The fickle weather could mean feast or famine for the upcoming year. The climate of Palestine is very different from our own. A peek at their calendar gives a new perspective on a man's everyday life.

CLIMATE

The climate of Palestine was as varied as its terrain. The expanse of territory where the Israelites made their home was comprised of hill country, where the winters were bitter cold; coastal plains, where the morning dews watered the orchards and fields even in the worst heat of the summer; and a river valley, where the climate was positively tropical. Though these variations affected the intensity of the seasons as they came and went, there was still a familiar rhythm to the year. Winters were cold and wet, for the rains would come in torrents. Summers were hot and dry, for the rains did not come at all. In between these two extremes were times of planting and tending and harvest.

MEASURING TIME

Methods of measuring the days and weeks changed from culture to culture, often developing and changing over time. During Bible times, a few different systems can be seen. At first, days began at sunrise. A twelve-month calendar of thirty days was in use, and five extra days were tacked on to the end of the year. Later, days were given their start at moonrise, and a whole day became "the evening and the morning." Along with this particular system of timekeeping, the nights were divided into three four-hour watches. When the Romans became influential, this was changed again to suit their standard. By New Testament times, the months began with the moon, and so lasted twenty-eight or twenty-nine days each. Nights were divided into four three-hour watches now, and sometimes an extra month had to be added at the end of the year to even out the calendar. Ancient calendars were often a plate made of bone in which holes were bored. A peg was moved along the holes to track the passage of time.

DID YOU KNOW?

- There were six seasons on the ancient calendar: seedtime, summer fruits, the hot season, harvest time, the cold season, and the bare season.

THE GEZER CALENDAR

Remember the simple saying "April showers bring May flowers." Or how about that poem, "Thirty days hath September," that helps you keep track of the number of days in each of the months. People have always used sing-songy nursery rhymes to help children remember. In ancient times, poems were used to help keep the calendar straight as well. A tablet was found with a kind of school-boy's rhyme to keep straight the farmer's year. It goes like this:

The two months are olive harvest (September/October)
The two months are planting grain (November/December)
The two months are late planting (January/February)
The month is hoeing up of flax (March)

The month is barley harvest (April)
The month is harvest and festivity (May)
The two months are vine tending (June/July)
The month is summer fruit (August)

It's called the Gezer calendar, and it was written around the time of King Solomon. By the way, the late planting in January and February was millet, peas, lentils, melons, and cucumbers. Not exactly great literature, but it probably loses something in the translation.

MUD PUDDLES

In a land where, for most of the year, the soil resembled the crackle finish of antique furniture, one thinks more of sand dunes than of mud puddles. While it is true that swaths of desert sands swept into the landscape of Palestine here and there, most of the land was covered, however thinly, with fertile soil. This pay dirt was inches deep in some places, but when tilled and seeded, it valiantly produced a rich harvest. However, before a crop could be harvested, it had to be planted. This is where the mud comes into play. During the winter months, rain fell in cold, unrelenting sheets. It did not take long for the hard-baked soils of summer to become an endless sea of mud. Getting about in the damp and the mire was nearly impossible, and yet this was planting time for the farmers. The softened earth yielded to the plow, and the seeds received the moisture needed to germinate. The farmer who wanted a good harvest had to be willing to muck about in the mud (Prov. 20:4).

THE EARLY AND THE LATTER RAINS

The phrase from the prophets, "the former and the latter rains" has an almost poetic quality to it (Jer. 5:24; Hos. 6:3). It also happens to be as concise a description as you will find of the weather patterns in Palestine. The "early rains" are the rains of October, November, and December, when the farmers allowed the weather to soften their lands before hitching up their teams to the plows. This was planting time for the wheat and barley, which would provide bread for a family throughout the upcoming year. The "later rains" arrived in March and April. These rain showers were the difference between feast and famine for a family. They blew in just in the nick of time for the crops that stood under the growing heat of the summer sun. The moisture of the later rains was just the thing to swell the heads of grain that were beginning to ripen. There were also dust storms in Palestine (Ps. 83:13).

STORMY WEATHER

"The Lord has his way in the whirlwind and in the storm" (Nah. 1:3). The Scriptures tell of enough wild weather to thrill any meteorologist's heart. Thunder rumbles and lightening flashes across the pages of the Bible (Ps. 77:18). Job tells of the winds, which caused the waves of the sea to roll and crash against the shores (Job 30:14). A tempest at sea leads to Jonah's plunge into the icy depths (Jonah 1:15). God commands the snows to fall (Job 37:6). Isaiah speaks of hailstorms and of floods (Is. 28:2). Yet in the midst of the fury, stands One who can calm it all with one word (Ps. 107:29; Mk. 4:39).

DROUGHT RELIEF

The lands of Palestine were dependant upon the rainy seasons. If the rains did not come, then the fields withered and the harvests failed. Drought could destroy all of a farmer's hard work, and leave his family hungry. The Jews understood drought to be a judgment of God upon a sinful people. When immorality ran rampant, rain was withheld (Hag. 1:9–11). When His people repented and walked in obedience, the clouds rolled in, thunder rumbled, and rain showers refreshed the land. There was one exception to these dry spells, however. Even if a rain cloud did not cross the sky for years, the dews could still roll in at night. It was not enough moisture to produce a crop, but the drops of moisture kept the land from total destruction. Dew was equated with God's mercy. When the people of Israel were especially naughty, God withheld even the dew (1Kin. 17:1; Hag. 1:10).

HARVEST TABOOS

Just as with everything else in the lives of the children of God, there were some strict dos and don'ts attached to the harvesting of crops. First of all, reapers were instructed not to do a thorough job. More specifically, they were never to reap to the edges of a field or to go through a field a second time. The corners of the fields were left standing. These bits, plus the gleanings, must be left for the poor and landless (Lev. 19:9). We find Ruth in this circumstance, as she follows the harvesters through Boaz's fields looking for dropped heads of barley. These rules extended to the owners of orchards and vineyards as well. During the harvest, a tree or vine could not be picked over twice. Any olives or grapes that were overlooked on the first pass were fair game for the gleaners coming behind (Lev. 19:10). Crops could be planted for six consecutive years, but on the seventh year the land must be left fallow for the soil to recover (Ex. 23:11). God promised that the harvest on the sixth year would be sufficient to provide food for the following year.

DID YOU KNOW?

• Elijah listened for the voice of God in the midst of a great storm, but found it instead in a still, small voice (1Kin. 19:11–12).

• Boaz and his workers slept at the threshing floor to protect the grain from thieves until all of their harvest could be brought into storage (Ruth 3:2).

OLIVE HARVEST

Deuteronomy 8:8 describes the Promised Land as a land of olive oil. From September or October to November, olives were harvested.

They were shaken from the trees onto blankets, sorted into baskets, then pickled, packed in salt, or pressed for their precious oil. Early on, oil was squeezed out by stepping on the olives or by pounding them with a rock (Deut. 24:20). Later on, an olive press equipped with a millstone was developed. When the olives were pressed, the oil ran down and was captured in great vats. Once it had been given time to settle, the precious oil was poured into jars. While David was king over Israel, he had a man in charge of the royal olive groves, as well as a man who saw to the storage of the olive oil (1Chr. 27:28). Olive oil was one of the chief exports of Israel in New Testament times.

FRUIT HARVEST

The summer fruit harvest took place in August and September. Fresh figs, pomegranates, grapes, and sycamore figs were plentiful. This was a busy time for the women, since much of the fruit had to be dried and stored away before it spoiled. The big event was the grape harvest. The grape gatherers made their way through the laden vines, plucking the fruit, but leaving enough for the gleaners (Jer. 49:9). Baskets of grapes were brought down the slopes and taken to small vats, where they could be stomped. Jars placed at the base of the vats caught the juices. Some of the juices were drunk fresh. Some were fermented in wine sacks. Some grape juice

was boiled down into a thick syrup, which was used as a sweetener when honey was unavailable. Though this was a time of celebration and plenty, the harvesters had to keep up their guard. Sometimes the summer fruit harvest brought in raiders and thieves, who would snatch what they could and carry off their plunder (Jer. 48:32).

FLAX HARVEST

In March and April, with the "latter rains," the grains received the growth spurt they needed to be ready for harvest. Flax was ready first. This plant was cut off close to the ground with a hoe and the stalks were gathered up and dried. Flax was a valuable crop, for it could be made into fabric (Is. 19:9). The flax stalks were dried on rooftops (Josh. 2:6), then soaked and beaten to separate the fibrous strands of the plant. Cords of flax were woven together to make wicks for the oil lamps in homes (Mt. 12:20). Thicker strands made cords and ropes. Better yet was the fabric that was made—linen. Fine linen was cool, crisp, and a soft off-white color. It was perfect for those hot, humid days in the delta. The entire nation of Egypt wore linen clothing.

DEATH AND TAXES

Benjamin Franklin declared that the only two things in life that were unavoidable were death and taxes. Even back in the "good old days" of ancient history, taxes were unavoidable. In fact, for the Jews of the New Testament, taxation was a touchy subject. They were twice taxed for the living they eked out of the land. They faithfully brought a tithe to God at the Temple, and the Romans who ruled over their land also levied a heavy tax. This section deals with the government of ancient days, which affected the everyday lives of Bible-time people.

THE KING'S OFFICIALS

Ancient kings were busy men, and they established a kind of cabinet of trusted officials to deal with the daily affairs of the kingdom. The "master of the palace" probably managed the king's personal properties. He would also have been known as the chief minister. There was also a royal secretary. He acted as personal scribe and secretary of state. There was also a royal herald, who was probably a kind of royal public relations official. He may have kept tabs on public opinion. Kings had a personal bodyguard and also employed military officers. Joab and Amasa vied for the title of general in David's army (2Sa. 17:25; 19:13).

SALE OF LAND

From the time the Israelites settled in Canaan, the buying and selling of land was not approved. Even if a property was mortgaged to pay a debt, it had to be returned to the family in the year of jubilees. People held their land in trust from God; they were not the owners. Each family had received a plot of land as its own inheritance. It should therefore remain as part of that family's property. One of the earliest business deals recorded in the Bible is Abraham's purchase of a field and cave from Ephron the Hittite (Gen. 23:17). That property remained in the family for centuries, so that the bones of Joseph were carried out of Egypt and buried there next to his ancestors (Josh. 24:32).

> **DID YOU KNOW?**
>
> • The Romans used locals to do their dirty work for them. The Jews hated the tax collectors, men who had gone over to work for the oppressors in order to turn a profit. Both Matthew and Zacchaeus were tax collectors (Lk. 5:27; 19:2).

BRIBERY

Bribery was a no-no in ancient Israel. If a man tried to bribe a judge, he was guilty of a crime against his entire community, for he had attempted to beat the system that God had established (Ex. 23:1–7; Deut. 19:16–21). Because of this, bribery was considered both a civil and a religious crime. Judges were expected to toe the line as well, for God had forbidden them to take bribes (Deut. 16:18–19). All defendants were to be given a fair trial. The system was not infallible, though. When a judge and jury had their own agenda, the defendant didn't have a chance. Jesus was rushed

PAUL
A Prisoner for Christ

Paul was always in trouble with the law. Overall, the Romans were a tolerant bunch. As long as citizens were peaceful and law-abiding, they could do as they pleased. In an empire where blending in was appreciated, Paul stuck out like a sore thumb. He just didn't blend. When Paul started to draw crowds, preaching in the synagogues and in the marketplaces, Rome ordered him to cease and desist. But, he wouldn't stop preaching. He wouldn't stop telling people about Jesus. Instead, he moved on to another city and repeated the process. He persuaded the people. He drew even larger crowds. And when Rome demanded that Paul stop, he still said no. The authorities did everything in their power to dampen Paul's enthusiasm for Christ. Paul ended up in all sorts of trouble. He was beaten with rods in Philippi (Acts 16:22), and again in two other cities (2Cor. 11:25). Once, the people stoned him, dragged him out of the city, and left him for dead in the rubble (Acts 14:19). Paul also had a fair understanding of Rome's prison system, having been given an inside view several times during his missionary career. He knew the mustiness of the cells, the scrabbling sounds made by vermin, the cold that sank into your bones at night. Once, he and his companion, Silas were arrested and put into a prison in Philippi. To put their discomfort out of their minds, they decided to fill their dreary cell with songs of praise (Acts 16:25). When he was imprisoned again in Rome, Caesar had Paul placed under house arrest, with a guard chained to him at all times. But even the imposing presence of a Roman centurion could not quell the zeal of Paul. He preached on. In fact, it became something of a joke, that in trying to hush up the mouth of Paul, Caesar managed to loose Christianity within his own household. In his letter back to the church in Philippi, Paul sends greetings "especially from those in Caesar's household" (Phil. 4:22).

through the system and found guilty even though the witnesses couldn't keep their stories straight (Mt. 26:59–60). He never spoke a word in his own defense (Mt. 26:63; 27:14). And when brought before a higher court, the judge determined that Jesus was innocent (Lk. 23:14). Even so, the death sentence was imposed.

TRIALS

When a dispute arose among the people of Israel, Moses heard the case and handed down his decision in the matter (Ex. 18:13). Judges did the same (Judg. 2:16). So did kings, like Solomon (1Kin. 3:9)—even government officials, like Pilate (Lk. 23:24). When criminal cases were brought before the authorities, witnesses were questioned (Num. 35:30; Deut. 19:15) and the defendant was called to answer for his actions. Sometimes a man was called upon to pay for the damages he had caused. At other times, his life was required of him because of the magnitude of his crime.

> **DID YOU KNOW?**
>
> • A Roman census was taken every fourteen years, for Caesar wanted to make sure that every inhabitant under his dominion was paying his taxes. During a census, people were ordered to their hometowns to be counted (Lk. 2:2).
>
> • God ordained that the tribe of Levi should live by bartering their services as priests for food and meat, which were brought to the temple for sacrifice (Num. 18:25-32).

EXECUTIONS

God's Law was never meant to be broken. But when it was, the penalty was usually death. Murderers, adulterers, and thieves were generally stoned. This form of execution was simple and effective: stand somebody in a pit and throw big rocks at them until they died. There was even a law on the books that allowed parents to have their disrespectful children stoned (Deut. 21:18–21). Achen was stoned for theft (Josh. 7:24–25), Stephen was stoned for his faith (Acts 7:58), and the woman caught in adultery was nearly stoned (Jn. 8:5). Other nations had their preferred forms of execution. Babylonian kings kept a pit of lions (Dan. 6:7) or utilized their fiery furnaces (Dan. 3:6). Romans nailed their criminals to crosses (Mt. 27:38).

TAXES TIMES TWO

As if taxes were not bad enough, the Jews were weighed down by a double taxation for much of their existence—first, they had a prior obligation to God. But then, Rome demanded their due as well. In New Testament times, Rome levied taxes on the entire known world in order to maintain its vast army, its building projects, and its emperor. Tax collectors who worked for the Romans were distrusted and despised, for they cheated taxpayers into paying more money than they owed. Zacchaeus was guilty of lining his pockets with extorted funds (Lk. 19:8).

TEMPLE TAX

The second tax to which Jews were subjected was the Temple tax, and it applied to every male over the age of twelve. This bounty, consisting of cattle, grains, fruits, oils, wines, spices, and other goods, was intended to sustain the members of the tribe of Levi, who served as priests in the Temple and did not own their own land (Deut. 10:9). The rest of the sons of Jacob had received an inheritance of property in the Promised Land, but the children of Levi were set aside for ministry in the Temple, and the rest of the family maintained their needs. When it came right down to it, the tribe of Levi had very little to complain about. The priests lacked for nothing. God had called His people to bring the "first fruits" of all their labors to the Temple. The seven first fruits—wheat, barley, figs, grapes, pomegranates, olives and honey—had a portion reserved for temple use. In addition to all these things, there were occasional dues during special festivals, thanks offerings, sin offerings, trespass offerings, and so on. Although the temple vaults were richly stocked, even the poorest Jews didn't complain about the demands from the Temple, for their gifts were in obedience to God's command.

ONESIMUS

The Runaway

In New Testament times, a life of slavery was not the life of misery in which the children of Israel found themselves in the Book of Exodus. Still, their lives were not their own, and some slaves chaffed under the fetter of servitude. Onesimus was such a man. Serving in the house of Philemon, Onesimus was disgruntled, dissatisfied, and determined to escape. With carefully laid plans, he watched for his chance to slip away unnoticed. When the opportunity arose, Onesimus seized it. With some pilfered cash in his pocket, Onesimus disappeared. In an attempt to get as far away from his former master as possible, he made his way to Rome. Bounty hunters were sometimes employed to track a runaway, and Onesimus wanted to put some distance between himself and home. Losing himself in the crowds of strangers, Onesimus began his new life as a free man. He never intended to give Philemon another thought.

It was in Rome that Onesimus heard a name he knew. His master, Philemon, had been a convert of the man called Paul of Tarsus. Onesimus learned that Paul was in Rome under house arrest. More homesick for a familiar face than he wished to admit, Onesimus trailed behind some men who were going to hear Paul speak. He slipped into the back row of one of Paul's discussions. He heard Paul's story and the message that he proclaimed. Onesimus became a Christian, led in prayer by the same man whom God had used to convert his master, Philemon. Paul calls Onesimus his son (Philem. 10), and Onesimus enters into ministry with Paul in Rome (Philem. 13). Suddenly, Onesimus realizes that he is in a predicament. He has sinned against Philemon by running and stealing from him. Assured of Christ's forgiveness, he is nonetheless convinced

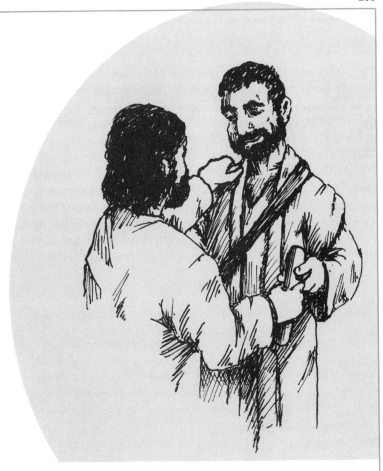

that he must seek Philemon's mercy as well. Turning to Paul for counsel in this matter, Onesimus receives a great gift in the form of a letter of reference from Paul, urging Philemon to forgive his slave and offering to repay the stolen money himself (Philem. 19). Paul assures Onesimus that the little scroll will pave the way towards reconciliation. With the prayers of the Christian church in Rome to uphold him, Onesimus returns home, a runaway no longer.

RENDER UNTO CAESAR

The Jews never grumbled over their tithes to God and the Temple. Unfortunately for them, taxation did not stop there. Sure the taxes went for good roads, waterways, bridges, and amphitheaters, but they also supported Caesar and his minions. These conquerors were hated for their dominion. There was a one percent poll tax, just for living in the empire. Then, there was a road tax, a property tax, a water tax, a city tax, and even a death tax. There was a poll tax of half a shekel just for being alive! Imports and exports were subject to duties, and there were tolls in the markets. Caesar Augustus went so far as to institute a sales tax that provided pensions for retired Roman soldiers. The religious leaders among the Jews reflected the general opinion of this drain on the nation's funds, but Jesus simply asserted that they should "render unto Caesar that which was Caesar's" (Mt. 22:21).

TAX EXEMPTION

Can you imagine serving your country so well, in such a time of great need, that in gratitude you were told that you and your family never had to pay taxes again? I heard that scoff! It has happened before! When the people of Israel were trembling on the brink of captivity to the Philistines, King Saul was desperate to find a hero. Hoping to lure a mighty warrior with a noble streak out of the woodwork, he put together a sweet little compensation package. The man who stepped forward and agreed to fight Goliath would receive not only his undying gratitude, but the hand of his daughter in marriage and tax exempt status (1Sa. 17:25).

WOOING THE MASSES

When a nation was conquered by Rome, it was still allowed to function independently, so long as the citizens did not try to rebel against Rome's authority. They could do their own thing, appointing their own governors and officials, if they were good. In return, Caesar expected the people to pledge allegiance to him. To this end, Rome attempted to influence the people. Plans were in place to woo the people of foreign lands so that they began to think and feel like Romans. With this agenda, the Roman armies marched in, not to plunder, but to build. Roads, aqueducts, temples, spas, arenas, schools, and office buildings were brought into the cities. Rome offered top-notch schooling in the gymnasiums, and edge-of-your-seat entertainment with the coliseums. With so many improvements, many newcomers to the Roman Empire walked willingly into their captivity.

IN MATTERS OF RELIGION...

The Jews were ruled by numerous foreign powers throughout their history. They became subject to the whims of Assyria, Persia, Babylon, Greece, and Rome. They were subjected to laws and tributes and taxation. Through all of it,

> ### DID YOU KNOW?
>
> • Under Roman authority, the Jews were given the right to discuss, evaluate, and vote on the laws that affected their people.
>
> • The Romans often buried their dead in underground tombs, or catacombs. Christians who suffered Roman persecution sometimes held their worship services in the catacombs during times of oppression.

however, the Jews maintained their spiritual identity. In religious matters, they clung tightly to God's supremacy. They appointed their own priests and elders, and kept their own religious laws and practices. In this way, the Jews maintained their identity as a religious community, set apart by God, despite the change of powers.

RULING AN EMPIRE

In New Testament times, the Jews were absorbed into the Roman Empire. The Empire extended into most of the known world, and keeping it in good working order took some organization. In essence, there were two sorts of provinces within Rome's control—peaceful ones and problematic ones. The Senate in Rome kept track of the cooperative people, appointing governors every year. These were the proconsuls of the Empire. When trouble was brewing in a province, the Roman emperor took charge, and troops were sent in to keep order. Deputies were appointed for four or five years at a time in trouble spots. These were the legates, prefects, and procurators of the Empire. If a region was especially compliant to Rome's wishes, they might be allowed to keep their own king on the throne, so long as they abided by the Empire's wishes.

"FREE CITIES"

As long as peace was kept in certain cities, they were allowed to remain self-governing despite Rome's ultimate control. Two such free cities were Athens and Ephesus. Certain cities were also allowed some control over their religious affairs. Jerusalem was such a city, for the High Priest and the Sanhedrin were allowed to oversee the needs of the Jewish community. Still, the Jew's authority was very limited, and Rome had the final say in important matters. An example of this would be the death sentence passed on Jesus. Only Pontius Pilate, the Roman governor, could hand down such a ruling (Jn. 18:31).

UPKEEP

Rome prided itself on efficiency and order. Part of keeping the peace was a vast maintenance program. The Roman Empire built roads, provided office buildings for local legislatures, and set up markets, bathhouses, sewer systems, and other little improvements. Roman soldiers had to be uniformed, fed, and paid, and retired Roman officers received pensions. Trade routes had to be patrolled and protected. Aqueducts were erected, providing reliable sources of water in dry and dusty lands. These amenities were paid out of Roman taxes—property taxes, sales taxes, poll taxes, death taxes, and so on. In each area of the Empire, tax collectors were hired to bring in the money.

HEROD AND SONS

King Herod the Great reigned in Judea for forty years. During Herod's reign, Jesus was born in Bethlehem, and Joseph and Mary were forced to flee into Egypt to protect the boy (Mt. 2:13). When Herod died, his three sons divided the land amongst themselves, establishing themselves as rulers in Palestine. Antipas grabbed the north country, where Galilee is located. Philip opted to govern the areas of Iturea and Trachonitis, further east. Archelaus gained control of Judea and Samaria, which included the city of Jerusalem. When Joseph returned to Judea and heard that Archelaus was in power, he detoured further north and settled in Nazareth (Mt. 2:23). Archelaus couldn't maintain the peace in Judea, and so it became a Roman province, under the supervision of the Emperor and his appointed procurators. Pontius Pilate was the fifth such procurator to govern Judea.

CENSUS

Every so often, a ruler could call for a census to be taken. Actually, the opportunity came up every fourteen years. Rome liked to keep careful tabs on its citizenry, noting births and deaths in each family tree. When census time came around, it was family reunion time. If children had grown up and moved away, they had to return to home base in order to register. This is why we find Joseph journeying from Galilee to be counted among his family in Bethlehem (Lk. 2:4). That is where the descendants of David called home. The census wasn't just for information gathering and data analysis though. The leaders had their eyes on the various billfolds, wallets, and coin purses throughout the empire. Rome conducted the counting in order to confirm that all the citizens were paying their taxes.

CITIZENSHIP

The officials of the Roman Empire had a carrot that they liked to dangle before the myriads of people who came under their control. Those who were submissive to new ownership could

DID YOU KNOW?

• Roman colonies were regarded as outposts of Rome itself, and were governed like the capital. Philippi was one of several colonies featured in the New Testament.

• Firstborn sons had to be bought back from God by way of a special offering at the Temple (Ex. 34:20).

• A king could call every able-bodied man in his kingdom to arms for protecting their homes or in conquest of other nations (1Sa. 8:11–12).

earn the right to become true citizens of Rome. This had its privileges. A true Roman citizen was spared the indignity of being bound, hand and foot, when being taken into custody. He could not be whipped. He was always given a fair trial, and could appeal to the higher court of the Emperor himself. Since such privileges were included with citizenship, it might be easy for any troublemaker to make such a claim when faced with a whipping block. However, these liars could be found out simply by checking the scrolls of the official registry in town. Paul was proud of the fact that he was a citizen of Rome (Acts 22:28). However, sometimes nobody bothered to check the credentials of an itinerant Jewish preacher. In Philippi, Paul and his companions were not only bound, but beaten and imprisoned without a trial (Acts 16:37–38). Imagine the amazement and then the distress of the city officials in Philippi when they discovered that they had mistreated a Roman citizen.

SPORTS AND LEISURE

"All work and no play makes Jack a dull boy." Hardly a proverb from King Solomon, but true enough nonetheless. Life was hard in ancient times, and work was a necessity. Still, God worked in times of refreshment for his people. Weekly Sabbaths were set apart for rest and worship. Festivals were sprinkled throughout the year, giving men a holiday from the daily grind.

TOYS FOR TOTS

Very little has changed over the centuries when it comes to children's toys. Small children played with rattles and whistles. Little girls had dollhouses, complete with little pottery furnishings. Some dolls had jointed arms and legs, with beads for hair. There were puppets on strings and pull-toys on wheels. Leather balls found their way into various games.

R AND R

Although the life of a Jew in the ancient world was a hard one, it wasn't all work and no play. The weekly Sabbath was a day of worship and rest (Ex.

31:15), and there were many special holidays and festivals throughout the year. These were the times of great anticipation. Adults and children alike were able to set aside their usual tasks, kick back, and relax. Though many of the prescribed activities during these days had profound spiritual significance, some things were purely for fun. So while the Jewish fathers in the land were passing on their knowledge of God to the next generation, there was time for some tussling as well.

> **DID YOU KNOW?**
>
> • The Greek people believed that it was just as important to be physically fit as it was to be educated.

PLAYING GAMES

Though games like Monopoly, Scrabble, and Uno were not yet bringing people together around the table on family nights, the Jewish people enjoyed many games. Hopscotch was a familiar pastime with the youngsters. So were marbles. These were rolled through a little course with archways, with pins to knock down at the end. There were no baseball bats or tennis rackets, but throwing games with leather balls were extremely popular. Dads and sons have been tossing the ball around after supper for centuries. Juggling was a popular diversion, as was target practice with a bow and arrow. Both adults and children enjoyed slinging stones. This was done with a simple slingshot, much like what David used to fell Goliath (1Sa. 17:50). A stone was put into the pouch of the slingshot, and the two strings were held to whirl the stone overhead. One string was released, and if the slinger's timing was good, the stone was sent hurtling into its target. There have been board games in people's homes since ancient times. Many of our games of strategy have their foundations in long-ago pastimes. Chess, checkers, and mancala were played by ancient families. Game boards were made of stone or clay, and in wealthy homes they might be overlaid with ebony and ivory. There were playing pieces for moving along the boards, and dice were rolled to determine plays. Dice games were taken very seriously, especially by soldiers in Roman times. A complicated gambling game that involved the casting of lots was like

the game of Life. Instead of going to school, getting a job, marrying, and filling the car with kids, players moved their pieces into positions where they could be robed, crowned, and sceptered. The first player to complete the ceremony was declared king and won all of the money that was put down on the game.

TOP TEN ANCIENT FAMILY GAMES:

- marbles
- hopscotch
- juggling
- archery
- wrestling
- bowling
- catch
- slingshot target practice
- foot races
- mancala

ROLLING DICE

In ancient times there were three forms of the die used in games. One sort was flat like a coin, with each side painted a different color. Usually these were black and white. Such die were used in divining the will of God, as with the Urim and Thummim (Ex. 28:30). When these lots were cast, two white lots meant "yes," two black lots meant "no," and a black and white combination meant that the people should wait. The next form of die which could be found in the gaming communities was used by the Egyptians. This was a four-sided die, shaped like a pyramid. The last sort of dice that have been found by archeologists were the familiar cubes. These six-sided die were popular with the Romans, and may have been a part of the game of lots that was underway at the foot of the Cross when Jesus was dying (Mt. 27:35).

ANNUAL ALL-SYNAGOGUE CAMPOUT

The Jews had their holy days and they had their festivals. One of the events that was very popular with the children was the annual Harvest Festival. It was called the Feast of Tabernacles, the Feast of Booths, or the Ingathering. Just like Thanksgiving, this holiday took place after all the summer's harvest had been gathered in and stored away. In an effort to remember and commemorate their past wanderings in the desert wilderness, the Jews camped out for a week. Tents were made from branches and cloth, either in the front yard or up on the rooftops (Lev. 23:42).

ATHLETICS

Sports were a form of grand entertainment in New Testament times. In Rome, barkers in the streets advertised the events held in the coliseums, and both concessions and souvenirs were for sale. Competitions were frequent, since Hellenistic thought deemed physical fitness to be as important as education. Periodically, however, the events organizers pulled all the stops, and men from the entire surrounding area were brought in for a competition of Olympic proportions. Each town and city would send their most promising athletes. Races were run, and competitors were tested in their abilities with jumping, wrestling, javelin, and discus. Sometimes there were also chariot races and boxing matches. As the competitions closed, a heralder would proclaim the name of the winner, as well as his hometown. His whole village received honor in his victory. Instead of a trophy, the young man was presented with a palm branch or a crown of leaves (1Pet. 5:4).

DID YOU KNOW?

• The sporting events mentioned by Paul in his letters are all linked to the Greek games. He writes of runners competing to win a prize (1Cor. 9:24; 2Ti. 4:7).

• The winners of athletic competitions were given a wreath of leaves to wear upon their heads. For all their work, they received a perishable crown (1Cor. 9:25; 1Pet. 5:4).

WRESTLING

The first sport we hear about in the Bible is probably as old as Cain and Abel, tussling as boys. Wrestling was an honorable sport, and an acceptable way for men to test their strength. In ancient Babylon, men wrestled while keeping hold of each other's belts. When two men squared off, the goal was to throw down and hold one's opponent. Then the triumphant one placed his foot on his opponent's neck. There were rules of proper conduct during a match. Jacob wrestled with an angel at Peniel, but he was not able to overthrow his supernatural opponent within the rules. Neither was the angel able to topple a determined Jacob, and so Jacob's hip was touched and he was unable to continue (Gen. 32:24–25).

PUBLIC ENTERTAINMENT

In later Bible times, people began to make a living by amusing others. Jugglers and jesters, magicians and mimes could be found on the street corners and in the king's courts. On a larger scale, sporting events were held in the great coliseums. This kind of entertainment became very popular in Greek times. These were hyped and advertised by barkers, who hoped to draw in large crowds. There were athletes of renown from faraway cities, and local boys trying to prove themselves. During Roman times, gladiators clashed against each other or against wild beasts. Souvenirs were being hocked. Marketing has changed little from the days of the Roman coliseum. Way back then, you could buy a drinking cup with your favorite gladiator painted on it.

READY TO RUMBLE!

Ancient times had its own version of the wrestling matches that can be seen today. Though nobody was being hit over the head with a folding chair, fans were promised an edge-of-your-seat performance by the competitors. These were the pankration contests. Pankration was hand-to-hand combat with a twist. When two men faced each other in such a competition, the usual rules of fair play were thrown out the window. These were knock-down, drag-out battles, and only two rules applied. Number one, no biting. And number two, no eye gouging.

The Women

A woman's work was never done. *Every new day sent her bustling about the home, tending to the needs of her family. Diapers had to be changed, and cooking was a time-consuming task. Then there were errands that needed to be run, and the family to clothe and care for. Trips to the market were needed, and daily ventures to the well, too. And there were the milestone events surrounding their family lives: babies, weddings, and funerals. Like the Proverbs 31 woman, "she watches over the ways of her household, and does not eat the bread of idleness" (Prov. 31:27).*

GOOD HOUSEKEEPING

A large part of a ladies day *was spent in household chores. Half of her day might be spent just in the process of making bread. Still, the simple houses of ancient times were homes, and a good mother kept hers well.*

KEEPING THE HOME FIRES BURNING

For baking bread and making vegetable stews, the women had to maintain the cookfires throughout the day. This was especially true in the winter months, when the fire also served to warm the home and drive away the dampness of the rains. She used sticks, thorns, stubble, or dried animal dung to fuel the oven. The children usually had the job of finding the fuel; but if they were not old enough to leave the house, the woman had to find the fuel herself. The fire was often kept in a shallow pit in the floor of the house, though ceramic fireboxes were also used. In the months when the weather was fine, the fire might be kept out in the courtyard. Part of the home fires was also the constant glow of the oil lamp. Although it had to be refilled every few hours, this light was never allowed to go out, even through the night. Keeping it filled was the woman's responsibility, and Proverbs says "her lamp does not go out at night" (Prov. 31:18).

COOKING

Mom rolled out of bed first each morning. She was up early, starting a fire in the hearth or oven. She had hungry children to feed, and a husband to pack a lunch for and send off to work. The main food in the Jewish diet was bread. In fact, the Hebrew word for food was a synonym for bread. One of the jobs that the wife and mother had, then, was to grind grain into flour. This involved several steps. She had none of the electrical gadgets that modern wives have, so all of this work had to be done by hand. Just the bread-baking took up the better part of a woman's day. Other mainstays of the ancient diet were goat's milk, which could be made into butter, yogurt, or cheese. Depending on where you lived, the meal could be spiced up with the addition of olives, dried fish, raisins, figs, and lemons. Most women supplemented their cooking supplies with their garden, and fresh greens, onions, leeks, cucumbers, and melons were welcome additions to their tables. Fresh meat was a luxury, often only enjoyed during special occasions and feasts. The cups at a meal were usually filled with water, wine, or a fermented beverage made from goat's milk. It was this potent milk-based beverage that put Sisera to sleep in Jael's tent (Judg. 4:19).

FETCHING WATER

Every family needed water. Sometimes a family built their own private cistern to store rain water, but most often the water came from a spring or well in the middle of the village. It was the woman's job to go and fetch that water every day. Large jars were used to collect the day's water, and a young woman had to be sturdy to balance a pot on her head. They often weighed as much as fifty pounds once they were filled. Far from being a drudgery, the women in a village looked forward to the trip to the well. They all timed it so that they could meet each other there. So, while the buckets were being lowered into the well to fill their jars, the women would stand together in tight groups, chattering and exchanging the news of their days. This was mom's big chance to get out of the house for a short time each day and see her friends and family.

CHANGING DIAPERS

Children were a blessing, and Jewish couples hoped to have as many as they could. This meant that young mothers often had several little ones underfoot at any given point in time. This added greatly to a woman's responsibilities throughout the day. While still expected to tend the fire, cook the meals, and fetch the water, she had to care for her little ones' needs. Small children had to be nursed, bathed, and diapered. This without the benefit of disposable diapers, washing machines, or running water. Children had to be spoon-fed, then potty-trained. As the children got older, the mother taught them proper manners. She also taught the older daughters how to cook, sew, and do the other things a good Israelite wife must know.

LAUNDRY

To do a proper job at washing laundry, a woman made her way to the moving waters of a river or creek. Garments could be soaked and laundered in large basins, but running water made swift work of the rinsing process. First, the clothing was drenched in the water, then treated with soap (Mal. 3:2). Next, the clothes were worked with the hands, stepped on, or beaten with rocks to loosen the soil that was trapped within the weave. This was an exhausting process. Next the pummeled outfits were brought into the swiftly moving waters, which would carry away the soil with the suds. Rinsed clothes were draped on the bushes or grass nearby to bleach and dry in the sun. Laundry day did not come very often for some people, who preferred a strong dose of deodorizing perfume to a good scrubbing. But young mothers with diapers to do had little choice but to rinse and wring nappies on a daily basis. David used the picture of washing clothes as a symbol of the action needed to cleanse away his sin (Ps. 51:2).

RACHEL
Fetching Water for the Flocks

Rachel was one of the younger daughters of Laban. Her older sister, Leah, was a great help to her mother in the kitchen. Rachel had been taught all the tasks that she would need when she married. She learned, at her mother's side, how to make bread, tend babies, spin wool, sew clothing, and do laundry. Her parents had taken care in making her a valuable asset in some man's home, worthy of a hefty dowry. But Rachel was not needed in the tight quarters surrounding the family's cookfire. Her mother could manage with Leah's help. So, her family put this energetic youngster to use elsewhere. It is very appropriate that Rachel's name meant "ewe" or "sheep," for Rachel worked as a shepherdess. Younger children in a family were often given this task (1Sa. 16:11). Her daily task was to watch over and water the family's flock of sheep and goats. This sent the girl out into the pastures and surrounding hillsides. The fresh air and exercise put a healthy glow on her cheeks and a sparkle in her eyes. She developed a very pretty figure, too (Gen. 29:17).

One of the daily chores that was set before young Rachel was the watering of the sheep. In the hot lands, the dry grasses did not supply much moisture to the grazing flocks, and there were no pools or streams handy. So, the village in Haran provided a well in the middle of a field where the local flocks could be watered. To protect the well from unsavory characters, they covered it with a heavy stone, which took a few shepherds with gumption to shift. Once the shepherds and shepherdesses had all herded their flocks into the pasture, the water was drawn and the animals were allowed to drink their fill. Rachel was in the midst of this task one evening when Jacob came up and introduced himself. A cousin! A son of her own

dear Auntie Rebekah. Within the month, Jacob asked for her hand in marriage. Another sister would have to water the sheep now, for Rachel would soon be minding her own cookfire and tending her own family.

ALABASTER

Alabaster had the corner on the market. Just as we call any "facial tissue" a Kleenex, the Greeks called any thin-necked bottle an "alabaster." This was because of the very familiar shape of the perfume bottles that were sold in the marketplaces. Actually, alabaster is the name of the stone from which these distinctive bottles were made. With its colorful streaked markings, alabaster was similar in appearance to marble. However, it was much easier to carve, and was made into beautiful jars, boxes, and vases. When finished, these carvings were partially transparent and could be highly polished.

DID YOU KNOW?

• The first sign that a home needed a new roof was the incessant dripping of water indoors. Proverbs compares this annoying invasion of wet and cold to living with a cranky wife (Prov. 27:15).

• In the nomadic tents, the woman's quarters housed all the cooking and cleaning apparatus—lamps, water skins, mills, pots, water jars, bedding, brooms, spinning wheels, etc. The men's quarters were for entertaining.

POTPOURRI!

There is a very special reason that alabaster was used for perfume bottles. They were not just little luxuries beautiful to look at, with their marble-like sheen. The woman who received such a treasure could use an unopened bottle of perfume much as we would use a sachet filled with potpourri! Alabaster is a soft mineral, with many tiny holes in it. When filled with a costly perfume, the bottle itself became saturated with the scent. An alabaster flask of a precious scent could last for years! When the woman came to Jesus and anointed his head and feet with perfume (Mk. 14:3), she broke open the alabaster bottle to pour out its precious scent. To the disciples' dismay, perfume, which could have lasted for years, was spilled out all at once.

SEWING

Many of the women in the Bible were praised for their ability to sew and made it their business to sew for needy people. Dorcas was one such godly woman who stitched up garments for the poor and needy (Acts 9:39). The Proverbs 31 woman was also acclaimed for her handiwork. "She stretches out her hands to the distaff, and her hand holds the spindle" (Prov. 31:19–22). It was expected that a mother provide for the clothing needs of her family, and it involved so much more than "back to school" shopping. Since families could be quite large, this became a daunting task. She easily added "seamstress" to her lengthy job description. Many women, especially wives of small town farmers, had to start from scratch. Even when mom purchased fabric in the marketplace, sewing was done the old fashioned way, with a needle. Her hands were kept busy in carding and spinning wool and weaving the thread upon a small loom. Thankfully, the patterns were simple, with no tucks, ruffles or buttonholes to fuss over. Tunics, robes, and girdles were practical items that left little scope for the imagination.

NEEDLEWORK

Even though patterns for basic clothing were simple, there were plenty of opportunities for a woman to show off her skill with a needle and thread. Much care was put into the embroidery around the neckline of her robe. Sometimes, embroidery patterns were traditional designs, unique to her family or village. Wedding garments were always given special attention, and could take several months to complete.

SPRING CLEANING

It was not always easy to keep the house spotlessly clean. Rooms were small and dimly lit, often having just one tiny window to let in the sun and breezes. Many women were accustomed to a floor that was simply the sand under the tent. Others had hard-packed earth underfoot. In some homes, rocks were used to make a kind of cobblestone floor, but this made it easy to lose things in the cracks (Lk. 15:8). Most country women

RUTH

Gleaning in the Fields

Widowed at a very young age, Ruth was uprooted from everything that she had known when she chose to follow Naomi into the land of Israel (Ruth 1:16). Naomi's husband, Elimelech, had also died, and the two women were left without any means in Moab. Naomi had heard that the land of Israel was through their recent famine, and so she began to make plans. They would be traveling to Naomi's hometown, in Bethlehem. Ruth loved her mother-in-law dearly, and was prepared to help provide for her well-being in whatever the future might hold. Once they had settled back into a small house on the lands of Elimelech, Ruth began to look for ways to make ends meet. The barley harvest had begun (Ruth 1:22), and it was the local custom in the Jewish community to allow the poor to glean in the fields while the crops were being gathered. Naomi and Ruth certainly qualified as poor, so there was food to be had. All that was needed was a strong back and a willingness to work. Ruth possessed both, and so the early mornings found her making her way out into the barley fields to gather grain.

Gleaning was a task for the persistent, because the small handfuls of kernels added up slowly. With a sharp eye on the ground, Ruth moved through the field, stopping only to stoop down and gather up a stray cluster of barley that had fallen from the reaper's bundles. During a lunch break, Ruth met the owner of the field. Boaz explained that he knew who she was, and he thanked her for her kindness to Naomi (Ruth 2:11). Ruth was invited to return and glean in his fields again tomorrow. As the day moved on, Ruth seemed be finding larger and larger bundles of stray barley, and thanked God for this added blessing. By the end of the day, Ruth settled herself on the edge of the field to evaluate her success. Rather

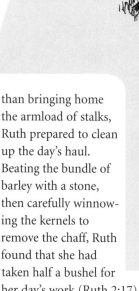

than bringing home the armload of stalks, Ruth prepared to clean up the day's haul. Beating the bundle of barley with a stone, then carefully winnowing the kernels to remove the chaff, Ruth found that she had taken half a bushel for her day's work (Ruth 2:17). At home, Naomi's eyes lit up at the bounty set before her. They shared the day's news as they weighed out the grain. Naomi had tended the fire in anticipation of Ruth's foray, and the women prepared to grind some of the precious barley into flour, which could be made into simple cakes of bread. As they worked, Naomi chattered on about the kindness of Boaz, and of his position of kinsman redeemer in their clan (Ruth 3:2). In the lonely home of Naomi and Ruth, there was celebration and even hope.

had to share their home with their animals. At any given time a donkey, some goats, sheep, and a handful of chickens might be in the same room where she slept. Still, bedding could be shaken out and aired. Dishes were kept washed. The ashes from the fire could be carried out to the garden. And any accumulating manure on the floor was trotted up to the rooftop, where it could dry in the sun and be stored away for winter fuel. With so few belongings, it did not take long to set them in order.

BRINGING IN THE SHEAVES

Wives often had to set aside their usual chores for seasonal tasks. So their daily routines had to be flexible enough to include these other jobs. Harvest times were especially busy, for the wife was expected to help in the gathering. Every hand was needed to bring the harvest in safely. In poor homes, harvest time sent the women into the fields to glean in order to supplement the family's meager pantry (Ruth 2:23). Ruth gleaned in the fields for Naomi, and brought home both barley and parched grain from the day's labor. There was enough to eat a little and store the rest away for the winter months ahead.

KEEPING THE FAMILY IN ORDER

Daddy, Mama, Junior, Sissy, and their dog, Rover were not the typical residents of a home in ancient times. Most homes grew right along with the family, and housed a multi-generational mix of relatives. Young couples moved in with the husband's family. Parents who were too old to care for themselves were given a room. Aunts, uncles, cousins, and second-cousins were frequently working and living together in a kind of mini-community within a city.

EXTENDED FAMILY

Essentially, Old Testament times saw little of the nuclear family. Extended families stuck together, and for very good reason. There was safety in numbers, for one thing. The more brothers and uncles and cousins there were to protect their encampment, the less likely they were to be invaded by thieves or raiders. Also, many hands made light the work. While the group of men worked together in the field to ensure a harvest, their several wives were busy in the tents, tending the meals, children, and sewing. A young bride was never at a loss in the kitchen, for she shared it with many. A young mother was never left in dismay with a mewling infant, for many were the hands of experienced mothers ready to coax and coddle the newest member of the family. Even later, in New Testament times, the women learned from each other. Mary traveled to be with her cousin, Elizabeth (Lk. 1:56). In helping to prepare for the coming of baby John, she was preparing herself for the coming of her own Son.

THE IDEAL WIFE

According to Proverbs 31:17, an ideal wife in the days of the Old Testament had strong arms. To be sure, a pretty face could turn heads, but in the long run, a man needed a wife who could work hard. Every day a young woman would fill her water jug at the local well and carry it home on her head. Preparing grain for the day's bread-baking was another back-breaking chore.

DID YOU HEAR THE ONE ABOUT...

An old Jewish story demonstrates how important the woman was in Israel. The story says that a good and righteous man once married a good and righteous woman. They were unable to have children, so they eventually agreed to divorce one another. The husband then married a wicked woman, and she made him wicked. The good woman married a wicked man, and she made him righteous. The moral of the story is that the woman sets the tone for the home. A mother holds an important place in the life of her family. She can be the key to a successful family, or the cause of its failure. She can have an incalculable influence on her husband and her children.

MOMS MAKE THE DIFFERENCE

In the long and sometimes boring Chronicles of the Bible, there is, occasionally, a reason to jump up and down. One such morsel of information just goes to prove how important a mother is to her family. In 1 and 2 Chronicles, each time a king is mentioned, we get the rundown of his life: when he began his reign, how old he was, how long he reigned, whether or not he was a good king, and who his mother was. The queen mother is mentioned in nineteen different passages, which list the kings of Judah. At her hand, a future ruler was raised up, and her influence in that prince's life was unmistakable. A good mother pointed her son in the right direction, so that the Scriptures record: "Amaziah, the son of Joash...reigned twenty-nine years in Jerusalem. His mother's name was Jehoaddin of Jerusalem. And he did what was right in the eyes of the Lord (2Kin. 14:1–3, RSV). Although we do not know exactly what the queen's role in government and society was during those days, she did wield influence in the household. Bathsheba, Solomon's mother, persuaded David to vow that Solomon would be king (1Kin. 1:30), and Solomon respected his mother for what she had done (1Kin. 2:19).

> **DID YOU KNOW?**
>
> • Strictly speaking, a girl's only value was in the work she did around the house when she was young and in the bride price that she brought when she was married off.
>
> • Mary may well have attended Elizabeth during the birth of John the Baptist, and prepared herself in this way for the arrival of her own baby (Lk. 1:56).

BUNDLES OF JOY

In ancient times, marriage had very little to do with love. It had everything to do with babies. The whole point of marriage was procreation. A Jewish couple wanted to be remembered, and only through offspring was this ensured. As part of the preparations for a wedding, the family of the bride would all gather together in order to bless her. They would declare their happiness for her, and wish her many children. We see Rebekah's family doing this: "Our sister, may you become the mother of thousands of ten thousands" (Gen. 24:60). Although new parents were happy to have a daughter, every couple hoped their newborn would be a son. You see, men stayed with a family and increased its size and wealth by bringing in their own wives, and still more children. Girls, on the other hand, were raised only to leave, becoming wives in others' families.

SWADDLING CLOTHES

It is a familiar enough line from the Christmas Pageants, "and this will be the sign to you: You will find a Babe wrapped in swaddling clothes, lying in a manger" (Lk. 2:12). And so, swaddling clothes are associated with the fuzzy flannel blanket we see wrapped around the doll used in children's plays. However, these clothes were not just an ancient onesie. There was a purpose to swaddling infants. You see, when a baby was born, the midwife gave it a good salt scrub (Eze. 16:4), which was thought to harden the skin. Then the little one was swaddled in yards and yards of white cotton or linen cloth. These bands of cloth were about five inches wide and six yards long. The Jewish mothers thought that if their baby was bound tightly in this way, its arms and legs would grow straight and strong.

ADOPTING AN HEIR

When a man in Palestine had no son to inherit his land and possessions, he needed to keep his eyes open for a strapping young up-and-comer. Usually the man would chose a likely candidate from within the clan, then give to the young man his daughter in marriage. The adopted son was then required to work in the household as if he had been born there. If a natural son was born later, the adopted son was cast aside in favor of the natural-born heir. It may be that Laban had intended to adopt Jacob as an

ESAU

Firstborn Son

Isaac had two sons—Esau and Jacob. The boys were a study in contrast. Jacob was a quiet boy who spent a lot of time hanging around his mother's tent. Esau was a man's man. He was tall and strong, and covered with thick hair. He was tanned from his days spent out in the surrounding hills, and his striking red hair glowed. Esau was the picture of health. He smelled of fresh air and green grass. Isaac loved Esau. Even though he had a twin brother, Esau had managed to be born first. Those few extra minutes of seniority made Esau the firstborn son and heir to Isaac's wealth. In ancient times, a man's land was not divided equally amongst all of his sons, for then it would dwindle into nothingness over the course of generations. Although younger sons were often provided for in some small way, the firstborn son received everything else. Esau, by birthright, was destined to be a patriarch. Most young men took their responsibility seriously, following closely behind their fathers, watching and learning. Esau, however, preferred to spend his days alone in the hillsides. He was a master huntsman. His skill with a bow was unparalleled in their part of the world. But he cared more for developing his skills than in caring about his family. In this way, he scorned his birthright. Esau wasn't one to worry about the future, but lived in the moment. So, when he came into the camp after a long hunt, he expected the usual "hail to the conquering chief" and a bowl of something hot to eat. He had anticipated the scene of his father's boasting and his mother's home cooking. Imagine his affront when the only person lurking about the tents was his brother. As a disgruntled Esau approached his brother, he had to grudgingly admit that whatever Jacob was stirring smelled

appetizing. Esau deemed his own immediate needs greater than those of his family, and he traded away his birthright for a bowl of stew. In the end, he lost the blessing of the firstborn to his brother as well. Jacob had grasped what Esau had disdained. Realizing what he had lost too late, Esau pleaded, "Bless me, too!" Once given, the blessing was irrevocable.

heir, marrying off both his daughters to him. There were sons born to Laban, though, and they may have been jealous of their brother-in-law (Gen. 31:1). This would account for the dissention between Laban's shepherds and Jacob's. Perhaps the natural sons of Laban feared that Jacob would try to claim inheritance.

LONGING FOR A CHILD

When a woman was barren in Bible times, she might be able to adopt the child born to her servant. The servant-girl was made a concubine of her mistress' husband, and the full-fledged wife got first dibs on any child the young woman bore. We see this with Sarah, who gave her servant, Hagar, to Abraham (Gen. 16:3). We also see this with the dueling sisters, Leah and Rachel, who had given their servant girls to Jacob in hopes of producing sons (Gen. 30:3, 9). When the birth of a child was imminent, the barren woman would be ready. At the birth, she would then take the child and put him on her knees to signify that she was adopting the child as her own.

> ### DID YOU KNOW?
>
> • The twelve tribes of Israel are named for Jacob's twelve sons, although Joseph's portion was divided between his two sons, Ephraim and Manasseh.
>
> • Lemuel thought so much of his mother's words that he actually wrote them down for posterity. Her good advice survives today–it is Proverbs 31.

WHAT'S IN A NAME?

Jewish people believed that they must first know a person's name before they could know the person himself. Because of this, the choosing of a name for a baby was not taken lightly. Mothers were normally granted the privilege of naming their child, and normally the name had some kind of special significance to the family. Because of this, it is very interesting to follow through the Scriptures looking at the meanings of names as they are given in footnotes and margins.

WHICH MARY?

In Amish communities, where so many large families have the same last name, women are often known by their husband's name. For instance, the Mary Yoder who is married to Amos Yoder would be differentiated from Andrew Yoder's wife, Mary, by calling the ladies Amos Mary and Andrew Mary. In a similar way, the close-knit communities and large families in Bible times had ways of letting each other know who they were discussing. One such way celebrated the all-important achievement of parenthood. At the birth of a new family member, the parent's names were adjusted slightly. For instance, when young Jesus entered this world, Mary would have become known by her friends as "Mary, mother of Jesus."

NEW NAMES

Changing one's name wasn't just a case of sweet little Billy coming home from school one day and wanting to be called Bill from now on. A person could request that their name be changed, but that usually signified some drastic change in a their character. For instance, Naomi, whose name meant "sweet," asked that she be called Mara, meaning "bitter," because of all of her troubles. The zealous Pharisee Saul, who had attempted to stomp out Christianity, renamed himself Paul once he, himself, became a Christian. On other occasions, someone else would give a person a new name. God renamed Abram ("exalted father") Abraham ("father of many"), and He renamed Jacob ("he deceives") Israel ("one who struggles with God"). In the New Testament we find that Jesus renamed his disciple Simon ("hearing") so that he becomes Peter ("rock"). Each of us will receive a new name as well, once we see our Savior face to face (Rev. 2:17).

BABY NAMING BASICS

Mothers were in charge of naming their newborns, and we can see that they followed some pretty basic criteria when doing their choosing. A child's name might signify the feelings or events surrounding their birth. We might name a baby girl born at sunrise "Dawn," or during a hurricane "Stormy."

In the Bible, Rachel originally named Benjamin "Ben-Oni," after her difficult delivery, meaning "son of my sorrow" (Gen. 35:18). The wife of one of Eli's sons went into early labor when she learned that her husband had been killed in the same battle in which the enemy had captured the ark of the covenant. Since this event meant that the glory of God had been taken from Israel, she named the son she bore that day Ichabod, which meant "the glory has departed" (1Sa. 4:21). Often the child's name referred to a personality trait that they hoped would describe their child as he grew. For example, Andrew meant "manly." On the other hand, suspicious parents would name a child something rather unflattering, because they believed that evil spirits would hinder the growth of a child that was too good. An example of this practice might include such people as Nabal (1Sa. 25:3), whose name meant "fool." The names that suggested imperfections would help prevent these demons' notice. Animal names were often used. For instance, Deborah is the Hebrew word for "bee." A mother naming her daughter Deborah might be hoping that her newborn would grow into a busy little bee about the house.

> ## DID YOU KNOW?
>
> • After the age of thirteen, a boy qualified to become one of the ten men who could constitute a synagogue.
>
> • Lot's two sons, Ben-Ammi and Moab, were also his grandsons, for the boy's mothers were Lot's own daughters (Gen. 19:32).
>
> • If a father wished, he could sell his daughter into slavery (Deut. 15:12; Joel 3:3). A disobedient son could be put to death (Deut. 21:18–21).

BIRTHRIGHTS AND BLESSINGS

There were some serious perks to being the first-born boy in an ancient family. So much was riding on the birth order, that when twins were to be born, the midwife was obliged to mark the first baby to make an appearance (Gen. 38:28). A man expected his oldest boy to follow in his footsteps and take care of the family's interests. He would inherit everything. A younger son would only receive what the eldest son gave to him.

BAR MITZVAH

In Bible times, a boy was a boy until he turned thirteen. Then he was considered to be a man. Part of this rite of passage was the bar mitzvah, when he became a son of the law.

LEVIRATE MARRIAGES

A levirate marriage provided a way for a woman to have a child to carry on her husband's name and to provide for her needs in her old age. Put simply, a young widow was given to her dead husband's brother. Any child conceived between them was considered to be the child of the deceased, and the heir carried on in their father's place in the family. An example of this is found in Genesis, where Judah's eldest son dies suddenly. The son's young wife, Tamar, is given to the next boy in line, but he refuses to do his duty by her. God strikes him down, and Tamar is passed along to son number three. Once again this boy won't do his part, and he bites the dust as well. Now, Judah is alarmed at his dwindling household, and asks Tamar to wait until son number four is a bit older. In the end, Judah himself provides Tamar with twin boys, who take the place of his eldest son in the line of Christ (Mt. 1:3).

POLYGAMY

Since children were such a blessing, and a way to leave your mark in the world, the more the merrier. In an effort to "be fruitful and multiply" exponentially, some men took more than one wife. As long as he could support the increased size of his household, this was completely acceptable in Old Testament times. The first case of polygamy involved one of the sons of Cain; a man named Lamech (Gen. 4:19). Jacob also took two wives—Rachel and Leah (Gen. 29:23, 28). Even men who only married one woman would sometimes take a concubine in order to increase the number of children in the household. Abraham did not marry Hagar, but was willing to use her to provide a son for Sarah to raise (Gen. 16:3). Kings liked to establish themselves and were often given wives as gifts from other nations. David had several wives and concubines living in his

BOAZ

The Kinsman Redeemer

Boaz was a leading citizen in his hometown of Bethlehem. Boaz was recognized as a good man, upright and godly in the eyes of God and man. He was also wealthy and influential (Ruth 2:1). He owned many fields, and employed many reapers during the harvest. Still, he did not leave the fields only in the hands of his supervisors. Instead, Boaz made it his practice to survey the progress each day. Approaching the laborers, Boaz called out a blessing to the workers, "The Lord be with you," which they returned to him respectfully, "The Lord bless you" (Ruth 2:4). He knew all of his reapers by name, and in the small community of Bethlehem, he knew the poor families who gleaned there as well. So, as he approached the harvesters and conferred with his overseer, it did not take long for him to spot, Ruth, and inquire after her. Boaz had heard the local gossip about the foreign girl. The ladies in town did not approve of her and were shunning her in the square. But, he had also seen how she loved her mother-in-law, Naomi, and how she was so willing to care for the older woman. Her work in the fields that very day was a testament to her faithfulness. Boaz admired that in the girl, and so he spoke to her. Thanking her for her care for Naomi, he invited her to continue gleaning in his field for the duration of the harvest. As she joined the other reapers, he gave special instructions to a few of his workers. "Drop a few extra handfuls in her path," he urged. Boaz knew that Ruth was bringing her harvest home to Naomi, and he felt a family obligation to make sure that the two widows would have enough food for the winter months ahead. Boaz was a member of their clan, and a very close relative. He had grown up with Naomi's husband, and had known Ruth's husband, Mahlon, since he was a baby.

Then came the night when the harvesting was over. Ruth came to him at the threshing floor, and she pleaded with him to fulfill the obligations of a kinsman redeemer with her. If Boaz was willing, then Ruth would become his wife, and she might be blessed with children. Her firstborn son would take the place of Mahlon, and carry on the family line of Naomi's husband, Elimelech. Boaz was able to secure the right to serve as kinsman redeemer from his relative, who did not wish to marry the foreign girl. Boaz took Ruth as his wife. Ruth gave birth to a son, and Naomi rejoiced over her grandson. Boaz had given the two widows a new lease on life, restoring their hope and their family line.

palace (2Sa. 5:13), and his son Solomon had seven hundred wives and three hundred concubines in his harem (1Kin. 11:3). This was in direct contradiction with God's previous command for a king not to multiply wives in his home (Deut. 17:17).

CLAN

In Bible times, extended family didn't just include a handful of uncles, aunts, and cousins. Relatives were coming out of the woodwork, because everybody belonged to a clan. Members of a clan were all descendants of some ancestor, and because of this, they saw each other as kin. A clan could be so large that members numbered into the hundreds (Gen. 46:8–27; Ezr. 8:1–14). Members of a clan looked after each other in times of trouble, offering assistance and protection to those in need. Men often sought a wife from within their own clan. That is why Abraham sent his servant to bring a wife for his son from his father's house (Gen. 24:4). Later, Jacob sought a bride from among his mother's nieces (Gen. 28:2). Esau felt his parents' disapproval in his choice of a bride from among the Gentiles, so he found a bride from among the descendants of Abraham through Ishmael in an attempt to appease them (Gen. 28:6–9).

> **DID YOU KNOW?**
>
> • A groom paid a bride-price to the bride's father, because by taking away a daughter, he was decreasing that household's workforce.

KINSMAN REDEEMER

Every clan had its appointed hero. He was the avenger, the rescuer, the protector. He was the kinsman redeemer. This man was able to help his family out of many difficult situations. When a clan member found himself in a financial pinch so that he needed to sell a parcel of land to pay off his debts, then the kinsman redeemer was called upon to buy the property so that it was kept within the clan (Jer. 32:6–8). If a man was taken captive by his enemies and sold into slavery, the kinsman redeemer was given the task of finding this unfortunate soul and trying to purchase his freedom

(Lev. 25:47–49). Should a man die childless, the kinsman redeemer was expected to marry the man's widow (Deut. 25:5–10). Any children born of this union were considered to belong to the deceased in order to carry on the family name. If a clansman fell victim to murder, the kinsman redeemer was sent to avenge the crime. In carrying out this justice, he was called the "avenger of blood" (Deut. 19:12).

SHOP 'TIL YOU DROP

Before the days of the Wells Fargo Wagon comin' down the street, there was still an arrival that would set the whole town a'buzz. In Bible times, every head would turn when a caravan rode into the village. Merchants in bright cloaks would ride into town astride their long-legged camels. As they neared the city, caravaners would break into song, accompanied by the bells that jangled from their saddles and the instruments they had carried on their backs. They drew a crowd as they entered the marketplaces and set up their booths.

THE SHOPPING EXPERIENCE

The shopping experiences in ancient times were vastly different from today's trips to the grocer. It was a bit more like a trip to the farmer's market. There was no one-stop shopping available, so fresh produce, eggs, cheese, and fish were all sold at different booths along the market square. Other booths might offer fine fabrics, sandals, jewelry, and perfume. A trip to the market was not quick. Such outings were fraught with time-consuming traditions and courtesies. Little price stickers and express check-out were unheard of, for the cost of an item was subject to a good haggling. Sellers called out to passers by, extolling the quality of their goods to anyone who would listen. Shoppers might find a cackling hen or a fresh fish waved in their face by eager vendors. Buyers picked through the stalls, feigning disinterest and dissatisfaction with the wares set before them. Bargaining was a game, as affable salesmen matched wits with shrewd housewives.

DAVID
Husband to Many

David began his years as the baby of the family. With seven older brothers to help around the farm, David was given the task of watching the sheep in the pastures. But, life in the hillsides did not last long. At the age of sixteen or so, he was sent on an errand that would change his life. His father, Jesse, sent him to deliver some cheese to a few of his older brothers who were in the army and bring back word of how they were doing. Once at the battlefield, David caught sight of the Philistine armies, and of the giant, Goliath. The confrontation that followed left the giant dead, the invading armies scattered, and the shepherd boy a hero. He was brought before Saul to receive his reward, and one of the prizes was the princess, Michal who became the first of his wives. Later, he married Abigail, a widow who had proved herself both wise and generous, and a woman named Ahinoam of Jezreel, who gave birth to his firstborn son, Amnon. Bathsheba was brought into his palace as a wife after David had her husband, Uriah, murdered. She became the mother of Solomon, David's future heir.

Polygamy was a common luxury of the wealthy. Royalty could afford the mounting costs that these women incurred better than most men, plus they wished to establish their bloodline by having lots of children. God had warned that a king should not multiply wives to himself, for the women could influence their husbands and turn them away from serving God (Deut. 17:17). Still, David didn't seem to think that three wives were a problem, and over the years he continued to add to his harem (2Sa. 5:13). The alliances that were made across a kingdom's borders were often sealed with his marriage to some foreign dignitary's daughter. His

wife, Maacah, was a princess from Geshur. David also had wives named Haggith, Abital, and Eglah. He then added several concubines and a whole passel of children within the palace walls.

BARTER

There are so many options for spending money today: discount stores and grocery stores, outlet malls and mega malls, coffee shops and barber shops. And all of them have the same question for you: "Will that be cash or charge?" Not so in Bible times. They preferred to haggle! Even today, we are not completely unfamiliar with the system of barter. It can be used at any age. "I'll trade you my peanut butter and jelly sandwich for your cheese sandwich." In Old Testament times, before a standardized system of coinage was worked out, barter was the only way to buy goods and services. It was the simple idea of fair trade! Trading wool for wine, fish for figs, chickens for cheese. Even a bride was bought from her father by the groom. Hosea exchanged grain and silver for a wife (Hos. 3:2). Rachel's bride-price was set at seven years' labor (Gen. 29:20). Though coinage made it into the marketplaces by New Testament times, small towns still used barter. Joseph, the carpenter, who lived in the small town of Nazareth, may well have been paid for his work with wool, olive oil, dried figs, or pickled fish.

ADVERTISING

The tradesmen who traveled in caravans served as the "grapevine" for regional businessmen. Of course this wasn't just chit-chat and gossip; this was advertising. They tried to tempt the housewives from each village with the wares that were crafted in the villages they had just left. Pretty and practical wares were displayed with a flourish in the hopes of making a sale. One village might specialize in blue dyes they obtained from their groves of pomegranate trees. "Just look at this wonderful shade of blue. No other town can boast of such a deep, heavenly color!" Another village might be home to several skilled potters. "The clay in that region is of quite an unusual color. See how these water pitchers are nearly red? And look, these bowls match them exactly!" When a caravan's route brought them close to a sea port, they were able to bring even more exotic goods inland. "Have you ever smelled such aromas? Such a lovely woman as yourself must have this perfume. It comes from across the sea, and is as rare as your beauty!"

THE JERUSALEM MARKETPLACES

Jerusalem boasted seven different marketplaces in New Testament times. A brisk business had built up around the Temple, which was certainly the most important factor in the city's business dealings. Much of the trade was in goods required for worship at the Temple, especially animals for sacrifice. Merchants sold goats, lambs, and doves as well as fine meal and oil for sacrifice. There were also moneychangers set up in the marketplace, who could—for a modest fee—exchange any foreign currency for the accepted Jewish shekels to pay the Temple tax. Jesus objected to the fact that this kind of trade was going on right in the courts of the Temple (Mt. 21:13).

CUSTOMER SERVICE

Service with a smile! In the marketplaces, the Jewish rabbis had strict rules for business deals, and there were market inspectors to see that they were carried out. Customer service was of the utmost importance, as was cleanliness. Scales and weights had to be cleaned regularly, and buyers had the right to complain. And although they could be heavily taxed, no interest was to be charged to fellow-Jews.

> **DID YOU KNOW?**
>
> • Personal belongings could be handed over as security against a loan. But essentials such as cloaks and millstones were not to be sold in the event of non-payment (Ex. 22:26; Deut. 24:6).
>
> • Much of Abram's wealth was counted in cattle, camels, donkeys, goats, and sheep. Livestock was a common form of money in ancient times.

IMPORTS AND EXPORTS

In New Testament times, imports increased in spite of Jerusalem's remote highland position. According to records, no fewer than one hundred and eighteen different kinds of foreign luxury goods were being sold there. This became possible because of the long period of peace under Roman rule, and the roads that connected them to the rest of the world.

JACOB

Bartering for a Bride

When Jacob scurried out of Canaan to avoid certain death at the hands of his angry twin brother, he sought haven in the house of his uncle Laban. Heeding his mother's advice to find a bride from among his cousins, Jacob approached Laban concerning his young daughter, Rachel. She was lovely, strong, and kind. Laban was thrilled. It would be a wonderful match. However, such a daughter carried a high price. Even for family, Laban could not part with Rachel for nothing. The bride-price must be set. Jacob turned out the proverbial pockets of his robe and came up empty. Still, he was willing to do anything to prove himself worthy of her hand. Laban agreed to allow Jacob to marry Rachel, but there was a catch. Jacob had to work for her. Seven years of tending the flocks was a small price to pay for such a girl. So Jacob willingly worked, anticipating the day when he could claim his bride.

Once the wedding day came, Jacob found the tables turned. Laban must have been reluctant to lose his best shepherd, for a way was contrived to secure several more years of service. Just as Jacob had deceived his father and cheated his brother, Jacob found himself deceived by his uncle and cheated out of his bride. (This devious nature must have run on his mother's side of the family!) The seven years that Jacob had logged were used in an unauthorized payment for big sister, Leah (Gen. 29:25). Laban smoothly assured the bitter young man that Rachel could be his—next week. All he had to do was agree to another seven-year tour of duty with the flocks. What could Jacob do? There had been no cash payment made for all of his previous labor. Coming full circle, he was again stuck without a bride-price for Rachel. Jacob must work for his father-in-law seven more years for the privilege of marrying two wives in one week (Gen. 29:30).

Merchants carried exotic and unusual wares throughout the known empire. The Jews exported increasing amounts of olive oil and linen while bringing into Jerusalem such luxury items as cotton, silk, Greek wines, salted fish, spices, glass bowls, apples, cheese, baskets, and slaves.

NEW TESTAMENT MONEY

Keeping your coins straight in New Testament times could be complicated, because there were three different currencies in popular use. There was the local money, which was of Jewish mint. This was used in paying the Temple taxes. There was provincial money, which was the Greek standard, leftover from the days of Alexander the Great. Lastly, there were coins of Roman origin. These were the official, imperial currency, accepted anywhere in the world.

ANOTHER DAY, ANOTHER DENARIUS

Imagine working for an entire day in the hot sun and receiving one coin at the end of the day for your efforts. A whole day's work in exchange for a bit of metal. In a growing empire, this became much more convenient than barter. Abraham's wealth had been counted in the number of camels, goats, sheep, and donkeys that were in his flocks. Job's blessings were translated into large herds as well (Job 42:12). As cities developed, precious metals took the place of flour, wine, and cattle. Coinage became standardized rather slowly. Copper discs might have the imprint of a village's chieftain. In large marketplaces, lumps of silver were weighed out during business transactions. Eventually, coins became miniature works of art, bearing portraits of powerful men and their gods (Mt. 22:21).

CHAPTER TEN

THEIR JOBS

The Butcher, The Baker, The Candlestick-maker! Not every person in the Bible was a shepherd or a carpenter. When the stories of the Scriptures are looked at carefully, an **amazing array of occupations** come to light. Farmers, merchants, artisans, scholars, and slaves all had their niches in the ancient world.

FARMERS AND HERDSMEN

In Bible times, the farmers were the real pioneer types: independent, self-sufficient, living off the land. There have always been farmers in Palestine, although the climate and soil made farming a life of constant toil and hardship. The herdsman's life was no easier, living out in the open as they followed their flocks in search of pastures and water.

A HARD LIFE

As a man living off of his land, the farmer worked hard and steadily through the seasons. The winter months, when the rains came, found him trudging through ankle-deep mud, pushing his plow through more mud. Although cold, wet, and miserable, a farmer had to work quickly to till and plant his fields while the ground was softened by the winter storms. Spring brought a wheat and barley harvest. Summer brought simmering heat. Then came the harvest of fruits of the summer: olives, and grapes, and melons. A farmer who owned vineyards or orchards would have been swamped with work. It was a hard life.

DID YOU KNOW?

- Pharisees often referred to those with no religious education as "people of the land," which showed their scorn for the common farmer.

THE FARMER'S FLOCK

The Hebrew word for cattle included a variety of animals: sheep, goats, oxen, and donkeys. The donkeys were kept for carrying loads, and oxen were used for plowing the fields and pulling carts. Sheep and goats were always kept together. The sheep were mainly raised for the wool that they provided. Goats were by far the most valuable animals. They provided milk, which was used for making cheese, yogurt, and butter. They could be used for meat, and their hair made a coarse cloth from which the nomad's tents were made. Goat skins were used to make wineskins and water bottles as well.

THE FARMER'S WIFE

By New Testament times, many women had the benefit of a local market at which to do their grocery shopping. However, the farmer's wives were the ones whose families provided the fresh produce used to stock those markets. So, while all women still had water to fetch and fires to tend, a country woman's day was long and busy. Goats must be milked, and the day's milk turned into fresh butter and yogurt. Cheeses were also prepared and aged. There was wool to spin, skeins to dye, and cloth to weave. Flour must be ground for the day's bread, and the fire tended so that the bread would bake properly. During harvest time, the wife joined her family in the field, gathering up the sheaves of wheat and barley. A garden of fresh produce, like cucumbers, onions, and melons needed to be tended. If the family owned a vineyard, there were grapes to stomp and wine to bottle. If they had olive trees, there was the olive harvest, and oil to press. Fresh fruit, like pomegranates and figs, must be gathered and dried. A very busy day did not end until sunset, when the whole family set aside their tasks for the day and joined together for the evening meal, which the woman had lovingly prepared.

GROWING UP RURAL

The children on an ancient farm were kept busy with little jobs to do. They gathered firewood and fetched water. During the harvest times, they were busy helping with the reaping and the threshing. Children could help tend the grapes in the family vineyard. They were expected to learn about every aspect of working the land, for it would be their inheritance someday. Most of the time, the children were put to work looking after the family's animals. They would take the sheep and goats to pasture each day and watch over them. David was a farm boy, and as the youngest son in his household, was given the task of tending the sheep (1Sa. 16:11).

DEW OF HEAVEN

A mist rolls in from the Mediterranean Sea in the evenings during the hot summer season. During these months there is no rainfall, so the farmers depend upon the heavy dews left by this mist to sustain their crops until the rains returned. In his two blessings in Genesis 27, Isaac mentions this as the "dew of heaven." Jacob's land was near to the coastal plains where the mists would sweep inland, but Esau's kingdom in Edom was too far inland to receive the dews. This fine night mist was also refreshing, as it cooled the evening air for people as well (Hos. 6:4). To take the best advantage of these dews, farmers constructed dew mounds around the bases of their trees. A pile of loose pebbles was built around the base of plants on which the dew could condense. The water would then trickle down into the soil beneath. Some of these dew mounds, that are thousands of years old, can still be seen in the midst of the Negev Desert. The trees are long since gone, but the rows of mounds remain where orchards and vineyards once stood.

> **DID YOU KNOW?**
>
> • The word for 'cattle' in Hebrew includes sheep, goats, oxen, and donkeys, but not pigs.
>
> • The generous farmer never gleaned his own fields or harvested the corners of his fields, leaving all of the missed grain for the poor to collect for themselves (Deut. 24:19).

IRRIGATION

In a land where there was no rain for months at a time, and droughts could last for years, people learned to prepare for the worst. Cisterns were carved out to capture and store precious rainwater, and wells were dug to tap into natural springs beneath the surface. Ancient peoples also learned to make the most of what was available. For example, a vast system of irrigation was developed: man-made dams, reservoirs, aqueducts, and canals. In ancient Egypt, extensive canal systems criss-crossed the land to harness the waters of the Nile to sustain the crops in their fields. Since a Pharaoh's second-in-command usually was overseer of the irrigation and distribution of water, Joseph probably filled this position when he was promoted in Egypt (Gen. 41:40).

MAKING ENDS MEET

Farmers in Old Testament times generally worked to provide for their own needs. Their fields and gardens and flocks were sufficient to sustain their family for the coming year, and nothing more. However, as centuries passed and large cities grew, enterprising farmers found willing customers in the busy marketplaces. Farmers who lived close enough to the cities to make a regular trip into town would grow more produce and sell it to the city-folk. Farmers would put in a few extra rows of melons and build up their herd of milk goats. Wives counted their eggs carefully and set their daughters to churning butter. When the fieldwork allowed, farmers could earn extra money by taking advantage of other resources on their land. A hive of honeybees was a veritable goldmine, and in New Testament times, farmers tended them. Also, a grove of wild figs could be carefully tended, and the extra harvest from them added to the pantry and to the market booth. Amos was a herdsman who also tended the wild fig trees (Amos 7:14). In a land where drought was a constant threat and harvests were uncertain, every little bit counted.

PLANTING TIME

During the late summer months, a plow couldn't be used to turn the earth because it was baked hard (Jer. 14:4). Farmers waited for the change in season. The beginning of the grain season was in October/November, when the rains came and softened the soil enough so that it could be worked more easily with the plow. Plowing and planting were accomplished at one time, with grain being scattered and then plowed under so

AMOS

Tending Wild Figs

Amos was a simple farmer, but he was chosen by God to bring his people a message. Astonished by God's intentions, Amos protests that he is unlearned, not having attended any of the prophetic schools. "I was no prophet, nor was I a son of a prophet." (Amos 7:14). Amos lived in the town of Tekoa, not many miles south of Bethlehem in Judah. He was a herdsman (Amos 1:1), who tended his flocks on the pastures that surrounded his home. However, like every shrewd businessman, he had diversified his sources of income and made the most of the resources available to him. Amos was a tender of wild fig trees (Amos 7:14). Every year during the early summer months, he would take his flocks into the sycamore groves with him. The increasingly hot days found him scurrying among the tree branches, tending a "bonus crop" from sycamore trees in the back forty. Amos had to be wary, for the fig trees attracted large numbers of wasps, which would bore into the fruit. In order for the sycamore trees to produce good figs, the top of each piece of fruit had to be carefully cut. It was a time-consuming, daily chore, which stained his already work-roughened hands. With a knife in hand, Amos trooped into the groves every day, until he was sure that the fruits of his labors were properly dressed. The wild figs ripened slowly, but the mature fruits were dark and sweet. As the baskets of figs were brought in from the woods, Mrs. Amos very likely had the task of preserving them. Since the fruit spoiled quickly, most figs were dried in the sun before they could be brought to the markets for sale.

that the birds could not take it away (Mt. 13:4). These early rains were called the "former rains" and they continued heavily and sporadically throughout the winter. The fields became a great mass of mud during these weeks, and the work was unpleasant. It was tempting to stay inside and wait for warmer days (Prov. 20:4).

GRAIN HARVEST

Wheat and barley were harvested in April, May, and June. Stalks were cut by hand with a sickle, and the bundles of wheat were tied into sheaves. When the harvesters were working quickly, it was easy for stray bunches of wheat to be missed and left on the ground. A generous field owner would instruct his workers not to be too thorough at their work, so that there would be grain enough for the poor gleaners who followed behind them (Deut. 24:19; Ruth 2:2). Once the sheaves had dried out in the field, they were loaded onto carts or onto donkeys and taken to the threshing floor. Once threshed, the grain was stored in large earthenware jars, dry cisterns, barns, or in silos that were dug into the floors of homes.

THE THRESHING FLOOR

At threshing time, grain from the fields was brought to the threshing floor. This was usually a clay-covered or rocky ground in a high spot, so that it could catch the wind. Stones were put around the edge of the floor, and the sheaves were spread out about knee deep over it. Let the threshing begin! Now, the goal of threshing was to shake all of the kernels of grain from their stalks. To accomplish this, the farmers could do one of three things. He could walk through the knee-deep stalks, beating them with a stick. He could lead his animals through the sheaves, letting their hooves do the work. Better yet was the use of a threshing sledge. This was simply a board which had bits of iron fastened into it. It was dragged through the grain to help grind the grain from their hulls.

WINNOWING

Once the grain had been thoroughly stomped, trampled, beaten and, in a word, threshed, it was time to winnow. This is the part of the process where the elevated location of the threshing floor comes in handy. Winnowing was scheduled on a windy day, if possible. The farmers would throw their beaten down stalks of grain into the air with a wooden fork or a shovel. The wind would cause the heavy kernels of grain to fall right back down at the farmer's feet, but the lighter straw and chaff was blown to the side by the breezes. The straw was collected and stored to feed the animals in the winter, and the grain was placed in earthenware jars for the year ahead. The fact that Gideon was winnowing in a valley instead of on a high hill shows the fear that the Israelites felt because of the oppression of the Midianite army (Judg. 6:11). Gideon was trying to hide his harvest so that the enemy would not confiscate it for their own use.

FIRST FRUITS

Every gardener knows the feelings of longing as they watch their tender crops ripening before their eyes. Oh, how they long for that first red, ripe tomato, or for that crisp, summer melon, chilled in a nearby stream— seeking out the first red strawberries of summer, or anticipating the sweet tang of grapes after the first frost. Surely the grower, who has worked so hard, should have first dibs on all these delectables? Actually, no! These first fruits belonged to God. Of course, God didn't exactly get to enjoy the bounty firsthand either. They were brought to the temple and presented to the priests, who were allowed to eat them (Num. 18:12–13). In this way, the farmer showed his thanks to God for his provision of this foretaste of more to come.

SHEPHERDS

Shepherds were hardly refined folk. They spent weeks in the wild with only bleating sheep and goats for companionship. It should be mentioned as well that sheep stink, and the smell rubs off on shepherds. They worked a kind of year-long, swing-shift that depended upon the availability of food and water for their critters. At first, when the winter rains had ceased and spring came to the villages, there was plenty of grass nearby on which the flock could feed. As a bonus, when the harvest was complete, the herds could be turned loose in the empty fields to graze on anything that had been left behind. However, once these options were exhausted, the sheep had to be guided farther and farther from home in search of green pastures. This is where shepherds were useful. Many times, villagers would pay the local shepherd to take their sheep and goats out with him. He kept them safe in the outlying countryside, and returned them to their owners once their long season of wandering was finished.

> **DID YOU KNOW?**
>
> • Sheep were occasionally eaten as meat (2Sa. 12:4)—in Palestine their distinctive fat tail was considered a delicacy.

GUARDING THE FLOCK

Although a shepherd carried a tent with him (Song 1:8), his life was no camping trip. Jacob rehearsed the hardships of thirst, cold, and lack of sleep (Gen. 31:40). When a sheep was tired or injured, the shepherd carried it on his shoulders (Lk. 15:5), and when a lamb became lost, the shepherd went out to find it (Ps. 119:176; Is. 53:6; Lk. 15:3–6). Sheep needed constant oversight because there were many dangers to the flock from the wild animals that came up from the jungles surrounding the Jordan river gorge. Lions and bears were common (Judg. 14:8; 2Kin. 2:25), and David's adventures protecting his own flock weren't out of the ordinary (1Sa. 17:34–36). Amos tells of a shepherd who actually tried to take a sheep from a lion's mouth (Amos 3:12). Hyenas and jackals also lurked nearby. The shepherd had to fight them off, because he had to repay any losses to the owners (Gen. 31:39; Ex. 22:10–13).

WATERING THE FLOCK

A shepherd in the countryside had to plan his daily circuit carefully. Water was a must on the route. Since sheep could get bogged down easily in moving water, still waters were preferable (Ps. 23:2). As summer months progressed and the availability of water dwindled, shepherds depended on wells to quench their flock's thirst. This meant driving the flock out into the pastures just so far, so that he could return them to the troughs at the well each evening. It was customary to cover the well with a heavy stone, which required several men to lift. Jacob was able to show off a little for Rebekah by moving this large stone by himself (Gen. 29:10). This large stone helped to protect water rights from wanderers and water-thieves. Once all the local flocks were gathered, the water was drawn for the animals.

KNOWN BY NAME

Spending weeks at a time out in the wilds, the shepherds had only two choices: talk to yourself or talk to your sheep! Inevitably, there was a very close relationship between the sheep and their shepherd. Shepherds would name their sheep based on personality and mannerisms, and the

sheep knew theirWinky! Come, Spitfire, Nimble-foot, Wrong-way!" The flock would turn their heads, bleat, and come ambling along behind their shepherd. Jesus said that his sheep also know him (Jn. 10:14), so that when they are called, they respond to his voice (Jn. 10:4–5). Shepherds knew their flocks so well, that there was no worry when several flocks arrived at once at a well to drink (Gen. 29:1-3). Even if a shepherd was responsible for sheep from master's voice. All it took was a call: "Here, Fluffy, Curly, more than one village, he knew exactly to which family each animal belonged.

KEEPING THEM ALL TOGETHER

Although sheep knew their shepherd's voice and willingly followed his lead, they just as willingly wandered off in some other direction. Sheep were pretty ditzy. When a shepherd led the flock, he would often have his dogs bring up the rear (Job 30:1). This would ensure that the sheep stayed together, and that wild animals could not come up from behind and take out the stragglers. Shepherds were also able to use their slingshots to keep the sheep in rank. A well-placed shot in the path of a wandering sheep could startle it into returning to the comforting safety of the crowd.

THE SHEEPFOLD

When night fell, the shepherd gathered his sheep together into a safe place and settled himself to keep watch (Lk. 2:8). A shallow cave was a good place to start, but the shepherds took the time to fortify it with an enclosure. A fence made from gathered stones would be built, and it was topped with thorny brush to dissuade predators. If no cave was available, shepherds might simply construct a kind of corral entirely from the thorny brush (Eze. 34:14). The sheepfold had just one opening, and it was here that the shepherd lay down. He became the door (Jn. 10:7). The villages often set up a sheepfold in the center of town to keep the flocks safe when they returned. This was built in a sunny spot, and had a low arched building attached so that the herd could be gathered indoors during stormy weather. This village fold also had to be guarded from attack, but this time from sheep-rustlers. The usual scheme was for the criminals to sneak over the wall, slaughter as many sheep as possible, and throw them over the wall to their accomplices. Jesus referred to this when he said that thieves and robbers do not use the door but climb over the wall (Jn. 10:1, 10).

SHEEP SHEARING

Sheep shearing took place after the summer grazing. Shearing-time meant payday for hired shepherds, for the animals were counted and the profits were distributed. The sheep were all gathered into pens, and one by one they were relieved of their wool. The work was turned into a giant celebration, with food and good-natured competition. The festivities could get pretty noisy, and the ruckus provided a good cover for covert activities. Absalom had his brother, Amnon, murdered during sheep shearing time (2Sa. 13:23–30). Jacob chose shearing time to make his getaway from Laban (Gen. 31:19–21).

CRACK SHOT WITH A SLINGSHOT!

Although the slingshot was a dangerous weapon, it also served as a means of entertainment for the long, lonely days spent in the pastures. The sling was simple, made from a small pouch of leather and two long cords. The pouch was loaded with any handy rock, then spun about at the end of the two cords. When one cord was released, the stone was flung from its pouch with amazing force. Since the shepherds had so much time to practice, they developed a lethal accuracy. Children received slings as a kind of toy in Bible times, and started practicing with them at a young age. Many ancient armies boasted whole battalions of slingers who could "sling a stone at a hair's breadth and not miss" (Judg. 20:16).

THY ROD AND THY STAFF

The phrase in Psalm 23:4, "Thy rod and Thy staff, they comfort me," gives us two very important pieces of the shepherd's equipment. The rod was a nice, big club. It was made from heavy wood, with sharp stones or nails embedded in the "working end." The purpose of this intimidating piece of weaponry was to pack a wallop! The shepherd used his club to beat off predators: lions, bears, wild dogs, hyenas. David spoke of taking hold of a lion and beating it off (1Sa. 17:35). The staff was the shepherd's crook that we usually picture. It was not a weapon, but a walking stick. It was about six feet long, and sometimes had a crook at the end. The staff could be used to nudge a wayward sheep in the right direction, and the crook could be used to lift or turn sheep who had gotten themselves into trouble.

COUNTING SHEEP

Before a shepherd could catch some Z's at night, he had to count sheep! The shepherd's staff was used to help him do this. When the flock prepared to pass through a narrow opening, like the door of the sheepfold, they were counted as they passed under the rod. This is how the shepherd in Jesus' parable could know that one sheep was missing (Lk. 15:4). Ezekiel uses this idea when he says that only those who had been loyal to God would "pass under his rod" (Eze. 20:37–38). The staff was also used to mark the sheep. The bottom was dipped into dye, and as the sheep passed under the rod, every tenth one was marked and given to God as the tithe (Lev. 27:31–33).

FISHERMEN AND SAILORS

Although the Mediterranean Sea was close at hand, the Jews of the Old Testament had very little to do with it. They generally left the sailing of great ships to other nations with other ambitions. However, the New Testament leads us into the fishing villages surrounding the Sea of Galilee, where sails and nets and anchors were a part of everyday life.

FISHERMEN

"I will make you fishers of men." Jesus spoke these words to his first two disciples, Peter and Andrew, who were fishermen by trade (Mt. 4:19). The entire fishing industry seems to have begun in Palestine, and it was a booming business during New Testament times. The Sea of Galilee was

surrounded by fishing villages, and boats were on the water daily to haul in their catches. In the Gospels, fishing is described as a family business. James and John worked with their father, Zebedee (Mk. 1:19), and Peter and Andrew were brothers who worked together as well (Mk. 1:16). Their days were spent hoisting sails, hauling in fish, mending nets, and repairing boats. Often they fished at night (Jn. 21:3–4). The catch of the day had to be cleaned and preserved and brought to the markets for sale. Fish from the Sea of Galilee found their way all the way to the seller's stalls in Jerusalem!

STORMS ON THE SEA OF GALILEE

Because of the formation of the hills surrounding the Sea of Galilee, storms could rush across the water with great intensity and suddenness. Seasoned fishermen like Peter would always keep a close eye on the skies for building clouds. Still, the disciples were caught by an unexpected squall in the middle of the lake (Mk. 4:37). The wind and waves were so fierce, that experienced sailors like James and John, the "sons of thunder," were knocking knees and turning green!

NETS FOR CASTING

Fishermen on the Sea of Galilee had a few different ways of bringing in the fish. One method was casting fishnets into the water. Peter and Andrew were casting nets into the water when Jesus called them away (Mk. 1:16–17). These nets were large and circular, with weighted edges and a long rope at the center. There was a knack to throwing this large net, making sure to put enough spin into the action so the weights on the edges would cause the net to unfurl. The fisherman would stand in the shallows with his carefully folded net poised. A well-flung net would drop over the top of a school of fish, trapping them underneath the mesh. Then the net was pulled into the shore. These nets would bring in everything it had trapped, so that some sorting had to be done once the net was ashore. The good fish were sorted into baskets, and the unwanted fish and rubbish were tossed back (Mt. 13:47–48).

JERUSALEM'S NAVY

Although located on a high hill, far from any significant body of water, King Solomon was determined to raise up a royal navy for Jerusalem! He wanted to establish his own fleet of trading ships, to bring in silks and spices and oddities from around the world. These merchant vessels brought in such things as gold, silver, ivory, apes, and monkeys (1Kin. 10:22; 2Chr. 9:21). Since Jerusalem was not a port city, and most of the Jewish people had little knowledge of sailing, Solomon called on the King of Phoenicia for help. King Hiram helped the Jewish people by loaning them his own sailors to man the fleet and train the new recruits (1Kin. 9:26–27).

ST. PETER'S FISH

A fish called the tilapa, which has since been renamed St. Peter's fish, is found in the miraculous story of Matthew 17:24–27. The tilapas carry their eggs and later the young fish in their mouths to keep them safe. The little fishies will vacate long enough for mom to eat, but as soon as she's done, in they go! As the youngsters grow, they become quite a mouthful, and mom gets tired of all the rumpus inside. When enough is enough, she will pick up an object, preferably a shiny one, and will keep it in her mouth to prevent them from returning. In the case of Matthew 17, the fish that Peter caught had picked up shekel pieces.

CRAFTSMEN AND ARTISANS

Ancient Jerusalem was never filled with great statues, painted masterpieces, or impressive sculptures. In Israel, craftsmen did not create things simply to be beautiful. Instead, usefulness was of foremost importance. The works of their hands were everyday objects that were needed for ordinary purposes. Still, a practical thing could be well made, and many villages during Bible times were renowned for their fine workmanship.

TRADE GUILDS

In Bible times, trade guilds were established in most towns. In fact, different craftsmen even had their own quarters within the business districts of a city. When the time came for Nehemiah to oversee the building of the walls around Jerusalem, he called upon the trade guilds. Each group was responsible for building up the walls nearest their neighborhood (Neh. 3). In New Testament times, the Roman Empire was familiar with the trade guilds, and even required them to be licensed to make sure that they were not fronts for covert anti-government radicals.

BASKET WEAVERS

Basket-weaving was hardly a summer camp activity in Bible times, and it was never done under water! It would have been a kind of cottage industry, practiced by housewives all over the land of Palestine. It was a necessary skill in ancient times, when reeds and grasses were woven not only into baskets, but into hampers, mats, and ropes as well. Jochabed wove the most famous basket in the Old Testament for her baby son (Ex. 2:3). It was surely made from the rushes of the papyrus plants that grew along the Nile. Baskets were used for harvesting, for storage, and for shopping trips to the market. In Deuteronomy, God is asked to bless the baskets in which women kneaded their bread (Deut. 28:5, 17).

CARPENTERS

Many Christians have a bumper sticker on their car that reads "My Boss is a Jewish Carpenter." The trade of carpenter is mentioned often in the Bible. Usually, the carpenter was a talented wood carver. although it may be hard to picture now, in the days of the Bible, Palestine was full of trees in many areas. Acacia, cedar, cypress, sycamore, oak, fir, fig, olive, and pomegranate trees provided wood for working. The carpenter's daily tasks might include the construction of common items like doorposts and stools, but a true craftsman might be allowed to do fine carvings for the local synagogue. Joseph was a carpenter in the city of Nazareth in Galilee (Mt. 13:55), so Jesus was trained as a carpenter as he grew into manhood.

THE TOOLS OF THE TRADE

Isaiah mentions the tools of the carpenter's trade: "Another workman uses a line and a compass to draw on the wood. Then he uses his chisels to cut a statue and his calipers to measure the statue…." (Is. 44:13). The "rule" was a measuring line, used just like a ruler or measuring tape today. The carpenter would use his rule to measure the correct lengths on a piece of wood, then mark it. Archeologists have discovered compasses throughout Egypt and Palestine, which were used for marking off circles and arcs. The carpenter's tools also included the adze, which was used to shape wood, and awls, saws, hammers, chisels, bow drills, and nails.

FULLERS

Even back in Bible times, you could take your shirts to the cleaners. Although "heavy starch" was probably not an option, wealthy people could have their laundry done by a professional fuller. The term fuller means "one who washes" or "one who treads." There was even an area on

LYDIA
The Seller of Purple

Lydia's hometown was Thyatira, a great center for the clothing industry. She had grown up on streets that were filled with the clatter of looms in a steady rhythm. Bleating sheep ran before their shepherds, on their way to the shearers. Fullers worked the new fleece with soap, rinsing the raw wool and spreading it in the sun to dry. Old women sat in the shade of their houses, with nimble fingers twisting yarn on their spinning wheels. Lydia was most familiar, with the steaming dye pots, which awaited the new skeins of wool. It was her family's business. Red dye was procured from a little bug that lived in the bark of an oak tree. A beautiful blue dye was concocted from the rinds of the pomegranates. The drying racks in front of the house of the dyers were always filled with an eye-catching array of wool. But, the current fad was for purple fabric. The purple dye was extracted from the shells of the whelks that were found along the seashore. It was said that, in Rome, only the Emperor was allowed to wear this rare color. The purple dye was very expensive, and the shade of purple made in Thyatira was especially lovely.

An unmarried woman with a knack for business, Lydia set up shop in Philippi. Business was good for her, for she was a dealer in the coveted purple. She headed up a large household, and her home was spacious enough to entertain travelers. Lydia was also a believer in the one true God, and had become a Jewish proselyte. So, when the band of Jewish missionaries came into town, Lydia went to hear their words. They preached about Jesus, the Christ, and God "opened her heart to heed the things spoken." Afterwards, Lydia opened her home to the men—Paul, Silas, and Luke. They enjoyed her hospitality (Acts 16:14–15, 40). Lydia, the seller of purple, became the first Christian convert in all of Europe (Acts 16:14).

the northern side of the city of Jerusalem called the "fuller's field." This location, outside the city, was preferable because the job was a smelly one. Clothes were rubbed with "fuller's earth" (cimolite) or with chalk, then stomped on or beaten with a stick in a tub of water. Soap was also used as a cleaning agent (Jer. 2:22; Mal. 3:2).

WASHING WOOL

Shearing time was a very busy time of year for both the shepherds and the fullers. Each spring, the sheep were dipped, then shorn. The new wool was sent to a fuller to be cleaned of its natural oils. The fuller did this by treading out the wool on a rock in the water. The freshly cleaned wool was wrung out and left in the sun, where it could dry and become bleached (Is. 1:18). Fullers were also employed to work with newly woven cloth in order to pre-shrink it before sending it to the clothiers.

DID YOU KNOW?

• Nearly all of the glass objects that have been found in Israel by archeologists were clearly imported from other countries.

• Lamps changed gradually over the centuries so archeologists use them when dating the sites they uncover.

GEM-CUTTERS

Although diamonds were not yet a girl's best friend in Bible times, there was a brisk business in semi-precious stones. The Bible describes such stones as jasper, sapphire, beryl, topaz, emerald, sardonyx, and amethyst (Rev. 21:19–21). Such jewels were used to adorn the rings, necklaces, and bracelets of women since the earliest times. Although birthstones were not yet assigned to each month of the year, a Jewish girl could choose to wear the stone of her tribe. God had assigned twelve different stones to represent the twelve tribes of Israel, and they were cut and set for the High Priest's breastplate (Ex. 28:17–21). Stones were also cut and polished to make beads, engraved with designs, or carved with the owner's names to serve as seals.

HUNTERS

Esau was one of these rugged, outdoorsy kinds of guys. His days were spent scrambling over rocky slopes as he tracked wild deer out in the hills. He would creep quietly down into the small valleys where there were waterholes. Armed with a bow and arrows, a day spent hunting could be long and tiring. It is no wonder he returned one afternoon so hungry that he was willing to toss aside his birthright for a bowl of stew (Gen. 25:30–34). Hunters tracked a variety of animals through the wilderness, including the roebuck, hart, and fowl that populated the land.

IVORY-CARVERS

The urge to accumulate ivory started early. Apparently, there was not the current uproar against taking tusks away from elephants. Jerusalem was receiving imported ivory from Africa and Syria on a regular basis. Women would decorate their hair with beautifully carved ivory combs. The furniture industry used ivory inlays to decorate expensive pieces. Small carvings and even board games were created out of ivory. King Solomon probably used ivory carvings and inlay in the decorations of the great Temple he had built (1Kin. 10:18). King Ahab had a palace in Samaria that he actually called the "Ivory House" (1Kin. 22:39). Could that have been an early version of the White House? Archeologists have found the largest collection of Israelite ivory in Samaria, consisting mainly of inlays, carvings, and sculptures.

> **DID YOU KNOW?**
>
> • Cotton was the poor man's cloth; it was more plentiful than linen and more widely used. The best quality cotton was raised in the humid climate of Upper Egypt.
>
> • Rahab's roof was being used for drying flax (Josh. 2:6), which is used for making linen, and she had a long red cord (Josh. 2:18). She and her family may have been dyers.

LEATHERWORKERS

The working of leather into useful goods actually involved a couple of different trades. Once the animals had been skinned, a tanner was employed to dry the hides, to stretch, and treat them until they became softened and supple. Then the finished leather was turned over to those who did the shaping and sewing of the leather. In this, there could be several different areas of expertise. Sandal-makers would cut several thicknesses of leather to create comfortable soles for their footwear. Tailors would create clothing and belts from the leather (2Kin. 1:8; Mk. 1:6). Men's phylacteries were made of soft black leather and bound with leather thongs (Mt. 23:5). Leather was also used as a writing material, so scribes were in the market for long lengths of leather to be made into scrolls. Whole skins of animals were carefully sewn and sealed to make bottles for wine, water, or milk (Josh. 9:4; Judg. 4:19; Mt. 9:17).

MOURNERS

A woman whose children were raised, whose eyesight had grown dim, and whose fingers were too stiff to be much good, could still provide a useful service to her neighborhood. She could become a professional mourner! In Bible times, one's love for the departed was shown in the amount of grief poured out at their funeral. In an effort to ensure a suitable din of weeping and wailing, professionals were booked for these occasions. The hired mourners would come in, find a good spot, compose themselves, then throw up their hands in anguish and begin to wail. At a really swell funeral, musicians were also brought in, to set the mood by playing mournfully on their instruments. When Jesus returned with Jairus to his home, the musicians and mourners had already set up in the living room (Mk. 5:38).

PERFUMERS

Perfume was an expensive product, and whole towns could be built around their industry. These neighborhoods smelled better than hot cinnamon rolls at the mall! From every door drifted the exotic fragrances of far-away lands. Preparations of rare ingredients like frankincense, myrrh, cinnamon, saffron, aloe, and nard were being infused into oils. Then the sweet essences were bottled into tiny vessels of alabaster and readied for export. Perfume was made by the Jews, who used it in their worship. Even while wandering in the desert, the children of God made oils and ointments "according to the art of the perfumer" (Ex. 30:25). The perfumer's special concoctions are the basis of Solomon's words "Dead flies putrefy the perfumer's ointment, and cause it to give off a foul odor" (Eccl. 10:1), which are the basis of our phrase "That's the fly in the ointment."

POTTERS

Potters were masters at the fine art of playing in the mud. Actually, a potter was quite fussy about his mud, and mixing the clay was considered highly skilled work. The clay was gathered from a local field and put into a pit near the potter's workshop. It was left in the sun and rain to give the worms a chance to escape, then trampled into a fine muck. Just the right amount of water had to be added to reach the proper consistency. Once this was done, the potter could wash his feet and choose some clay for shaping. Potters worked their clay in three different ways. It could be pressed into a mold, as were most lamps of Old Testament times. The clay could be shaped freehand, athough this was generally a method only used to create toys and some kinds of ovens. And, of course, the clay could be shaped on a wheel—the favorite way to play with clay!

THE POTTER'S WHEEL

The earliest potter's wheel was a disc that spun on an upright shaft. Around the time of the Exodus, potters found that by mounting a second disc below the top one, they could increase the speed of rotation. Then, in New Testament times, somebody rocked the pottery world by unveiling an entirely new model! He had reinvented the wheel! The lower disk was dropped to the floor, and the foot-powered potter's wheel was born.

ROYAL POTTERY

In Old Testament times, there was a royal guild of skilled potters that worked exclusively for the king. They tried to keep up with the needs of the entire palace—lamps for every room, a new set of plates and platters for an upcoming banquet, flower pots for the queen, giant water pots, storage jars for the kitchens, toys for the royal toddlers. The list could be endless! Archeologists have found jars with words stamped into the handles: "belonging to the king." Several potters would have worked together, along with their apprentices, to make sure that the royals were on the cutting edge of new designs, colors, and glazes.

PRETTY POTTERY

To embellish their pottery, the Israelites had three main options available to them. First of all, they could water down clay of an unusual color. This could then be applied with a brush to the entire jar in order to deepen its color, once fired. This also resulted in a pretty contrast between the color of the inside and outside of a piece of pottery. Another popular form of decoration was to paint a line of either black or red around the middle of a jar. The third option was to burnish the pots. Once the clay of the potter was dried, but before it was fired, it could be rubbed carefully with a piece of bone or wood or stone. Any areas that had been burnished would shine after they were fired.

SMITHS

The village blacksmith was an asset to the ancient community. His trade provided the farmers with sharp blades on their plows and kept their pitchforks and hoes in good repair. When invasion threatened, he provided the weapons of war. Without a blacksmith, the people would be defenseless. This is why the Philistines would not allow the Jews to have their own blacksmiths. Not one of the Jews owned a sword, and none could be made. They even forced the farmers

DID YOU KNOW?

- The firing of objects in a kiln was the ultimate test of a potter's art, for different clays needed different temperatures.

- Craftsmen were held in high regard by the Jews in New Testament times. Craft workers were exempt from the rule that everyone should rise to their feet when a scholar approached.

to pay Philistine blacksmiths to sharpen their plows (1Sa. 13:19–21). These smiths were also known as "hammerers" (Is. 41:7; 44:12) because they flattened and smoothed metal by pounding. When working with gold, smiths were able to hammer it into thin sheets, which could then be used to cover objects like the altar in the tabernacle (Ex. 37:26) or the royal throne (1Kin. 10:18).

METALWORK

Smiths would take metal ore, melt it in a clay pot over a fire, then pour it into a stone mold. This process lent itself best to providing useful objects to homeowners: plow points, chisels, needles, tweezers, safety pins, and bracelets. Smiths were also capable of fine works of art. Metal bowls, pitchers, urns, and lamps were created. Delicate jewelry was wrought to tempt the ladies. Metalworkers also provided the army with needed ammunition: arrowheads, lances, spear tips, swords, and daggers.

COPPER SMELTING

Copper was the most plentiful metal in early Israel. When copper is mixed with a little tin, bronze is created, which is stronger and harder than copper. Goliath wore bronze armor (1Sa. 17:5–6). It's not clear just when the Israelites started using bronze instead of copper, because the Hebrew words for the two metals are the same. Copper and bronze were used for kitchen utensils, and women had mirrors and powder boxes made from the metals. Most musical instruments were also made from copper. When David began making plans to build a temple for God, he began hoarding large quantities of copper. He needed more copper than the land could provide, so he began to demand it as part of the tribute from other nations (1Chr. 18:10). Solomon's finished temple had beautifully shaped bronze pieces—the great bronze basin resting on twelve bronze bull-calves (1Kin. 7:44), and the bronze pillars, whose tops were decorated with lilies and pomegranates (1Kin. 7:41–42).

Stone Masons

In Galilee, the stone was normally black basalt, and on the coast, yellow sandstone; but for most of the country in the limestone area, the stone was white. The temple that Solomon built was made from the white limestone, which was quarried in the nearby hills. During construction of the temple, the neighboring communities didn't have to put up with the constant noise of hammer and chisel, for the stone masons finished the stones at the quarry and then shipped them to the building site ready to put in place (1Kin. 6:7).

Making Clothes

The clothes-making business involved many tradesmen. Shepherds raised the sheep and sheared them every year. Fullers were hired to wash the wool. Women would card the raw wool and spin it into thread. Dyers dipped the skeins of wool into steaming vats to color them. Weavers wove the threads together on their looms, creating long widths of fabric. Tailors cut and measured and sewed the fabric into garments. Embroiderers embellished the necklines with decorative threads. Merchants sold the finished garments in the marketplaces.

Tanners

Tanning was one of those dirty jobs that somebody had to do. Although tanned hides were vital to the clothing industry, the tanners were forced to work on the edges of a city, preferably downwind. It was an admittedly smelly job. The tanner would take the skins of animals and rub them with a fragrant mixture that knocked all the hair off and softened the hide. The skins were then stretched and worked and rubbed until the final product was soft and supple. The Jews considered the tanner's trade to be disreputable, because the tanners defiled themselves by handling dead animals. Peter ignored this prejudice by staying with a tanner named Simon while traveling through Joppa (Acts 9:43).

DYERS

The process of dyeing is described in detail on Egyptian monuments. The Israelites were also familiar with the art of dyeing cloth, for their tabernacle was decorated with blue, scarlet, and purple tapestries (Ex. 26:1, 14; 35:25). The natural dye colors used by the Jews were black, red, yellow, and green. A lovely indigo blue could be achieved using the rinds of pomegranates. Red, which was very popular for Hebrew clothing, came from an insect that was fond of oak trees. Most famous was the purple dye, which came from a species of shellfish in the Mediterranean Sea. Purple was valued highly, and it was often reserved for royalty. In the Old Testament, Rahab was drying flax on her roof, which is used for making linen, and had a long scarlet cord (Josh. 2:18). It is very possible that Rahab and her family were dyers.

In the New Testament, Lydia is described as a seller of purple in the city of Thyatira (Acts 16:14). Thyatira was famous for its cloth dyers. Lydia may have dealt in the purple fabric, or in the dye itself.

DYE VATS

One of the centers for the dyeing industry was discovered in a city called Debir. The excavations showed that about thirty homes had rooms especially made for the dyeing process. Each contained two stone vats with small openings on top. Both vats would be filled with colorful dyes, for the wool had to be given two baths. The second vat would also contain potash and lime, which would set the dye into the wool. After drying, the beautifully tinted wools would be ready for spinning and weaving.

EMBROIDERERS

The Hebrew people excelled in decorative needlework. Some say that they picked up some of their technique while living as slaves in Egypt. The

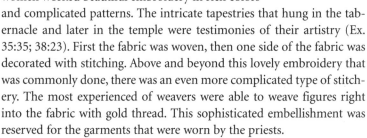

women worked beautiful embroidery in rich colors and complicated patterns. The intricate tapestries that hung in the tabernacle and later in the temple were testimonies of their artistry (Ex. 35:35; 38:23). First the fabric was woven, then one side of the fabric was decorated with stitching. Above and beyond this lovely embroidery that was commonly done, there was an even more complicated type of stitchery. The most experienced of weavers were able to weave figures right into the fabric with gold thread. This sophisticated embellishment was reserved for the garments that were worn by the priests.

WEAVERS

When it was time for fabric to be made, the warp and weft of the weaving process were handled by experts. Weavers spent their days in front of a loom. Thread was attached to the beams of the loom (this was the warp), and a shuttle was used to weave cross-threads through them (this was the weft of the fabric). Various textures and patterns could be produced, and color combinations were also possible. One popular fabric that was made alternated threads made from brown camel's hair and black goat's hair, creating stripes. The Bible speaks of the weaver's wares: woolen garments (Lev. 13:48), embroidered priestly garments (Ex. 28: 4, 39), and twined linens (Ex. 26:1).

LOOMS

There were two basic models of looms in Bible times—the vertical loom and the horizontal loom. The basic vertical loom had an elevated beam from which hung the many threads that made up the warp of the fabric. These dangling threads were weighted with stones and blocks to keep them from getting tangled with each other. As the weaver worked the threads crossways, they were pushed upwards. Several threads could be worked on at a time, so intricate patterns could be produced in the finished product. The benefit of this style loom was that the weaver could move along its length easily, so very wide pieces of material were possible. The horizontal loom was much smaller, and it was stretched out on the ground. Two beams secured the ends of the warp threads, and the weaver sat in front to do the weaving. This loom could be no wider than the reach of the weaver's arms, so a narrower piece of fabric was created. A horizontal loom was no doubt used when Delilah wove Samson's hair into it (Judg. 16:13–14).

> **DID YOU KNOW?**
>
> • The beam of the loom is mentioned in Scripture as the weapon wielded by Samson against his ambushers (Judg. 16:14).
>
> • The writing of the rabbis mention such trades as nail-makers, bakers, sandal-makers, master builders, and tailors.

LINEN

Linen was a popular fabric in Palestine. Rather than being woven from animal hair, like wool, it was made from the long fibers of a plant that farmers could grow right in their fields. Flax, which grew especially well in the coastal plains and in Galilee, was cut and dried (Josh. 2:6). Then to soften it, flax would be soaked and then dried again. As the fibers of the plant began to separate, it was ready for spinning and weaving. Egyptians wore linen clothing almost exclusively. Linen was also a popular fabric from which to make ships' sails.

BUSINESSMEN

The men who lived in the cities of Bible times did not have to scrabble in the dirt to make their living. Indeed, these were the "white collar" workers of ancient times. These businessmen were mostly the shopkeepers who lined the marketplaces in cities. They made a reasonably good living, providing goods or services in their neighborhoods.

BAKERS

While most women in the outlying countryside made their own bread every day, city-folk were able to buy their bread if they chose. In large cities, the bakers all lived in one section of town, and their large dome-shaped ovens could bake dozens of large loaves at once. These ovens consisted of a large chamber in which a fire was laid. Dried grasses were often used for fuel (Mt. 6:30). Once the fire had burned down a bit, the walls of the oven and the coals retained much of the heat. At this point, the oven door was opened and the loaves were placed inside. Flat, hard, unleavened cakes or small yeast breads (Ex. 12:39) were baked in a matter of minutes. The larger ovens of the professional bakers allowed for great loaves of bread to be formed. Round loaves that were a foot in diameter and three inches thick were brought steaming from the ovens after forty-five minutes of baking (1Sa. 17:17; 2Sa. 16:1). These large loaves were the sort used as the showbread in the temple (Ex. 25:30; 35:13; 39:36).

BANKERS

Men have been able to keep banker's hours for centuries! The old "Savings and Loan" was a regular part of main street business in the larger cities. Archeologists have found the records of a family of bankers who lived over five hundred years before Christ. Naturally, their offices were swamped with paperwork! Over seven hundred clay tablets were found, recording both commercial and real estate transactions. These documents included land leases, business contracts, loan contracts, and receipts. In a wealthy city, the Jews who established themselves as bankers became very prosperous.

ZACCHAEUS
The Tax Collector

Zacchaeus was a wee little man, and a wee little man was he!"
In his day, Zacchaeus was not looked down upon simply because he
was short. He was spurned by his neighbors, and hated by his
debtors. For a "wee little man," Zacchaeus wielded a lot of power.
You see, he worked for the Roman government, and that put him
squarely in the middle of political mayhem. The Romans thought
little of him, for he was just a lackey who was paid to do their dirty
work. To the Jews, he was a traitor, who had sold out to the enemy
and turned his back on his people. Zacchaeus cared little for this, for
after all, business was business! The Romans paid him to do a job,
and collecting taxes had a tremendous perk. While working out the
income taxes of regular folks, Zacchaeus could play with the numbers a little and overcharge them. These extra funds then found
their way into his own purse. The position of tax collector was such
a lucrative one, that a man would bribe his way into the appoint-
ment. Zacchaeus ran a successful little business in the great city of
Jericho until he was confronted by Jesus. In fact, he was a chief tax
collector, with underlings whose takings he skimmed as well.
Although the Law required that a thief must return double what he
stole (Ex. 22:4), Zacchaeus offered to pay the full price four times
over (Lk. 19:8).

THE LOCAL BARBERSHOP

The tools of the barbering trade were familiar to the Jews. Razors and mirrors were common enough (Is. 7:20). The Jews in Old Testament times did not often cut their hair, but there were times when the services of a barber were needed. Men who took a Nazarite vow before God let their hair grow until their promise before the Lord was fulfilled. Once this was completed, he would shave his head (Num. 6:18). There were also cases when the whole body was shaved for purification purposes (Num. 8:7). These instances did not make for brisk business though. The real place to set up shop for the barbers in ancient times was Egypt. Egyptians were meticulous about cleanliness, and so they bathed often, shaved daily, and cut off all of their hair. All Egyptian men shaved both their faces and their heads. The trade of barber was very common in Egyptian neighbor-hoods, and their shops were found in every neighborhood! When Joseph was mourning the death of his father, he let his hair grow out, according to Jewish tradition. But because he had done this, he was not "decent" to present himself before Pharaoh until he had shaved again. Instead, Joseph had to send word to Pharaoh by messenger (Gen. 50:4).

BUTCHER

There were no butcher shops in the times of Genesis. If a family wanted a nice steak or some mutton, they did their slaughtering right in their own yard. Since poultry, fish, vegetables, and bread formed their principal food, perhaps there wasn't sufficient demand to warrant butcher shops. It took a celebration of great proportions to warrant killing the fatted calf (Lk. 15:23). Since there was no way to preserve the meat in those days, the animal was not killed until it was time to cook it. (Gen. 18:7;1Sa. 28:24). By New Testament times, however, the meat market was as easy to find as the local temple. So many offerings of sheep and cattle were brought to the temples of false gods, that their priests made a brisk business selling the meat they couldn't use up in a day. This is why the Corinthian church struggled over the issue of eating meat that had been sacrificed to idols (1Cor. 8:1–10; 10:18–21, 27–29).

HIRED WORKERS

Cracking whips over the backs of sweating slaves was outmoded by New Testament times. When the big building projects came up on the city schedule, workers were hired by the day until the project was completed. Jesus' parable speaks of men waiting in the city square for someone to hire them for a day's work (Mt. 20:1–8). Their day's work was worth a day's wage, which in New Testament times was a denarius. Stone masons, carpenters, metal workers, and brick layers were all put to work on the temple built in Jerusalem by Herod. The giant building took years to complete, and when it was done, more than 18,000 people were out of a job.

INNKEEPERS

The position of hotel manager has become famous because of its place in the story of the nativity. The gruff innkeeper said "No room!" but then allowed a desperate young couple to take shelter in his stable (Lk. 2:7). In Bible times, inns were built wherever two major roads crossed paths. For a small fee, travelers could rest and water their animal, get a bite to eat, and sleep without the threat of thieves or wild animals overtaking them. Innkeepers heard all the news

DID YOU KNOW?

- People who exchanged money were also able to make loans. In fact, the table over which money was passed was called a "bank."

- Night watchmen guarded the streets of large cities at night, and the hours after dark were divided into "watches" (Mt. 14:25; Mk. 6:48).

- In New Testament times, pagan temples opened up butcher shops to sell off the extra meat that came in for sacrifices. This was the "meat offered to idols" that the Corinthian church was so worried about (1Cor. 8:4).

of the outside world from their guests, and enjoyed many a story by lamplight. In the deserts, these safe houses might be found in a natural oasis. In the cities, they were sprawling structures. In one city, archeologists found an inn that was built into a hillside. The stables ran along a lower street level, but the household itself was built above the stables, with the doors and windows facing the opposite direction on a street further up the slope. The Good Samaritan left the wounded traveler in the hands of an innkeeper, paying generously for meals and for care (Lk. 10:34–35).

MONEYCHANGERS

When festival times came around for the Jews, Jerusalem was the place to go. The law required that Jewish men should leave their homes and make their way to the temple three times a year in order to celebrate and worship. Men would climb the slopes to the holy city, bringing their offerings to the temple. There was a catch to making an offering, though. You had to have the temple currency. Most people by New Testament times had either Greek or Roman coins, but the Jews minted their own money, and theirs was the only currency accepted by the priests. So, outlanders had to find a moneychanger before they made their way into the temples. Now these moneychangers had the corner on the market, so their exchange rate was outrageous. No wonder Jesus was so filled with indignation that he drove them out. They had turned the holiest of places into a "den of thieves" (Lk. 19:46).

TAX COLLECTORS

The job of the tax collector was both the goal of ambitious men and the object of common scorn. Men actually bribed their way into the position, for it was a unique position of power. A tax collector calculated and gathered the Roman taxes, and Rome cared little if the collectors overcharged the people. Any extra funds that were extracted quickly found their way into the tax collector's pocket. As a result, these men were both hated and feared when tax time rolled around. It was like using the words "audit" and "Internal Revenue Service" in the same sentence. Zacchaeus was a tax collector in Jesus' day, who repented of his thieving ways and promised to make restitution to his clients (Lk. 19:8). Matthew, one of Jesus' own disciples, was employed as the tax collector in a small town in Galilee. He left his position immediately when Jesus called him (Mk. 2:14).

MEDIUMS

A city-wide celebration in a Jewish town was filled with good clean fun. Pronto pup stands and ferris wheels had not yet put in an appearance in Bible times. Barkers did not offer to guess the weight of a passer-by, nor did fortune tellers gaze into crystal balls. The Law strictly forbade the practice of fortune telling, and mediums that dabbled in the occult did so in great secrecy. During the early days of his reign, King Saul had enforced the Law that banned the practice of witchcraft, putting all the mediums and spiritists out of the land (1Sa. 28:3). However, when he became desperate enough, Saul sought out a witch and paid her to perform a séance. He wished to speak to his dead mentor and guide, the prophet Samuel (1Sa. 28:7–12). The witch of Endor was naturally suspicious of his request, for fear of the consequences of breaking a royal edict.

> **DID YOU KNOW?**
>
> • Tamar wasn't a prostitute, but she pretended to be one to trick her father-in-law, Judah, after he broke his promise to make her his third son's wife. Judah had good reason to hesitate. His first two sons had married her then died (Gen. 38:6–23)!

PROSTITUTES

Although not truly the oldest profession on record, prostitution was nonetheless a common part of Bible-time societies. Many cities kept bevies of these women in their temples, since worship of their gods often included sexual indulgence.

Other women were forced into prostitution as a last resort. If a woman lost her husband, and had no son to provide for her needs, she found herself in desperate circumstances. A widow woman who lost her only son was truly bereft (1Kin. 7:17). Rahab, who is listed in the "Hall of Faith" in Hebrews 11, was a prostitute in Jericho (Josh. 2:1). Tamar, the daughter-in-law of Judah, played the part of the prostitute as well (Gen 38:14–18). Both of these women are found in the genealogy of Christ.

> **DID YOU KNOW?**
>
> • Although King Saul banned witchcraft, he tricked the witch of Endor into conjuring the spirit of Samuel so that he could seek his counsel on military matters (1Sa. 28:3–19). It was a desperate measure taken after God refused to help Saul because of his disobedience.

TENTMAKERS

Tent making has become rather famous considering its humble nature. A missionary who works on the side to provide for his own livelihood has come to be known as a "tentmaker missionary." This term hearkens back to the days of Paul in the Book of Acts. In those days, even Pharisees had to make a living, and so most of them were trained in some useful trade. Paul was raised in Tarsus as a tentmaker. His days were spent working with leather and sinews, stitching together animal skins to make the waterproof coverings of nomadic homes. When Paul's journeys took him to the city of Corinth, he met two fellow tentmakers, Aquilla and Priscilla. He set up shop with them in order to earn his keep in a strange city (Acts 18:3).

MINERS

Metal ores and precious stones could be found in abundance throughout the Middle East. The demand for bronze and silver and gold sent men burrowing into the earth after it. Of course, this was hard work, and the laborers were not all union men. Most countries employed prisoners of war and slaves for their mining operations. Copper and turquoise mines have been found in Egypt, where the enslaved workers scratched prayers to their gods into the walls. When King David was accumulating precious metals for the construction of a temple, he exhausted the local supplies of bronze and had to import more.

ROBBERS

Thievery was a viable career option for the people of ancient times. The desert dwellers planned annual raids on outlying villages, divesting them of their harvests and their flocks. Guards had to be posted in sheep folds, where rustlers would sneak in over the walls and quietly make off with part of the herd (Jn. 10:1). Travelers only set off in large groups, joining caravans whenever possible, for fear of bandits on the roads (Lk. 2:44). Some paths were known to be dangerous, like the road down from Jerusalem to Jericho, where outcropping rocks made ambushes possible. It was on this road that the Good Samaritan came upon the traveler who had been left for dead (Lk. 10:30). The penalty for a life of crime was high in Bible times. In Old Testament times, a thief or an enemy might lose his thumbs or big toes if captured (Judg. 1:6–7). The two men crucified on either side of Jesus are described as robbers (Mt. 27:38, 44).

SCHOLARS AND SPECIALISTS

Although the number of men with a formal education was few in Old Testament times, there were several occupations that required one. Magicians, doctors, priests, secretaries, and astronomers all received thorough training.

AMANUENSIS

Before the days of radio broadcasting and tape sets, there was only one way for a man of God to get his message out—letters! However, many a prophet and disciple lacked the training or finesse to put pen to paper. Whether it was writer's block or bad penmanship, they needed help. When this was the case, they relied upon companions who were better suited to the task at hand. In other words, they had an amanuensis—a secretary, if you will—write for them. Luke was a famous amanuensis, taking dictation for Paul as he paced behind prison bars (Col. 4:14; 2 Th. 3:17). It is speculated that the Gospel of Mark is really the story of Peter, put to paper by his friend.

Astrologers

The stars held men in fascination from early times. The skies were divided into segments, and the paths of the stars and planets were studied. Each change in the night sky was deemed a portent, which would affect the lives of the men below. Kings would employ an entire staff of astrologers, sooth-sayers, and magicians, who were to advise him. Joseph was considered wise in these arts, for he was able to interpret dreams. Daniel was also trained in the stargazer's skills, and served as an advisor in the king's palace.

Magi

The Magi of the ancient world were specialists in their day, often employed by powerful men for their insights and advice. Magi were scholars and information gatherers, and were sometimes sent to other countries, representing their employers or the royal family. The magi gathered for the big social events of the season: coronations, funerals, grand openings. In the Book of Matthew, we find them congregating because of the birth of a great king. Magi, as a rule, were fascinated by scholarly topics—time keeping, calendars, the tides, medicine, alchemy, and religion. Their particular interest though was in the night sky, for it was believed that what they saw there reflected in the events upon the earth. By studying the movements of the heavens, they believed they gained insight. Such information was essential when advising the kings of great nations. The Magi are mentioned in the story of the nativity (Mt. 2:1). These "three wise men" from the East were no doubt men who spent their nights studying the stars. Traditionally these fellas—Melchior,

Casper, and Balthasar—hopped aboard their camels and trucked across the desert just in time for Jesus' birth. There is no indication from the Scriptures that there were merely three men, but that number works great for Christmas pageants since there are three gifts to carry. Their gifts of gold, frankincense, and myrrh are said to signify Christ's kingship, priestly office, and death.

HEALTHY ATTITUDES

Israel had a unique attitude towards illness in ancient times. Surrounding nations blamed evil spirits and wrathful gods for sickness and death. They wore good luck charms to ward off disease and depended on the chanting and potions of their priests to bring healing. The Jews maintained that God was in control. Health and sickness both came from God's hand (Job 2:10). Health was

> **DID YOU KNOW?**
>
> • At one time, state doctors were employed in Greece. They were paid a salary and had to give free medical attention.
>
> • Surgical instruments and prescription labels have been found in excavations of Roman cities.

considered a divine blessing. Sickness and disability were signs that the spiritual relationship between a person and God had been broken. This is why Job's comforters urged him to repent (Job 5:17) and why the disciples wondered who had sinned so that a man had been born blind (Jn. 9:2).

MEDICAL PRACTICES IN JESUS' DAY

Much of the medicine that was practiced in New Testament times was greatly influenced by the Greek physician, Hypocrites, for whom our Hippocratic oath is named. He laid down certain principles that were to be followed by all doctors. The life and welfare of the patient should come first. Male doctors were not to take advantage of female patients. Abortions were not performed. Any information that the patient revealed was considered confidential. In Palestine, rabbis insisted that every town have a physician, and preferably a surgeon as well. There was also a doctor for all of the temple priests. He looked after them because they were more susceptible to certain diseases since they worked barefoot.

MEDICINES

In Bible times, most medicines were home remedies that used a variety of herbs and a good deal of superstition. If a child came running in the house with teary eyes and a skinned knee, the cure was a dab of olive oil. Olive oil, as well as a spicy resin called balm, were pretty normal ointments for soothing the scrapes and sores of everyday life. Jeremiah speaks of the balm of Gilead (Jer. 8:22, 46:11, 51:8), and the Good Samaritan poured oil on the wounds of the injured man (Lk. 10:34). Wine was another common remedy in Bible times. The alcohol content made it a handy antiseptic, which is why the Good Samaritan also poured wine over the injured man's wounds. Paul urged Timothy to take a little wine for his stomach (1Ti. 5:23). Certain herbs may have been used as painkillers. Wine mixed with myrrh was offered to Jesus on the Cross, for it could numb his senses (Mk. 15:23).

CAREER WOMEN

Not many women stepped out of their roles as wives and mothers in Bible times. One accepted role that a woman could fulfill was that of a midwife. Some women were even able to keep busy full-time helping new mothers throughout their neighborhood. In Exodus, we hear of the midwives of the Hebrew slaves, who were called before the Egyptians because they would not kill the newborn boys

(Ex. 1:18). A midwife was the woman's coach and comfort during delivery. She aided in delivery, and if twins were born, it was her job to keep track of which baby came first (Gen. 38:27–30). The midwife cut the umbilical cord, then rubbed the child with salt or salt water. Next, the baby was rubbed with olive oil and wrapped tightly in clean clothes. Once the midwife handed the infant to the mother for a first feeding, her duties were completed.

> **DID YOU KNOW?**
>
> • Ancient midwives must have been very skilled, for Tamar successfully gave birth to twins who seem to have been locked in a difficult position (Gen. 38:27–30).

BLINDNESS

Blindness is mentioned often in the Scriptures. There were three types common in ancient times. There was a sudden blindness that was caused by flies and aggravated by the constant presence of dirt, dust, and glare. There was the blindness that came gradually, brought on by old age. And there was blindness that was from birth (Jn. 9:2). The blind were often forced to beg in order to sustain themselves. Jesus responded to the calls of the blind beggars, like Bartimaeus (Mk. 10:46), and restored their sight. God placed a curse upon those who would cause the blind to wander out of their way (Deut. 27:18).

RABBIS

"Rabbi" was a title given to Jewish teachers. They were well versed in the Scriptures, and had mastered entire passages of the Law. The title was a way to honor them for the position they had achieved, much as we would say "Doctor" today. There were even degrees of honor. Lowest was rab, which meant "my master." Next would be rabban, meaning "our master." The highest compliment was paid by calling a man rabboni, meaning "my great master." This is the term of endearment used by Mary (Jn. 20:16). Unfortunately, the rabbis became a bit prideful about their honorable titles. Not only did they walk through the marketplaces each day just to be greeted and bowed at, they were deeply offended when someone

NEHEMIAH
Cupbearer to the King

Nehemiah held the office of royal cupbearer, or butler, to the king of Persia while the Jews were in captivity. The cupbearer held a place of great honor in the Persian court. He was the food-taster and wine-tester. By running everything by his cupbearer first, a king could determine if his meals were safe to eat without any personal risk. This cupbearer had to be with the king constantly throughout the day, for whenever the monarch wanted a bite to eat or a drink, the cupbearer had to taste it first. This unique position gave the butler opportunities to make small talk with the king, and a trust was formed. In a sense, this servant risked his life to protect his king. Sometimes, the cupbearer could obtain special favors from the king, which might be denied to any other. God was able to use Nehemiah's position in this high office to bring the Jews back to Israel. On the job, Nehemiah would taste the wine before serving it to the king. The most proper way in which to test the wine was for the cupbearer to pour the wine from its container into the king's cup, then pour some from the cup into the palm of his left hand and drink it. In this way, Nehemiah was responsible for keeping the king safe from the poisons of would-be assassins, but he also saw to the king's comfort. In ancient artwork, cupbearers are depicted as holding a cup in their left hand, and a fan made from palm fronds in their right hand. He could swish the fan to create a nice breeze and keep insects away. He was also the royal napkin-holder. Nehemiah would have worn a long, richly embroidered and fringed napkin over his left shoulder. This was for the king to wipe his mouth on after drinking from his cup.

neglected to salute them! They had a saying that "he who salutes his teacher, and does not call him Rabbi, provokes the divine Majesty to depart from Israel." Jesus rebuked the religious leaders for their showy pride in these things (Mt. 23:13–33).

MISSIONARIES

When Jesus ascended into heaven, He left instructions with his followers to bring the Good News to the whole world. This was a mammoth mission, but the men and women who were soon nicknamed "Christians" took it seriously. They raised money to support those who were sent out. Philip is credited with being the first missionary, for he reached out to the Ethiopian eunuch and baptized him (Acts 8:27–39). The church at Antioch in Syria sent out missionaries—Paul and Barnabas (Acts 13:1–3), and later John Mark, Silas, Silvanus, Luke, Timothy, and Titus. Apollos, too, would travel from city to city preaching (Acts 18:24–25), although Aquilla and Priscilla had to update him on the finer points of his theology (Acts 18:26–28).

SLAVES AND SERVANTS

The Jewish people spent centuries in slavery to one nation or another, and each time, God rescued them. Because of this, God required that the Israelites who were hired by their countrymen as workers be treated well. Although they served their masters, they were not slave to them. Then, after seven years, these workers were released from their obligations, and allowed to take their earnings away with them.

BRICK-MAKERS

The Israelites moved into the outskirts of Egypt to get away from the famine in their land. The Pharaoh welcomed them because they were the family of his second in command—Joseph. However, time passed, Joseph died, and the Egyptians began to resent their new neighbors. Before long, the welcome guests had been pressed into slavery. The Egyptian Pharaohs were always trying to outdo their predecessors in building projects, so there was a constant need for bricks. The Israelites became brick-makers and brick-toters and brick-layers. The clay soil was mixed with water and straw, then spread in wooden frames on the ground. After setting up, the frames could be lifted and moved along for the next batch of bricks, and the formed bricks were left in place to bake hard in the sun. In some cities, the bricks were baked in a kiln, which made them stronger. Babel was built of kiln-baked bricks (Gen. 11:3).

BUTLERS

A butler was always close to the king's side, and he ate from the king's table and drank the finest wines. Still, his was an unenviable job. Many an ancient king died under mysterious circumstances. Assassination was rather commonplace, and so the royalty learned to be cautious. Since poison was a favorite way to dispose of an unpopular dictator, every king employed a butler. Basically, the butler tasted everything that was brought before the king. There was a pause as all eyes turned towards him. If the butler did not turn colors, foam at the mouth, or collapse to the floor, everyone proceeded to eat. Other names for this job were wine-taster and cupbearer. One of the servants who asked for a dream interpretation from Joseph while in prison was a butler (Gen. 40:5). Nehemiah served as royal cupbearer to the king of Persia (Neh. 1:11).

DID YOU KNOW?

- Eliezer, the chief servant of Abraham, would have inherited his master's great wealth if Ishmael and Isaac had not been conceived late in Abraham's life (Gen. 15:2).

- The institution of slavery is often mentioned in the parables (Mt. 21:34; 22:3) as an analogy for the Kingdom of God.

GOVERNESSES

When Rachel traveled to Canaan to become Isaac's bride, she traveled with the woman who had been her nurse since childhood (Gen. 24:59). Although she was probably no Mary Poppins, Rachel was saddened when

BLIND BARTIMAEUS
The Beggar

Blindness was common in the area of Palestine. Some were born into it (Jn. 9:2, 20), but more often blindness was the result of blowing sands, glaring sun, and a disease spread by flies. Blind Bartimaeus was a social outcast. He could not read, work, marry, or enter the temple. He could not even make sure that his hair was neatly combed. This left him in a life of abject poverty and loneliness and forced him to rely on the compassion and pity of strangers in order to survive.

Bartimaeus spent his days crouched in the dust on the side of the street. A small bowl was cupped in his hands, extended towards the sounds of passing feet. The few mites and sheckles that clattered into his possession were spent on coarse barley bread, and perhaps a bit of cheese or fruit. By placing himself in the midst of the marketplace crowds, he was able to listen in on the day's business. Bartimaeus was a fixture on the corner amidst the stalls, and his ears were sharp, even if his eyes were not. No doubt he had heard the stories that were being told around the market about a teacher named Jesus. Some talked of the uprising he might lead against Rome. Some asserted that his pedigree was royal—he was of the line of David. Some declared that he was a wise teacher, and maybe even a prophet of God. Although a few scoffed at tales of miraculous events, more spoke with unabashed amazement at the healings they had witnessed. Bartimaeus felt the stir of hope in his heart, for the gift of sight could transform his whole life. A man who could see could work, worship, and even wed! As the murmurings of the crowd grew, so that Bartimaeus knew Jesus was in his very city and close at hand, he could not contain himself. Stumbling after the crowds, he called out in a loud voice to the One who could transform a beggar's life with the touch of his hand.

she had to say goodbye to her governess, Deborah (Gen 35:8). Another famous nurse in the Old Testament was Jocabed, Moses' mother. The Pharaoh's daughter hired her to care for Moses, the baby she had just taken from the Nile River (Ex. 2:7–9).

VOLUNTARY SLAVERY

When debts became overwhelming and there was no hope of paying off one's creditors, there was one way to come up with the cash as a last resort. A man could sell himself, and his whole family if necessary, as slaves. Their hard work was accepted as payment against the money that they owed. If a poor Jewish man became so indebted that he had to sell himself as a bond servant to another Jew, he was to be treated fairly as a hired servant. He technically remained a free man, and was to be freed in the Year of Jubilee (Lev. 25:40).

FORCED LABOR

Say you are a king, and you want to erect a new palace or temple. In Old Testament times, some building projects needed enormous numbers of workers in order to see them accomplished in a lifetime. In order to amass the needed workforce, slavery was considered an acceptable option. This usually entailed putting prisoners-of-war to work. Also, men and their families could be forced into slavery because they were unable to pay off their debts (Mt. 18:30). David forced POWs to work on his building projects. King Solomon organized a system of forced labor that put the Israelites themselves to work as well. God had warned them that a king would expect these things (1Sa. 8:10–18). The Jews were called, as loyal citizens, to leave their homes and work for their king one out of every three months. Solomon's methods enabled him to lay roadways and build fortresses and the temple for which he was famous.

> **DID YOU KNOW?**
>
> • Slavery was a class distinction that became meaningless in the church of Christ (1Cor. 7:22; Gal. 3:28).

New Testament Slaves

In New Testament times, slavery still existed in Palestine, but it had become more refined. Slaves were not forced to do heavy work. Instead they were servants in the houses of wealthy people or in the palace courts. On a larger scale, slavery was thriving throughout the Roman Empire. Peter and Paul both gave advice to Christian slaves in their letters to the growing church. They were urged to serve their masters faithfully, and live out their Christian faith before them (Eph. 6:5–9). Paul even wrote a letter of reference for a runaway slave named Onesimus, who had become a Christian and wished to return to his master. That letter is the New Testament Book of Philemon.

Beggars

The industries of Bible times were hardly equal opportunity employers! If a man was not hale and hearty, he was unemployable. What's more, he was looked upon with suspicion, for the Jews assumed that the sickly were being punished by God for some sin in their lives. Lepers, epileptics, paralytics, along with the lame, deaf, and blind were outcasts of the word-a-day world. Although allowances were made for the poor, like permission to glean in the fields and orchards during harvests, these bounties lay just out of reach for the handicapped. These men were forced to rely on the compassion of strangers, pleading for the mercy and generosity of passers-by. Jesus healed beggars who suffered from leprosy, paralysis, and blindness. Once freed from their various impediments, they could get normal jobs within their communities.

Gatekeepers

When a city or a large household buttoned down for the night, the gates were closed and the outside windows were barred. Latecomers were forced to deal with the gatekeeper if they wanted to get into the city after dark. This security measure kept raiding nomads and cat burglars at bay. In the homes of the wealthy, a locked gate faced the street. Here, a gatekeeper or porter was employed. He served as a kind of human doorbell.

When a guest knocked at the gate, the porter would open the door, lead the visitor into a waiting area, then go and announce the arrival to the master of the house. Rhoda had been assigned the task of watching the door when Peter came knocking (Acts 12:13), but she forgot to let Peter in before announcing his arrival!

GLADIATORS

The coliseums of Rome were the Hollywood of ancient times, and game shows were big. Spectators were lured by a free seat. Gladiators were kind of like professional wrestlers in Roman times. The big fights were scheduled regularly, and audiences flocked to the arenas for the show. Fans in the coliseums always had their favorite gladiators, and souvenir plaques and drinking cups were sold with their likenesses on them. Gambling flourished, and bookies took bets on the outcomes of the fights. The gladiators were slaves and prisoners, who fought to save their own lives at the cost of another's.

CHAPTER ELEVEN

THEIR TRANSPORTATION

When we think of transportation, the first phrase that pops into mind is **"planes, trains, and automobiles."** However, the lands of the Bible operated at a much slower pace. For most of the Old Testament time and beyond, transportation meant "walk, jog, or run." Still, there were other means to get about. Elijah traveled by fiery chariot. Jonah traveled by whale. Then there was Jesus, who could walk upon the water! It all makes planes and automobiles sound downright dull.

By Land

A lot of Bible men and women had to pick up and move. Their journeys are described in the Scriptures. In the Old Testament alone, Abraham and Lot move into Canaan, Jacob and his household transfer to Egypt, and the Israelites wander for forty years through the desert. The New Testament recounts in some detail the travels of Paul and other Christian leaders, and Jesus must have covered considerable distances during his public ministry.

WALKING

By far, the most popular mode of transportation in ancient times was simply walking! Most people couldn't afford a pack animal, so when they needed to make a trip they put on their sandals. In Old Testament times, roads were simply well-worn footpaths and cart trails. A man could kick up a lot of dust between point A and point B. Although more formal streets were laid by New Testament times, travelers still arrived at their destinations footsore from their trek. That is why a traveler's feet were washed when they were welcomed into a home (Jn. 13:5).

A SABBATH'S DAY JOURNEY

Travel was forbidden on the Sabbath (Ex. 16:29), for the journey would involve work. Work was a big no-no during the Sabbath rest. However, some moving about was unavoidable. How far could one go before they had been said to actually travel? The Jews set about to determine how far was too far. The number was set at 2,000 paces, or about six furlongs from the wall of the city. That is just under a half-mile. If a man traveled 2,000 paces and no further, he did not violate the Law. The Mount of Olives was a Sab-

---

DID YOU KNOW?

• Distance was often measured in the number of days it would take to journey to a place (Gen. 30:36; 31:23).

• In 1Kin. 18:27, Elijah taunts the prophets of Baal by suggesting that their god is away on a long journey, and that is why he did not answer their prayers.

bath day's journey from the walls of Jerusalem (Acts 1:12). Tradition holds that this was the distance between the Tabernacle of God and the surrounding tents in the Israelite encampments (Josh. 3:4).

A CLOUD BY DAY AND FIRE BY NIGHT

Wandering in the desert wilderness was no fun. During the day, the heat was unbearable as it shimmered off the sand and stones. Bodies sweated. Eyes squinted. Mouths were parched. There were little annoyances, like getting sand in your eyes and pebbles in your sandals. Bigger problems included things like sand fleas, vipers, and scorpions. At night, the temperatures would plummet, and the sweat from a long day in unrelenting heat would suddenly chill you to the bone. Families huddled together in their tents, trying to keep warm. Men would linger near the fire, with backs hunched against the cold. When the children of Israel faced a forty-year journey through the wilderness, God provided for them in a special way. His cloud overshadowed their days, and His fire warmed their nights (Ex. 13:21).

FALL IN!

When the children of Israel left Egypt, it actually took a while. This was the caravan to top all caravans. There were thousands upon thousands of men, women, and children. The lineup was longer than the Macy's Thanksgiving Day Parade, and by the time everybody was moving at the back end, the kids in the front end were asking, "Are we there yet?" In order to help keep this big crew in order, a few rules were established for organizational purposes. The people were divided into family groups, with the twelve

JOSEPH AND MARY

Looking for an Inn

The governor had called for a census at the most inconvenient of times. Mary moved slowly towards Joseph, ready to resume their journey after a short rest. Joseph fretted over his young fiancé as they eased back onto the road. They had started early to allow for a slow pace and for the frequent potty breaks, but they were not making good time. He had hoped to be settled in a room by now. Joseph had planned to find a midwife for Mary, and then stay in Bethlehem doing odd jobs until after the baby came. He had been watching carefully, and Mary's discomfort was evident. Her baby might come before they even reached their destination. They made it though, and he sighed in relief as they entered the city's marketplace. But, his relief was short-lived. Bethlehem was overrun! As they made their way to the largest of the inns, he was stopped in his tracks. The inn boasted several rooms in its two-story complex, with mattresses on the floor and a lampstand provided. The smells of baking bread and stew were carrying from its kitchens. But the family just ahead of him was being turned away, so Joseph moved on. In a couple of the smaller establishments, where guests had to provide their own bedding, he was told that even the space on their floors had been sold to people coming in for the census. If people were already crowding together to sleep on the floors in the inns, what were the chances of finding a private place for Mary to give birth? Despite his extensive inquiries, he could not find a single inn or boarding house that had any vacancies. Even private homes were filled to overflowing with extended family who had come to town to be counted. Joseph glanced back at Mary, and he knew he had to hurry. His shaky smile did little to ease the nervous look in her eyes. The child was definitely coming now, and Mary could

not be expected to give birth in the marketplace! Their only hope was to go door to door, begging for shelter. The first couple of inns were packed. Each room had two or three families sharing the space. The floors were spoken for in the hallways, and single men were sleeping with their pack animals in the stables. Joseph stopped asking for rooms, and asked instead for anything. He offered to pay cash for their stay, or to do some carpentry in exchange for a safe place for Mary to lie down. Finally, a man relented, and allowed them to use his stable for shelter. There, in humble surroundings, Mary brought forth her firstborn son, Jesus!

tribes traveling together in units. When camp was set up, everybody had assigned campsites arrayed around the tabernacle, which stood in the middle of the encampment. When it was time to pick up and move on, the signal was given on silver trumpets (Num. 10:2) and the people would fall in. First came the tribes camped on the east, then came the camps on the south, and so on. It was like the instructions for a serving line at a church potluck supper. "This table will go through first, then once they are in line, this table can follow them, and so on around the room."

SETTING THE PACE

When a caravan was being formed, one of the jobs of the caravan master was to set the pace of the trip. Traveling businessmen or merchants, who were all riding on camels, could make pretty quick work of a road trip. Camel's had a long stride, and endured the heat of the day well. However, if a caravan included large flocks of sheep or goats, the pace was slowed considerably. These smaller animals had to be herded to keep them going in the right direction, and their legs couldn't keep pace with a camel at full speed. The caravan master had to decide whether to take on extra travelers. They were sometimes approached by families who needed to make a trip and wanted the safety of a large group. However, the money that they offered might not offset the change of pace that their presence required. When Jacob departed from Laban with his wives and his flocks, he set an easy pace for them. Not only were there young children in the group, but there were also lambs among the ewes. "I will lead on slowly at a pace which they are able to endure" (Gen. 33:13–14).

ALL ROADS LEAD TO ROME

In the ancient world, it was true that all roads led to Rome. That's where they all came from! As the Roman Empire expanded, they literally paved their own way through the nations. It was their way of connecting the farthest reaches to the center and unifying their world. The Romans had the audacious expectation to be around forever, and so when they made stuff, they built it to last. Their road systems are a fine example of their craftsmanship. They

> ### DID YOU KNOW?
>
> • According to Jonah 3:3, it took a three-day journey to travel from one end of the city of Ninevah to the other end!
>
> • Jesus commanded his disciples to travel light—no luggage, no change of clothing, no provisions, and no money (Mt. 10:10; Mk. 6:8).

didn't just throw a load of gravel down in a straight line and call it a road. No, they actually dug in and laid a foundation of gravel, rock, and cement under their stone pavements. Many roads were raised above the level of the surrounding land, and had ditches on either side. Near large cities, the roads were wide enough to allow wagons and chariots to pass each other. There are roads in the Middle East still in use that were built by the Roman Empire.

ROAD CONSTRUCTION

A Roman road was well built. Two or three layers of foundational materials were paved with flat stones. Sometimes blocks of stone were cut specifically to be

JACOB
Journey by Oxcart

Jacob was giddy with anticipation. His son, Rachel's boy, that had been lost to him for decades was alive! In his old age, the memories of sweet Rachel were often with him. She had died so young, and he had believed Joseph to be gone as well. And now, an amazing revelation. Joseph was in Egypt, and he was a leader among the people there! Joseph was wealthy and powerful, and he offered them a place to settle. Joseph had grown up, married, and was a father now. He still shook his head in wonder and disbelief every few minutes. But here were the oxen and the carts before him. They were solid enough evidence of Joseph's well-being. The arrival of the oxcarts had caused quite a stir in the area. The land had been languishing under a famine for years now, and any cattle left in their area were all weakened from lack of food. The teams of Egyptian oxen seemed strangely out of place—strong beasts with sleek sides, snorting as they leaned into their yokes. The wagons themselves were a wonder of foreign design, with bright paint and strange letters. Such richness for a family of simple shepherds! All the boys were busy with the packing. He still thought of them as boys, although most of them were grandfathers by now. They emptied tents, packed belongings, loaded wagons, and gathered their flocks. The journey would be long for a man of his age. He had worried over the family's survival for more months than he could recall now. Some of the wells had run dry, and the rains had not come in time to save their crops. Their flocks had dwindled in the unrelenting heat, and there was little of the scrubby grass on the hillsides left to graze upon. Their survival depended upon this move. The family was desperate, and the path before them had opened up quite miraculously. Leaving the lands that God had given to his ancestors,

Jacob leaned forward, straining his eyes toward the horizon. He could not wait to behold his son again. Would he still look the same? Jacob wanted to see for himself the kind of man that this favorite son had become. The creak and sway of the oxcarts were rhythmic, but too slow for the heart that beat quickly for an impossible reunion. Then, a cloud of dust was spotted. A chariot could be made out in the distance. A shout of excitement was heard in the ranks. And then, he was gazing into the face of his son, Joseph. Jacob's son was brought back from the dead, and the boy had made a way of salvation for them. God had indeed provided a miracle.

used as pavers. When road construction was set to begin, they called in the troops. Many a young man entered the glorious service of the Roman army only to be put to work in a chain gang, digging roadbeds and laying rock. No obstacle was too great for the relentless Roman engineers. If they came to a river, they built a bridge. If they encountered marshy lands, they hauled in the materials to make a raised roadbed across the muck. If they came to a mountain, they tunneled right through the rock.

STREET SIGNS

In New Testament times, the road systems were quite advanced, thanks to the efforts of the Roman army. The streets that ran from city to city were fitted with carefully laid stones to smooth the passage for travelers. They had all the conveniences of a freeway system, with less advertising. "Have a Date in Jericho, City of Palms" or "One More Mile Laodicia, Visit our Hot Spring Spas!" were not plastered to billboards along the way. "This Way to Damascus" or "Thessalonica, three furlongs" might be more realistic roadside indicators. One actual amenity of this network of roads was the mile marker. Carved stones were set along the path to let passengers know how far they had traveled from one city or how far it was to the next. This came in handy for the Roman soldiers, who could nab civilians to carry their packs for them. It was within the rights of the military to use reluctant passers-by this way, but only for one mile. Jesus urged his followers, "whoever compels you to go one mile, go with him two" (Mt. 5:41).

OASIS

On a long journey, the oasis was a little bit of paradise. There, the water table was just high enough so that a pool or a spring formed. The water nourished a ring of lush vegetation in the midst of the surrounding

desert. The oasis was a dependable rest stop for the ancient caravans. There was all-you-could-drink water and shade under the branches of palm trees and low shrubs. If caravans managed to come there in the proper season, the date palms would also offer their fruit to the weary travelers. In the Scriptures, one oasis that is mentioned was at Kadesh Barnea, in the Sahara Desert. There is still an oasis there today. The children of Israel, wandering in the wilderness, took some rest at the oasis in Kadesh Barnea (Deut. 1:19).

LITTERS

When the wealthy of ancient times wished to get out in the streets to see and be seen, traveling by foot just didn't cut it. Mingling with the less fortunate was unthinkable. Merely walking was beneath their social status. But, to get into the shopping quarter and visit their favorite boutiques, 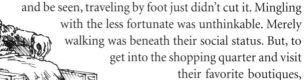 a chariot proved too wide. The streets that wound through the cities were crowded and much too nar-row. The solution

SOLOMON

Importing Horses

No king ever compared with King Solomon of Israel (1Kin. 3:12). Nor was there ever a king as wise or wealthy as Solomon. Foreign dignitaries traveled long distances just to hear him speak (1Kin. 10:1) and silver was so commonplace within his city that it was like rocks on the ground (1Kin. 10:27). He was a handsome fellow, with ruddy and good-looking David for a father (1Sa. 17:42) and beautiful Bathsheba for a mother (2Sa. 11:2). He amassed a fortune in gold, silver, and ivory and collected a menagerie of strange and exotic animals (1Kin. 10:22). He also married princesses from neighboring nations (1Kin. 3:1). Solomon had strengthened the borders of their land, and the Israelites knew a season of peace and prosperity (1Kin. 4:24). His words were so profound, that people actually wrote down his proverbs in order to pass them on to future generations (Prov. 1:1). He kept several palaces and established his own fleet of ships (1Kin. 9:26) to bring in more of the silks and spices and perfumes that delighted his harem of wives and concubines (1Kin. 11:3). God had promised Solomon a wise and understanding heart, as well as riches and honor (1Kin. 3:11–13). He had it made!

A man with this kind of background could afford some pretty expensive hobbies. Although a garage full of classic cars was not an option for Solomon, there was the ancient equivalent. Horses were a luxury that drew admiration from men. They were strong, spirited, and sleek. No two were alike. Horses had to be imported from far away countries like Egypt. They were a collector's dream! Solomon imported hundreds of horses (1Kin. 10:28; 2Chr. 9:28), and bred them in his stables. There was a practical aspect to the equine species as well, for horses just happened to be the backbone of an army

in those days. A mounted cavalry was the sign of a powerful army from a wealthy nation. War chariots, pulled by two horses, were the tanks of ancient warfare. Solomon had both. The army of Israel boasted 12,000 mounted troops and 40,000 horses for his chariots of war (1Kin. 4:26). How did a king manage to stable that many noble steeds? Solomon actually had entire cities built to house and care for his horses. They were called chariot cities, and the barns there were enormous (1Kin. 9:19). One city in particular had 4,000 stalls to house Solomon's horses and chariots (2Chr. 9:25).

was a litter. A couch or chair was set on a platform, which was carried by poles on the shoulders of four or six slaves. Sometimes a framework draped with curtains shaded the seat. The passenger could view their surroundings from an elevated position, or slip into seclusion behind flowing fabric.

GIDDY-UP!

When it was time to saddle up and hit the road, the main riding animal in Bible times was the donkey. These little long-eared pack animals were domesticated long before either the horse or the camel. They were very popular as a means of transportation. Now, the nomads of the desert kept camels, and as international trade became more developed, camels became more widely used by the merchants. Camels were perfect for desert travel, with their long stride and saucer-like feet. Both camels and donkeys were dependable and sturdy, able to haul heavy burdens over long distances. Horses were another matter! In Old Testament times, horses were usually kept by a king's army for war. They were swift and maneuverable in the battle fray. However, horses were much more expensive to care for than camels and donkeys, and were considered a luxury. It wasn't until New Testament times that horses became more common, and accessible for civilian purposes.

TRAVELING SALESMEN

When man decided to go onto the circuit as a traveling salesman, he had to start by drumming up his own business. He'd look around and find some appealing merchandise from his hometown and take it on the road with him. Then, as he traveled, he carefully watched for more products with potential. Part of a caravaner's business was finding undiscovered talent and marketing it to the world. In one town, he might find some particularly beautiful pottery. After some friendly haggling, the potter might trade his beautiful pots for the special blue dye that was only found in a village some miles away. The resulting blue pottery might later attract the attention of villagers from further down the way, who were willing to sell their intricately woven baskets for the aromatic balm that another village harvested from their trees. On went the cycle of products to sell and customers to buy them. So the traders planned their routes, hoping to tempt villages further down the trail into buying wares that were not available in their own hometowns.

INVENTION OF THE WHEEL

We tend to think of the horse and buggy as an old-fashioned way to get around, but in Bible times, it would have been a luxury afforded by the very wealthy. In Old Testament times, bundles were carried on one's back and water jars were balanced on women's heads. Pack animals were used for moving stuff around. Donkeys and camels were the backbone of a good merchant caravan. The first wheels

> ### DID YOU KNOW?
>
> • Traders gave little thought to the time involved in the travel. Sometimes the whole family spent a year or more on the road and in other countries buying and selling along their way.
>
> • In order to make a profit, merchants used strings of pack animals to move large amounts of goods over long distances.

were not chiseled from rough stone, but carved from wood. Wealthy farmers had ox carts to help with their work. Jacob was loaned several ox carts to help transport his family from Palestine to Egypt during the seven-year famine (Gen. 45:21). Countries with chariots were considered advanced, and their militaries were feared. Chariot wheels were made of wood and had spokes like a wagon wheel. Joseph rode in chariots in Egypt (Gen. 41:43), and David captured the chariots of his enemies (2Sa. 8:4). Solomon had so many chariots and horses to pull them that he established entire cities in which to house them (1Kin. 9:19).

CHARIOTS

A chariot was like an ancient humvee. It was used almost exclusively for the armed forces of the day, but was occasionally driven by civilians as well. These chariots were made from a wood framework with a curved dashboard, and covered by leather and metal ornamentation. A proud soldier kept his chariot oiled and polished, buffing the bronze until it shone like a chrome hubcap. A war chariot was equipped with special features to make it comfortable. Since the passengers stood while driving a chariot, the floors were made from criss-crossed ropes to serve as shock absorbers. Wheels were low, to prevent tipping, and set with razor-sharp blades that knocked down the competition in the heat of a battle. The sides of a chariot were fit with quivers for arrows, and there was a convenient bow rack. Hooks for water skins were ancestors of modern-day cup holders!

SAFETY IN NUMBERS

In the early days of long distance travel, safety was a big issue. While caravaners made a living by transporting goods from city to city, other men made their living by mugging them en route! A lone man was an easy target (Lk. 10:30). Any bend in the road or narrow pass was a likely place for an ambush. The priest and the Levite who left the wounded man on the road and hurried on were suspicious of an ambush. Such attacks were feared, and so men have always prayed for travel mercies. A safe journey was a matter for thankfulness: "The hand of our God was upon us, and he delivered us from the hand of the enemy and from ambush along the road" (Ezr. 8:31). Safety in numbers was a rule of thumb, and so a wise traveler set out with several companions. When Joseph and Mary came down to Jerusalem with Jesus, they traveled with a large enough group of people that they did not immediately realize that Jesus was missing (Lk. 2:44).

PROVISIONS FOR THE JOURNEY

Travel food was not very exciting. Trail mix hadn't become popular yet, and so the ancient version of hard tack was mostly used. This was a kind of hard, cracker-like bread that could either be gnawed or soaked in water to make porridge. It wasn't very exciting, but it wouldn't spoil during a long trip. After a few weeks on the road, fresh food was an appealing thought. David nearly attacked a farmer who wouldn't give his men provisions, but his wife averted the fight by sending David and his men some food anyway (1Sa. 25:18–19). They were appeased at the sight of fresh mutton, bread, wine, roasted grains, raisins, and figs. The road food of the Israelites was manna, which is described as tasting like "white coriander and honey" (Ex. 16:31). But even with such heavenly fare, they still complained about the fresh food they used to have in Egypt—fish, cucumbers, melons, leeks, onions, and garlic (Num. 11:5).

ANCIENT TRUCK STOPS

Where two roads intersected, the ancient equivalent of a truck stop sprouted up, offering travelers food, water, bathing places, and supplies for a small fee. Some were real "Mom & Pop" family businesses, offering room and board to strangers who were just passing through. In a land where thieves were abundant and ruthless, these safe houses were essential for safe travel. In New Testament times, Rome even posted soldiers at these stops along their roads, guaranteeing safe passage throughout the empire. Rest areas sprouted up in the deserts as well, usually at an oasis. Shade and water revived the spirits of dusty travelers. These waysides catered especially to the needs of the caravans that would rumble through. When a string of camels was sighted in the distance, the proprietors would fill the water troughs, give the stew a quick stir, and lay out the mats upon which meals were shared. Under the shade of a goatskin tent, newcomers would be offered bread and salt and water. After the animals were cared for, the men would gather to share an evening meal. Merchants were like traveling salesmen, and they were a source of stories from far away places. Their news was anticipated as much as the business they brought!

HOTELS AND MOTELS

The oldest inns were much like the desert truck stops but smaller, with fewer perks for the traveler. These were no-frills establishments that only provided a safe place to sleep. By New Testament times, customer service began to pick up a little, and inns could be large buildings with two stories and several private rooms. They had stables for animals and provided meals for a modest fee. In Jerusalem, the inns were filled to capacity during the Passover, when the population of the city nearly tripled! Smaller towns like Bethlehem were less equipped for an influx of visitors. When the census was called for and the homeboys returned to their old stomping grounds, the inns were packed. Many families made some extra cash by allowing the visitors to sleep on their floors. By the time Joseph got to Bethlehem with Mary in tow, inns and homes were full, and all that was available were the barns (Lk. 2:7).

TRAVELING AMONG GENTILES

As far as the Jews were concerned, Jews and Gentiles did not mix. To come into contact with a Gentile was to become unclean, and this was avoided at all costs. This led to some creative segregation over the centuries. For instance, when forced to travel abroad, Jews managed to keep themselves separate from Gentiles even in the smallest details. Jews carried large baskets with them on trips. In these they carried their provisions, which would prevent them from the horror of eating Gentile food. They even carried large amounts of hay with them on journeys, which they slept on at night. In this way, they separated themselves from the Gentiles in both food and lodging.

RUNNERS

In the days before telegraphs, telephones, fax machines, and instant messaging, people still wanted to get the news. Communication was vital, especially for kings who were waging war against other nations. The royalty anxiously awaited news from the front lines. This meant finding young men who could run like the wind! They brought the latest news from afar. Glad was the messenger who was the bearer of good news. More often their news was unwelcome. Hence the saying, "Don't kill the messenger!" Eli learned by messenger that his two sons had been killed in battle (1Sa. 4:17). In David's time, a messenger was sent from the general on the front lines to inform him that Uriah the Hittite was dead (2Sa. 11:19–21). Years later, a messenger brought word to David that the people had voted against him in favor of his son, Absalom (2Sa. 15:13). Jezebel sent word by messenger to Elijah, letting him know that she intended to kill him (1Kin. 19:2). Jesus learned by messenger that his good friend Lazarus was dead (Jn. 11:3).

DO NOT TRAVEL!

Once upon a Bible story, there was a man who was commanded not to travel. Solomon warned a man named Shimei that he should never leave the walls of Jerusalem (1Kin. 2:36). So long as he obeyed the royal decree and spent his days close to home, he would be safe. If for any reason he was discovered outside the city perimeter, it would cost him his life! Why such a harsh command? Well, Shimei was guilty of cursing King David, kicking up dust and hurling stones along with his foul words. At the time, David had vowed not to kill the man. On his deathbed, however, David urged Solomon to make Shimei pay for his misdeeds. Solomon granted Shimei a measure of mercy as well by commanding the man's confinement rather than his death. Shimei himself stated that Solomon's decision was a good one (1Kin. 2:38). For three years, Shimei kept his word and dwelt within the walls of Jerusalem. But eventually he slipped up, was found out, and Solomon had him executed (1Kin. 2:46).

DID YOU KNOW?

- In Solomon's Temple, ten identical carts of gold were embellished with angels, lions, oxen, and wreaths (1Kin. 7:29). Later in Scriptures we see that invaders destroyed these pretty little golden wheelbarrows (2Kin. 16:17; Jer. 52:17, 20).

- Entire towns would specialize in one trade, exporting their commodities for a profit. Some areas almost exclusively produced wine, pottery, dyed cloth, or jewelry.

TRICKY TRAVELERS

When Joshua led the children of Israel into the land of Canaan, they began to methodically kill off the previous owners. God had commanded that all of the Canaanites be killed, lest they lead the Israelites astray. The people of Gibeon did not wish to sit around, waiting to be exterminated like the inhabitants of Jericho or Ai, so they devised a clever plan. Men of Gibeon disguised themselves as ambassadors from a far away land. Attention to detail was vital here. Their props were carefully planned. The men dressed in shabby clothing, old and patched. Their wineskins were torn and mended. Their sacks were well-worn, and their provisions dry and moldy. Then they came before Joshua and told a convincing tale of their great journey and of their fear of their God. They put their moldy bread on display, and explained that it was hot from the oven when they left home. Their clothing and baggage had been brand new, but the long journey had left them in shambles. Without consulting God, Joshua proceeded to make a covenant with the Gibeonites. When the truth was known, Joshua was embarrassed and furious. He could not kill off the tribe of Gibeon, as God had commanded. Instead, he enslaved them. The Gibeonites figured that they got off easy!

"Make Way for the King"

When a king took a road trip, he sent messengers ahead to book all the best hotels. He had his men alert the various governors of his schedule, and he let them know how long he would be stopping over in their city. This news invariably sent entire towns into a dither, for rooms had to be prepared for the king and his royal entourage. Grand feasts must be planned and entertainment had to be arranged. The local gardens were pillaged for their best flowers and for fresh produce. Vintners gave up their best wineskins, and housewives contributed their fresh butters and cheeses. Singers polished up their repertoire. And in the midst of this entire flurry, one special detail was not to be overlooked. It was a small thing, but a matter of civil pride that the roads be ready for the royal entrance. In Isaiah it says, "Every valley shall be exalted and every mountain and hill brought low. The crooked places shall be made straight and the rough places smooth" (Is. 40:4). The bumpy roads were graded, the potholes were filled, and the stones were swept aside to make way for the king.

BY SEA

The Bible tells of journeys that bring people across the water—from the parting of the Red Sea to the exciting tale of Jonah and the whale. People took to the water to explore the world beyond their horizon, to shop in exotic locations, and to get from one place to another. They crossed seas, lakes, rivers, and creeks. Revelation even describes a river of crystal-clear water in heaven, flowing from the throne of the Lamb (Rev. 22:1).

The Ark

The first boat in history was built on dry land, without a drop of water close by upon which to sail it. Its construction took nearly a hundred years. Only four men worked on it—Noah, Ham, Shem, and Japheth.

JONAH

Ship's Passenger

When God tells his prophets to preach, he expects them to say "How long?" However, when God put in orders for Jonah to relocate to Ninevah and preach to the city's heathen population, he met with resistance. Jonah's reaction to God's command was more of a "Yikes!" Jonah packed a bag and assessed his travel options. The camel caravan could take weeks, and a nice, fast chariot was far too expensive. What's more, he wasn't so sure that he wanted to go. The city of Ninevah was the capital of the Assyrian empire, and Assyrians were tough customers. They were fierce, merciless, and unstoppable! Most people sent the Assyrians tribute, not prophets! On second thought, Jonah decided that the best way to handle this dilemma was "to flee from the presence of the Lord" (Jonah 1:3). Now Joppa, on the coast of Palestine, did not lend itself to docking facilities, but Johah was able to find a ship whose hold was not completely filled and talked the ship's captain into taking him as a passenger. A price was agreed upon, and money exchanged hands. Hoping that God wasn't looking just then, Jonah hid himself on board. Down in the cargo hold, Jonah made himself comfortable, and fell asleep while the men on deck prepared to set sail.

Although it wasn't the season for storms, the crew watched nervously as the clouds gathered and headed straight in their direction. Since sailors were a superstitious lot, they began to pray to their gods as the winds whipped around them. Somebody's god was really upset about something, so there was a whole lot of confessing going on! To avoid being capsized, the captain attempted to steer into the winds. When nothing else seemed to be working, the command was given for everyone to start tossing the cargo overboard. It was then that Jonah

was discovered. The crew looked on with disbelief as the captain shook him awake, "What do you mean, sleeper? Arise, call on your God!" (Jonah 1:6). Somehow knowing that the storm wasn't quite natural, the crew decided amongst themselves to cast lots to determine who was the guilty party. One crewman after another was found innocent. Finally, Jonah was singled out, and the crew demanded to know what he had done. Jonah confessed that he was running away from God. The storm grew worse, and although the crew tried valiantly to row against the waves, they could not make any headway. Jonah convinced the crew to throw him overboard. Immediately, the ship was becalmed, and the crew stared in wonder at the clearing skies. Indeed, the God of the Hebrews was powerful!

They felled the timber, stripped the bark, planed the planks, pounded the nails, and painted the whole kit and caboodle with pitch to make it waterproof. Built to God's own specifications, it was a seaworthy vessel, fit to endure its yearlong voyage. Three stories tall, and longer than a football field, Noah's Ark was hard to miss. It was the talk of the town— something you brought visiting relatives around to see. It was an absurdity, and Noah was the laughingstock of the world. In the end, the ship only carried eight passengers, along with representatives of all the animals of the earth.

A BOAT FOR BABY MOSES

At four months old, Moses was definitely the youngest solo sailor in history. With a basket for a boat, he drifted away from his mother's trembling hands and into the heart of a princess (Ex. 2:3, 6). The basket that Jochabed wove was made from the papyrus reeds that were plentiful along the banks of the Nile. To waterproof the tiny ship, she brushed its sides with pitch. Under the watchful eye of his older sister, the baby reached the quiet waters near the steps of the palace, where the women would come down to the water and bathe (Ex. 2:5). Even the little traveler's name was appropriately given, for Moses meant, "to draw out."

PARTING THE WATERS

Sailing across the sea could really shorten the mileage of a long trip. However, water could be a real obstacle as well. When the children of Israel were marching away from Egypt, the stragglers took note of a cloud of dust rising in the distance. When the clatter of chariots could be discerned, and the glint of sun on metal could be seen, panic worked its way up to the head of the line. However, the back end of the procession couldn't see what the front end knew. They were between a rock and a hard place—actually an army and a wet place. The Red Sea stretched out before them, and there was nowhere to turn. But God provided a miracle, and the Red Sea was crossed without means of a raft, boat, or ferry. The children of Israel crossed as if on dry land (Ex. 14:21). Again, in Joshua we find the Israelites standing at the border of the Promised Land. A river flows before them, and some of the men are calculating how many rafts they will have to build in order to get the carts across. But God speaks to Joshua, the command is given, and the people cross the Jordan without wetting so much as the hem of their robes (Josh. 3:17)!

ISRAEL'S FLEET

Jerusalem was landlocked, but King Solomon wished to maintain his own fleet of ships for bringing in exotic goods from overseas. Ships from various points of call brought him things like gold, silver, ivory, apes, and monkeys (1Kin. 10:22; 2Chr. 9:21). He asked for the help of King Hiram of Tyre in Phoenicia, and Hiram was able to give Solomon the help he needed in building up a merchant fleet. Hiram also agreed to give the would-be Israelite sailors a crash course in sailing. Most of the Jews had never set foot on an ocean-going vessel before, and they had a lot to learn. Solomon kept Israel's fleet anchored in a town called Ezion Geber, in the Gulf of Aqaba.

> **DID YOU KNOW?**
>
> • The great seafaring nations of the Old Testament period were the Egyptians and the Phoenicians. Their fleets included both trade vessels and warships.
>
> • When God sent Jonah to the people of Ninevah, Jonah ran straight to Joppa to book passage on a ship—but then he sailed off in the opposite direction (Jonah 1:3)!

SHALLOW SHORES

Palestine just wasn't set up for sea trade. The long stretch of beaches along the Mediterranean Sea were completely unfit for harbors. Shallow waters prevented ships from being able to draw near and dock without running aground. There wasn't a good place on the shoreline to build a major port city. Eventually, the Canaanites managed to build a seaport where a river flowed into the sea. Small bays were developed into ports of call as well. One famous little port was at Joppa. It was to the harbor at Joppa that Jonah booked passage in Tarshish (Jonah 1:3).

LUKE

Shipwrecked with Paul

Luke was a real trooper. Here he was, an educated man, a historian, and a doctor. He was a gifted writer, able to compile the various stories of the disciples and of Mary into a history—a gospel—of the life of Jesus Christ on the earth. He also wrote the Acts of the Apostles, which is a best-seller in its own right. Yet, we find Luke tagging along with Paul during his travels. He was handy because of his good penmanship. Luke served Paul on his missionary journeys as an amanuensis—secretary, really. Paul wasn't much with a pen in hand. His letters were large and his writing was slow. Paul wasn't able to keep up with his own thoughts, and he wasted a lot of paper! So the writing fell to a man who was quick with a pen. Luke wrote while Paul paced. All of Paul's epistles to the different churches they had visited were captured in ink as he gave dictation to Luke. So, wherever Paul was led by God, Luke followed faithfully. He was with Paul in the midst of many difficulties—beaten with rods, lashed by whips, imprisoned, stoned, mugged, hungry, sleepless, cold, and thirsty (2Cor. 11:24–27).

One of Luke's most memorable experiences with Paul came on board a ship (Acts 27). Paul had been taken prisoner, and was being transported to Italy to stand before Caesar. He was under the charge of a Roman centurion named Julius, and Luke was allowed to travel with him. Julius took the men, along with some other prisoners, to the harbor and hired a ship to take them across the sea to Rome. They might just reach the far shore before the winter storms set in. It was slow going, against uncooperative winds, but they made it halfway. Landing on the island of Crete, they rested and watched the skies. It was late in the season for sailing, and the decision

to continue was a difficult one for the crew. Paul tried to dissuade
them from risking the trip. Finally, though, the captain sent word
that the anchors should be lifted. On a day when warm breezes were
blowing, the ship put out to sea. It didn't take the crew long to realize
their mistake. A furious storm came up, waves crashed, they lost control of the ship, and were driven before the waves. For fourteen days
the men on the boat went without food, so busy were they trying to
stay afloat. Then Paul came to them and said, "Let's eat!" He had heard
from God, and had been assured that all two hundred seventy-six
men on board would live if they just hung in there a while longer.
Heartened by the news, everybody dug in, ate a good dinner, and
threw the leftovers overboard. The next morning, they ran aground
near an island. Some of the soldiers on board wanted to kill all of the
prisoners, so that they couldn't escape. Julius intervened, however, so
everybody survived the wreck!

SHIPWRECKED!

Sailing across the sea in ancient times was a tricky business. It was wonderful to plan a voyage that could take months off of the time taken in a road trip, but there were no guarantees that the wind and the waves would be cooperative. Not all journeys went smoothly. Paul did a bit of sailing in his time. His missionary journeys took him to many seaports, and even a few islands in the midst of the Mediterranean Sea, like Crete and Cyprus. On one of these journeys, Paul was shipwrecked, and had to flounder in the sea for a day and a night before he was rescued! But, Paul was not a man to be kept down. He returned to the sea when the need arose. In fact, Paul says that in the midst of all his travels, he was shipwrecked three times (2Cor. 11:25)!

CROSSING THE SEA OF GALILEE

Boat traffic on the Sea of Galilee was mostly fishing boats. The cities along the edge of the lake did a brisk business in the fish markets up and down the whole of Palestine. Many of the men that Jesus befriended in Galilee were fishermen by trade. There were some vessels that made the trip across the Sea of Galilee to get from place to place. Jesus traveled in this way during his ministry in the area (Jn. 6:1). Although often placid, the waters of the lake could be stirred up suddenly in a squall. The winds that raced down the surrounding hillsides would whip up waves that could dash a small fishing vessel to pieces. Even experienced sailors like Peter despaired of their lives in the face of such a fury (Mt. 8:25).

WALKING ON WATER

Travel by sea generally necessitated a ship of some sort. Even Paul, floundering in the Mediterranean Sea, needed to hang on to a bit of wood to keep afloat (2Cor. 11:25). But Jesus was just plain amazing, and he has all the other seafarers beat. Only the Son of God was able to walk on the water (Mt. 14:25)! According to Matthew's Gospel, he was moving along so well that he was even ready to pass the disciples on the left and keep on going.

CHAPTER TWELVE

THEIR
TRADITIONS

Y ou can almost hear Tevye singing it, can't you?

"Tradition!" Much of the Jewish life seems veiled

in tradition. **Things had to be done just so,** and

that was that.

WELCOME!

In Old Testament times, men especially prided themselves on their generous hospitality. It was an almost sacred duty. Friends and strangers were all welcomed, for in such a harsh environment, survival often depended upon the kindness of others.

TRAVEL COURTESIES

Joseph went out to meet his father (Gen. 46:29). This appears natural enough, but it was actually an Eastern courtesy. The farther a host journeyed toward his guest to "bring him in," the greater the courtesy. It conveyed the anticipation and excitement in the host's heart, as well as his respect for his guest. The walk together back to the host's house gave them some extra time to catch up on the latest news in each other's lives. Joseph's chariots arrived while Jacob was still far in the distance. They were both anxious for reunion! The father of the prodigal son ran to meet him while he was still a long way off (Lk. 15:20). Even Esau, when he learned that Jacob was returning to Canaan, set off to meet his brother (Gen. 32:6).

GREETING YOUR GUESTS

Next time you invite some friends over for dinner, consider reviving some old traditions of Bible-times hospitality. Now, most courteous guests will leave their shoes at the door. Won't they be stunned when you insist on removing their socks as well and washing their feet for them! Then, of course, comes the anointing. Liberally pour olive oil over each of your guest's heads. As a sign of courtesy and hospitality, perfumed olive oil was used to anoint an honored guest. Oil was used to make the face and hair shine, and was considered quite the beauty treatment. Perhaps in our case, it would be wise to skip to the third step of welcoming a guest Bible-style: offer them a glass of cold water.

HOSPITALITY

Bedouin hospitality was extended to friend and stranger alike. As a guest approached the nomadic tents, the man of the house greeted him.

Through the centuries, the traditional greeting has remained unchanged. Abraham would have welcomed his guests in the same manner used today. With his head erect, he would incline forward slightly and raise his right hand to touch his forehead, lips and heart. The guest was so welcomed, and immediately water and towels would be brought for the washing of feet (Gen. 18:4). Food was prepared—roasted goat in gravy, bread, butter, and sour camel's milk. Even though he was a wealthy sheikh, Abraham waited on his guests himself. The meal was slow-paced, allowing time for leisurely conversation.

FIVE COURSE DINNERS

During the days of Israel's kings, people stopped sitting on the floor so much. Tables and chairs, or even couches, were in style for dining rooms. At a formal dinner party, where the wealthy entertained important guests, meals were served in five courses. A banquet began with an aperitif—wine with honey stirred into it. Then three entrées were served at a leisurely pace, giving ample opportunity for conversation. The platters were carefully arranged and beautifully decorated, in hopes of impressing the dinner guests. Oohs and ahhs were mumbled as each course made its appearance. The final course was dessert-usually fresh fruit and honey pastries.

ARRANGING FOR ENTERTAINMENT

When a big dinner party was being planned, there was much more to consider than the menu. Entertainment had to be considered, and every host wished to surprise and impress his guests. Between the courses of the meal, poetry readings or stories were told. Sometimes they were put to music or included dancing. At a royal banquet,

PHARAOH'S BIRTHDAY FEAST

An Elaborate Display of Wealth

Egyptians took birthdays seriously, especially those of their Pharaohs! Men kept track of births down to the very hour so that a birth chart could be drawn up. They thought that the positions of the sun, moon, and stars held omens for the royal newborn's whole life. Astrologers claimed to be able to chart out a child's destiny, its character, its personality, its health, its talents and the happiness of its future marriage. These were early horoscopes. Oddly enough, the early Egyptians almost feared the coming of a birth anniversary, for the special day was thought to open the door for evil spirits to make mischief. To prevent any harm from coming to the celebrant, friends and relatives would gather, bringing gifts and well wishes. Birthday parties were held in most noble homes in Egypt. In fact, a part of every family's budget was set aside to purchase the party decorations and the animals used in sacrifices for the day. For the Pharaohs, these birthdays became feast days. Egypt's Pharaohs would order businesses to close on their birthdays so that everyone could observe their special day. They would throw elaborate parties for all of their hundreds of servants, often giving extravagant gifts. Cleopatra gave a birthday dinner so elaborate that some of the guests arrived at the party as poor men and left as wealthy ones. Some Pharaohs would grant pardons and forgive debts during their birthday parties. Festivities were accompanied by feasting, and oxen, camels, and donkeys were sometimes on the pagan menu, barbequed in huge pits. Hundreds of small cakes were baked and handed out to partygoers.

Joseph was languishing in prison when the Pharaoh's

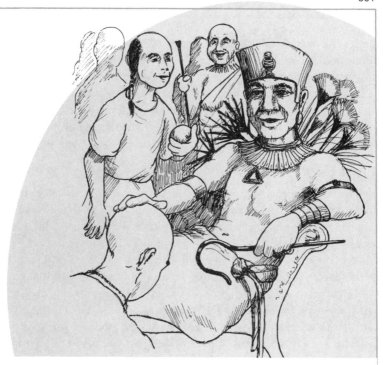

birthday celebration rolled around. His coat of many colors was a
mere memory, and he spent his days serving the jail-keeper with
the running of the prison. He knew every inmate within those walls,
and so when the two newcomers arrived, Joseph was curious. As he
came with the day's ration of bread and water, he prepared to introduce himself. The two where huddled together on the floor, heads
bent in anxious conversation. Before long, they were pouring out
their stories to Joseph's sympathetic ear. He was able to tell them
the meanings of the dreams that were troubling them. It was a case
of good news and bad news—one would be released, but the other
would die. Sure enough, the Pharaoh had a birthday feast three
days later, and as a part of the proceedings, he had his baker executed and granted a pardon to his butler (Gen. 40:20–22).

these displays could take on the characteristics of a full-scale musical. The locals would creep close to the brightly lit windows of the homes, hoping to catch a glimpse of the performances. Once the entertainment was completed and the dishes had been whisked away by servants, conversation ruled the remainder of the evening. Favorite old stories were shared, and proverbial sayings were recalled. Visiting went on long into the night, for after such an evening, it would have been an insult to leave too soon.

PLACE CARDS

Seating arrangements were vital at dinner parties. Where you were placed in the dining room indicated just how important you were to the host. In large homes, the dining hall had a raised platform on one end. This dais was for the head table, where the most honored guests were seated. At most wedding receptions, there is still a head table for the bridal party. Even if there was no platform seating, there were other coveted positions. The chief guest sat to the right of the host. This is why Mrs. Zebedee tried to get preferred seating for her two boys in heaven (Mt. 20:21). Such honored guests always received the choicest foods and the largest portions. Jesus tells of a man who arrived at a party and managed to snag a good seat up front, only to be humiliated when he was escorted to the back of the room. Much better to take a humble chair and be led to the head table at the host's urging.

RECLINING AT THE DINNER TABLE

From the elegance of Persian palaces to the banquets of Roman times, a fad in formal seating developed and stuck. Originally, most folks sat on

the floor during meals. Sometimes a wealthy homeowner could boast a stool or two. But when the wealthy wined and dined, they did so in the finest of fashion-lying down. Mind you, this wasn't breakfast in bed. It was more of a low lounge chair, pulled up so that the guest's head rested near the table. Guests reclined, propped on an elbow with one hand free to reach their plate. The disciples were probably relaxing around their dinner table in this fashion during the Last Supper. That is why John was able to lean back against Jesus to whisper to him (Jn. 21:20).

FOOT WASHING

A considerate host always provided for the comforts of his guests. After a long journey along dusty roads, a guest's sandaled feet became hot and dirty. Washing off the dust of the road was a way of making one's guests feel at home. Jesus reprimanded his host for not providing such a basic consideration at his dinner party (Lk. 7:44–47). Later, on his last evening with his disciples, he rolled up his sleeves and performed the duty of foot-washer himself (Jn. 13:5).

WEDDING AND FUNERALS

Weddings and funerals were the biggest events in town. Weddings were the social events of any season, and families looked forward to the festivities. Funerals drew them together as well, to say goodbye to one of their own. Even the children of the cities played at weddings and funerals (Lk. 7:32). They were the stuff of life.

"First Comes Love, Then Comes Marriage?"

For the Jews in Bible times, it was marriage first and love afterwards. Arranged marriages were customary, and sons and daughters were expected to go along with their parent's choices for them. Imagine choosing your own daughter-in-law. Consider meeting your husband for the first time after the ceremony. Although this seems very strange to us now, it tended to make for very stable marriages back then. Children who were contrary to the wishes of their parents found themselves in trouble. Esau's marriages to foreign women were against the wishes of his parents (Gen. 26:34–35).

Father Knows Best

Arrangements for a future marriage were made by the father, and were sometimes planned while the bride and groom were still very young. Of course, this does not mean that parents ignored their children's feelings entirely. Rebekah was asked if she was willing to travel from her home to marry Isaac (Gen. 24:58). Sometimes a son was able to make his preferences for a mate known to his parents. Love was even known to bloom before marriages occurred, as we see in Jacob's devotion to Rachel (Gen. 29:10–20).

Engagement Rings

In Bible times, marriage was rarely the result of a boy meeting a girl and falling in love. Marriages were contracts that were established by a child's parents, often before those children reached a marriageable age. Matrimony was more of a business arrangement, and the best offer won! Prospective grooms had to market themselves well. With that in mind, a marriage proposal was often brought to a girl's parents in the form of gifts. Eliezer gave Rebekah a nose ring and two bracelets during their meeting beside the well, and she recognized them for what they were—betrothal gifts. A girl who was betrothed often sported a nose ring which had been given by her intended. When Eliezer visited Laban's home, more gifts were brought forth—silver, gold, jewels and clothing (Gen. 24:53). This was an impressive offer, and a generous bride-price. Although she had never seen Isaac, Rebekah was willing to leave her family behind in order to marry him.

PLEDGED TO MARRY

A betrothal involved a promise made and even a legal contract. As the bride approached marriageable age, she would receive gifts from the groom, and a betrothal ceremony would take place. This was like an engagement period and lasted for one year. However, this engagement could not be carelessly broken. If the betrothal was to be broken, it had to be done by divorce. Betrothal was considered the beginning of the marriage, but marriage was not consummated until the groom came for his bride and the wedding took place. Mary was pledged to wed Joseph when she was found to be with child. Since this was a sure sign that the girl had committed adultery, Joseph troubled over whether or not to divorce her (Mt. 1:19).

BRIDE-PRICE

A man did not let his daughter go for nothing! The prospective groom needed to haggle with his future father-in-law over a bride-price. Dad was losing some of his household help, so the groom had to make an exchange. The bride-price could be paid in the form of physical labor. Jacob agreed to work for seven years in order to marry Rachel (Gen. 29:18). When the bride-price was paid in cash, a special rule applied. Apparently, the father of the bride couldn't just spend that money. It was set aside as a nest egg. Dad could keep any interest earned on the money, but the sum was kept in trust. It was like a little insurance policy. If the girl's husband died or if her parents died, the bride-price was given to her, so that she had some means to live.

DOWRY

There was some give and take in the whole arranged marriage game. The groom had to pay a bride-price for his wife. On the other hand, the father of the bride had to provide a dowry. The dowry, in appreciation for the money he received was a wedding gift to his daughter and her new husband. This could come in the form of land or servants. Laban sent Rebekah to Isaac with Deborah, Rebekah's childhood nursemaid (Gen. 24:59; 35:8).

DID YOU KNOW?

• "A friend who attends the bridegroom" (Jn. 3:29) negotiates on behalf of the prospective bridegroom and his father with a representative of the bride's father.

BRIDAL ADORNMENTS

When a young woman became engaged, she had a year to prepare herself for her wedding day. In this time, the groom spent his time in readying their new home. Once that was done, he would come for his bride. Carrying torches, he and his friends would travel through the town to the home of his girl. She was ready and waiting, veiled and in her wedding dress. The primary adornment was a strand of ten silver coins that hung across her forehead. These coins were precious, given to her either by her groom as a wedding gift, or by her mother as a part of her dowry. Such headbands were sometimes passed down from mother to daughter for generations. These coins were like a diamond engagement ring—the most valuable thing she owned. To lose even one coin would be devastating, and send the woman into a frantic search (Lk. 15:8).

THE WEDDING FEAST

Entire communities shared in the celebrations surrounding a new marriage. This was no mere reception dinner at the country club! Everybody met in front of the couple's new home, where they were seated under a canopy (Song 2:4). Festivities were planned that lasted for seven days (Judg. 14:12), and sometimes longer. Food was served, and wine was provided. For so much feasting, great quantities of food had been laid aside. The hosts did much planning, for the food had to last until all the guests went home. At the wedding at Cana, Jesus saved the host family from the embarrassment of running out of wine (Jn. 2:3–10). The guests served as witnesses that the marriage was properly consummated (Gen. 29:22–23). Often the family of the bride brought out the blood-stained bedding to prove that their daughter had been a virgin (Deut. 22:13–21). In very wealthy homes, everyone on the guest list was provided with special wedding clothes to wear for the party (Mt. 22:12).

CAPTIVE BRIDES

When a city was conquered, most of the population was put to the sword. Men were always killed, and so were many of the women, for it was feared that they would bring their false religions with them into their captivity. Even the youngsters were divided. Boys were killed as a matter of course, for they would only become rebellious men. Little girls were the only ones who were spared (Num. 31:18). These young virgins made good servants and good brides. They could be taught about God and learn how to serve Him. However, these little captives were given some time to adjust to their new circumstances. A girl was allowed to shave off her hair and mourn for her dead parents. After her mourning, she could become a bride, but the husband was commanded to treat her with gentleness because of her humbled state. What's more, if the man could not win her heart, he was to set her free (Deut. 21:10–14).

A TIME TO MOURN

When a dear loved one died, it was customary to grieve with emphasis. A proper show of mourning was expected in order to indicate how much the loved one would be missed. Some folks even hired mourners to create a regular din of dismay. Customarily, the close relations of the deceased were left alone to mourn. They would throw themselves onto the ground, toss dust in their hair, don sackcloth and ashes, and cry a lot.

This was deep mourning, and it was expected to last for seven full days. After the week, the mourner's friends and relatives would go to them, make them eat something, lead them to a good bath, and set out fresh clothing for them. Deep mourning was followed by a lighter mourning, which lasted for another month. During this time, it was okay to bathe and go about daily business again. King David did the opposite when he cleaned himself and ate something as soon as he learned about the death of his newborn son (2Sa. 12:20).

FUNERAL PROCESSIONS

Whenever somebody passed away, their family made preparations for the funeral right away. Before the heat and flies could do their worst, the body was prepared for burial. The Jews anointed their loved ones with oils and spices, then bound the body in linen clothes (Mt. 27:59). A piece of cloth like a handkerchief or a napkin was draped over the face (Jn. 11:44; 20:5–7). Ideally, the funeral procession and burial took place just hours after death. Many different men from the community would take their turn as pallbearers, for they all wished to help in shouldering the burden of sorrow. The women and the professional mourners led the funeral procession out of town to the burial site.

DID YOU KNOW?

• Mourners were hired to weep and wail on behalf of the family. These professionals helped to send off the deceased with a proper degree of sorrowfulness.

• Christians often inscribed the Alpha and Omega letters upon their tombs. These were to symbolize their trust in Jesus' promise and their hope in His return.

LAID TO REST

Each culture had its own traditions surrounding burial. We all have heard of the Egyptians and their mummies. Their deceased were embalmed and buried with food, cash, and favorite things in their sarcophagus. Both Jacob and Joseph were embalmed (Gen. 50:2, 26) because they were in Egypt at the time. Generally, the Israelites didn't use coffins at all. The dead were wrapped in linen cloths, with spices and oils and laid in tombs. Abraham purchased a cave to use as a tomb when his wife Sarah died (Gen. 23:9). Nicodemus used a hundred pounds of spices, along with the linen cloths to prepare Jesus for burial (Jn. 19:39).

WHITEWASHED TOMBS

The Jews kept their burial plots outside of town (Mt. 8:28; 27:7, 52–53). The tomb in which Jesus was buried was a short distance outside Jerusalem's walls (Jn. 19:41). Part of the reason behind this was that dead bodies and cemeteries were unclean. Usually, sepulchers were carved out of rock on a hillside, or placed into caves (2Kin. 23:16; Mk. 5:5). Everybody knew where they were, and avoided them. However, if a body was found in a field, it was to be buried right on the spot. In that case, a stone was set up to mark the grave, warning Jews to stay away, lest they become ceremonially unclean. When Passover drew near, the people spent the month beforehand making various preparations for the holy festival. Everybody was cleaning house, preparing their hearts, and making ready for the thousands of pilgrims who would soon enter Jerusalem. Lest any of the festival pilgrims unwittingly picnic on somebody's gravestone and become unclean, a custom was initiated. Every year, on the fifteenth of Adar, the Jews would go out and whitewash all of the gravestones and tombs, effectively marking them as "full of dead men's bones and all uncleanness" (Mt. 23:27).

MAKING MUMMIES

Egyptians were under the impression that bodies needed to be preserved in order to ensure an enjoyable afterlife. This drove them to perfect the process of mumification to such a degree that Egyptian mummies remain in excellent condition after thousands of years. The embalming process was long and complicated, taking seventy days to complete. Joseph had his father, Jacob, embalmed when he died (Gen. 50:2), and later, Joseph, himself was embalmed (Gen. 50:26). The children of Israel had promised that, when they left the land of Egypt and returned to their home, they

would bring the bodies back with them and bury them in the home plot. Their departure was delayed by four hundred years of slavery, but in the end, Joseph was laid to rest with his fathers (Ex. 13:19).

CATACOMBS

The Romans didn't allow bodies to be buried within the city limits. It was their own custom to burn bodies and sprinkle the ashes. However, the Jews who made their way to Rome, and later the early Christians, kept their own traditions of burial. They made sepulchers in the rocky hillsides outside the city walls. As time passed, and the Christians fell into disfavor, they began to dig catacombs. With a great deal of money and effort, the Christian church created winding labyrinths underground, about an hour's walk outside the city. Roman law protected all burial places, and so they were safe places to gather. Here, Christians were able to lay their dear ones to rest, with the hope of seeing them again at Christ's return. Bodies were laid in the niches of the walls, and then tiles were placed over the opening. Inscriptions were etched onto the tiles. The anchor, the palm, the dove with an olive branch, a fish, the Good Shepherd, and J.C. for

Jesus' initials, were all popular symbols on the walls of these catacombs. During decades of terrible persecution, the catacombs became a safe haven for Christian worship services.

ELISHA'S BONES

When the Jews buried their dead, they were laid in sarcophagi that were lined with little alcoves. These alcoves contained the bodies of previously interned bodies that had decayed over time. The older bones were simply pushed aside to make room for the new guy. In one astonishing turn of events, some men carried their friend to a tomb, but when they tossed him into place, he jumped back to life! He had been laid to rest upon the bones of God's prophet, Elisha (2Kin. 13:21), and was miraculously restored to health and life.

JUST BECAUSE

Why do you do it that way? Just, because! Sometimes that's the only answer you can give for a long-held tradition. It's just the way things are done.

ROCK PILES

Whenever ancient people wanted to remember something special that had occurred, they made a pile of rocks there. Sometimes one large rock was set on end. Jacob did that on the spot where he saw the stairway to heaven (Gen. 28:17–19). Other times, the rocks were formed into an altar, and sacrifices were made (Ex. 20:25). The Israelites left a pile of twelve stones where they had crossed over the Jordan into the Promised Land

(Josh. 4:3–7). Now, this wasn't just a compulsion with them. There was a method behind the madness! The stones were erected as memorials, and they gave opportunity for fathers and mothers to tell their children about God's mighty deeds (Josh. 4:6–7). These landmarks were testaments to their history and to God's faithfulness to his people.

BURIED TREASURE

During times of war, and if a family faced the prospect of being exiled in a distant country, certain precautions were made to protect family treasures. Rather than see precious heirlooms taken as booty by enemy soldiers, men and women would hide them. An inconspicuous spot in the back field or a hidden cave might be chosen to hide the family's gold, silver, and jewelry. The hope was that they would be able to return for it someday. The location of the buried treasure became a guarded family secret, passed down from generation to generation. Since this was really quite common, treasure hunting became popular (Job 3:20–21; Prov. 2:3–5).

Jesus even speaks of a man who finds a buried treasure and sells all he has
in order to purchase the field in which it is found (Mt. 13:44).

LONG LIVE THE KING!

Every king kicked off his reign with a coronation ceremony. The coronation usually took place in the Temple, on a raised platform for all to see
(2Chr. 6:13). A crown was placed on the young man's head, and then he
was anointed with oil (1Kin. 1:39; 2Kin. 23:30) in order to place him in
favor with God (1Sa. 24:6). Once this was accomplished, a trumpet was
blown and everyone cheered. "Long live the king!" The actual ceremony
was usually followed by a great feast, which could last for days. David's
celebration lasted for three days (1Chr. 12:39).

BOWING

As a matter of courtesy, bowing was
a part of proper greetings (2Sa.
15:5). This only needed to be a
forward inflection of the head
with a slight bend at the waist.
Those who wished to show
more deference to a great
person would bow more
deeply. Joseph's brothers
bowed before him, for he
was the governor of the
whole land of Egypt (Gen.
41:43). This greeting could even
become an act of prostration, with the greeter falling at the
feet of his companion (Mt. 18:26). Men were scolded by angels for this,
for it looked like an act of worship! Mordecai got in trouble with
Haman when Haman decided that Mordecai wasn't showing proper
respect to a man of his position (Est. 3:5). Jacob bowed to Esau, hoping
to show his respectfulness and to defuse any anger remaining in his twin
brother's heart (Gen. 33:3).

SIMEON
Dedicating the Child

Simeon was a modern-day prophet in New Testament times. God had told him that he would see the face of the Savior before he died. That had been years ago, and he was growing quite elderly. Each morning, he prepared himself and walked up the slope to the Temple. With anticipation in his heart, he watched and prayed. The man of God's choosing might walk through the Temple courts at any time. Jerusalem's Temple was a busy place. On any given day, hundreds of Jews came and went, bringing their offerings and making their sacrifices. Simeon watched as farmers brought in baskets of vegetables and grains—the firstfruits of their labors. He saw the men of Jerusalem coming and going in their prayer shawls, participating in the morning and evening prayers. The smell of smoke and incense and roasting meat filled the air. Doves cooed in their cages. Goats bleated as their owners laid their hands upon their heads before making sacrifice. Fringes swept the marble floors. Coins rattled in the cone-shaped openings of the offering boxes. It was all a part of the rhythmic ebb and flow of every day.

Then came the day when time seemed to stand still. A young couple, like so many other young couples, was coming into the Temple to make a sacrifice for their firstborn son. This was not so unusual. Every child was brought to the Temple for dedication. But God seemed to be prompting him to look upon this child. Then it dawned on Simeon. This was the Messiah. This little babe was the Savior for whom he had been waiting! How unexpected! He laughed within himself, even as he wondered over it all. He had been expecting a man, but even the Messiah had to begin as a child! Boldly, Simeon approached the couple, greeting them with a smile. Then he

gathered the boy into his arms, pronouncing a heartfelt blessing for the baby who would save the world.

A KISS

When two men met, and they were either good friends or family members, it was customary to plant a kiss on each other's cheeks. This was the greeting of equals, and was a mark of respect. Laban greeted his kinsman Jacob with a kiss (Gen. 29:13). With a hand on Jacob's left shoulder, he would have kissed both cheeks, beginning with the right cheek. Then, Jacob would have returned the salute. In large gatherings, there was a whole lot of kissing going on! A kiss could also cover up a scheme. On the pretense of a courteous kiss, Joab drew close enough to Amasa to grab him and thrust his knife into his belly (2Sa. 20:9). Judas' infamous kiss of betrayal is also recorded on the pages of Scripture (Mt. 26:48).

INHERITANCE

The birthright was a special privilege that belonged to the firstborn son. Just for being born first, he was due to inherit the bulk of his parent's entire estate for he was heir. Some men were only blessed with daughters (Num. 27:1–4), but for special cases, there were instructions for the exceptions. Daughters could inherit, but if there were no children, then the land would go to a man's brother. If there weren't any brothers, then the man's uncles were to inherit. This ancestral property was kept in the family this way (Num. 27:8–11). Abraham was dismayed because, despite his great wealth, he was without an heir. His trusted servant, Eliezer of Damascus, was due to inherit all he possessed (Gen. 15:2).

> **DID YOU KNOW?**
>
> • In situations of adultery, both the man and the woman were stoned. It is strange that no man was brought to Jesus along with the woman, since she had been caught in the very act of adultery (Jn. 8:4).

GUEST OF HONOR

Dinner parties were popular in ancient times. They gave people the chance to get together at the end of the day and enjoy one another's company. In New Testament times, low tables were brought out for feasters. They were spread with cloths and surrounded by cushions and pillows. Oil lamps provided ambiance. Silverware was not fussed over, for men ate with their fingers, tearing pieces of bread from flat loaves to use as edible spoons. Seating arrangements were carefully planned out, and guests were often led to their seats. Wealthy homes had a dais at one end of the dining hall on which the head table was placed. In general, the closer you sat to the host, the more favored your seat. The closer you sat to the back of the room, by the door, the lower your position. There were several ways to mark the guest of honor at any banquet. He was invariably seated at the host's side. Traditionally, the guest of honor was given a double portion of food in order to show special favor. And, at the close of a meal, it was traditional for the host to take a bit of bread and use it to sop up the last bit of gravy, and then place it into his friend's mouth with his own hand. This morsel was referred to as the sop,

> **DID YOU KNOW?**
>
> - In Egypt, peons kissed the hand of their superior as a token of respect. To show special favor, they kissed the hand twice, once on the back and once on the palm.

and it was a way of expressing love and friendship. Jesus hosted the Last Supper in an upper room that had been made ready. At this Passover meal, Jesus placed Judas by his side. Jesus spent some of his last hours on earth in dinner conversation with his enemy. It was Judas who received the sop. Knowing full well what the betrayer's plans were, he showed Judas love and gave him honor, right to the very end (Jn. 13:26).

DOUBLE PORTIONS

In the many countries surrounding the Promised Land, there was a universal tradition. When a guest came to dine, he was treated with impeccable generosity. The host never scrimped, never stinted, and wouldn't think of holding back the best he had. A guest was always served more food than he could possibly eat, and an honored guest was served a double portion of food. Joseph honored his little brother, Benjamin in this way, heaping his plate with good food (Gen. 43:34). Elkanah showed his special love for Hannah by giving her a double portion over his other wife, Peninnah (1Sa. 1:5). Elisha asked that a double portion of Elijah's spirit be upon him (2Kin. 2:9).

THIRTY PIECES OF SILVER

Most people do not try to put a price on human life. Each individual on the earth is unique, and therefore priceless. However, many nations knew the price of a man, for slaves were a possession. In ancient times, the going rate for a slave was thirty pieces of silver. This was the compensation provided to a man whose slave had been killed by the carelessness of another man (Ex. 21:32). This was the same price that Judas was paid for betraying Jesus (Mt. 26:14–15).

NECESSARY IMPLEMENTS

Thanks to God's no-nonsense approach to cleanliness, the Jews were spared from many of the diseases that ran unchecked through other civilizations. Even while they were wandering in the wilderness, the people thrived. One key factor in this glowing health report was a very necessary implement that every household kept handy. Quite simply, it was a little shovel used for digging a hole and burying one's own fecal matter. Believe it or not, it's right there in the Bible (Deut. 23:13).

DIVIDING BOOTY

There was a formula to follow when on the battlefield. If looting was permitted, then each soldier was allowed to ransack the vacant cities for booty—gold, silver, jewels, clothing, young women, and livestock. Sometimes, everything was to be destroyed. Disobedience to this stipulation had dire consequences (Josh. 7:20–26). At other times, the soldiers were allowed to keep what they found. In that case, all that was captured was divided in half. Half belonged to the soldiers who did the fighting, and they were to tithe one of every five hundred items to the Levites. The other half was divided among the whole congregation of the Israelites, and they were to tithe one of every fifty items to the Levites (Num. 31:25-30).

EXECUTIONS

God ran a tight ship, and in his theocracy, sin did not go unpunished. The ground could actually open and swallow you whole if you crossed him (Num. 16:32). Many a man dropped dead (2Sa. 6:7), burned to a crisp (Lev. 10:2), or writhed in the grips of a deadly disease (Num. 14:37) at his hand. If death was not instantaneous, a trial was called. Guilty parties were then stoned to death, often with their whole family, for good measure (Josh. 7:20–26). Stoning was the favorite method of execution for the Jews. The guilty party was placed in a pit, then baseball-sized rocks were hurled at him until the task was completed. When a man was found gathering sticks on the Sabbath day, he was brought before Moses and Aaron. The infraction may have seemed small, but it was disobedient, nonetheless. Moses inquired of God what was to be done with the man, and the answer sobered the whole congregation. The man was brought outside the camp and stoned for his sin (Num. 15:32–36).

ARMY EXEMPTION

Marriage had its perks, and this was true especially during times of war. When a young man took a bride, he would first fulfill the bridal week (Gen. 29:27). This was sort of a honeymoon period, except the whole village was invited to the party. Once the feasting was over and everyone went home, life was normal. If the king then called for a draft of young men to serve in the army, the newlywed was passed over. For a whole year the young man was exempt from military duty so that he could stay home with his new wife. This was so that he would "be free at home one year, and bring happiness to his wife" (Deut. 24:5).

> **DID YOU KNOW?**
>
> • In an act of groveling submission, especially when asking favors, a man would throw himself down and kiss the feet of another.
>
> • Birthright involved the inheritance of clan leadership. Heirs would take their father's place in the leadership and protection of his immediate and extended family.

GREETINGS

Small talk could really cut into a travel schedule. When two men met on the road, it was not enough just to nod and pass. That would have been rude! There was a ritual to saying hello and goodbye. The questions and polite answers were established. Men had heard the same conversations since they were boys, and they knew the routine. To sway from the program would have been an insult. And so, a casual meeting might well take a few hours to accomplish. That is why Jesus urged his disciples to put their blinders on, their heads down, and keep walking (Lk. 10:4).

DIVINATION

Every royal court had its staff of magicians, soothsayers, and diviners. Divination often involved the study of animals' innards. Cheaper alternatives involved the study of drifting smoke or the patterns that oil made when dropped into water. The most famous divination involved the interpretation of dreams. Whole books were written on what the images in a dream meant for the dreamer. God showed a good deal of creativity in the dream that He sent to the Pharaoh, for all of the royal diviners were completely stumped. The seven fat cows and seven skinny cows didn't show up anywhere in their books. And who had ever heard of heads of wheat eating each other? When Joseph was brought in and asked to interpret the king's dream, he was careful to explain that the interpretation was from God. The Old Testament forbids divination as an abomination (Deut. 18:10; Lev. 20:6; Eze. 13:6–8).

LEPROSY

The life of a leper was lousy. In order to keep the disease from spreading through a community, a leper was effectively quarantined. He had to leave his family and move outside of the city walls. When he took a walk, he had to keep his hand in front of his face, ring a bell, and call out "Unclean! Unclean!" (Lev. 13:45). This warned passers-by that he was diseased, and others should give him a wide berth. It was hard to make friends this way, which explains why lepers ended up hanging out

with each other (Lk. 17:12). Still, it was a lonely existence. That explains the utter joy of the men who were healed from their leprosy (Lk. 17:15). All they had to do was show themselves to the Temple priests, and then they would be declared clean and could go home to their families again (Mk. 1:44).

LOTS

When a big decision needed to be made, sometimes it was entrusted to the roll of the dice. Actually, it was more of a casting of lots, and in this case, the casting of sacred lots. The Urim and Thummim were the sacred lots, and the high priest used them to determine God's intentions. The sacred lots were cast in order to choose the first king of Israel (1Sa. 10:21). Saul knew his name would come up, so he found a way to make himself scarce. Later, by process of elimination, Jonathan was singled out by lot as the offender who had broken Saul's vow that nobody should eat (1Sa. 14:42).

NAKEDNESS

Nakedness was shameful in ancient times. As soon as Adam and Eve realized that they were naked, they blushed and tried to find a way to cover themselves. The Ammonites shamed some of David's men by shaving off half of their beards and cutting their tunics off at the buttocks (2Sa. 10:4).

DID YOU KNOW?

- Sitting on the ground was a sign of grief or repentance. Sitting in an ash heap indicated even greater distress (Est. 4:3).

- Laban and Jacob erected a pile of stones to mark a boundary line, and they both promised never to cross it (Gen. 31:51–52). They had no desire to see one another again!

In a state of semi-nakedness and complete embarrassment, the men slunk back into town. When David saw them, he allowed the men to travel out of town until their beards grew back again.

REMOVING THE SANDAL

It always seems an odd part of the story-Ruth goes to Boaz, apparently hoping for a marriage proposal. Boaz drops the bombshell that there is another man who is a closer relative. There is a meeting at the town gate, and the exchange of the sandal takes place. What's up with the whole sandal thing? Well, it was a custom, of course! When a woman's husband died, and she was left with no son, it was the duty of the dead husband's brother to take the young widow as a wife. The children they had would carry on the name of the deceased. In Ruth's case, the close relative did not wish to do this. By shirking his duty in this way, Ruth could have taken him before the city elders, told him off, spit in his face, and taken away one of his sandals (Deut. 25:6-10). This practice evolved, so that by Ruth's time, the sandal-thing was more symbolic than insulting. Boaz took care of the matter himself, leaving Ruth out of the confrontation, but the shirker still had to walk home without one of his sandals (Ruth 4:7).

TAKING HOLD OF THE BEARD

In a land where personal space is minimal and men kiss one another in greeting, there is one real no-no. It was considered very impolite to touch another man's beard. A close friend or relative might give an affectionate tug when coming in for the traditional peck on each cheek, but overall, such an action was discouraged. When Joab came to Amasa, he took hold of his beard. Under the pretense of a friendly greeting, he plunged a dagger into Amasa's stomach instead (2Sa. 20:10). With his beard firmly held in his adversary's grasp, Amasa could not pull away or even attempt to defend himself. The Roman army made their soldiers shave every day. That way, the enemy could not take hold of their beards in the confusion of hand-to-hand combat.

> **DID YOU KNOW?**
>
> • A cubit was the distance from a man's fingertips to his elbow, or about eighteen inches.
>
> • Elisha had served Elijah, and was known as the man "who poured water on the hands of Elijah" (2Kin. 3:11).

SMUGGLED MERCHANDISE

When Jacob told his two wives that it was time to start packing, they were not sorry to leave their old home. They said that Laban treated them like strangers, and the bride-price which was to be held in trust as their inheritance had been squandered. There was nothing for them there, and so they prepared to make a run for it. Rachel decided to make one little addition to her luggage, and snuck her father's household idols into her baggage. When Laban caught up to them, Jacob was outraged at being accused of stealing. He knew nothing of what Rachel had done, and so made the rash offer to execute whoever was supposed to have taken Laban's property. Rachel thought fast. She concealed the idols she had stolen from Laban by sitting on them. Then, when the pack on which she sat was the last thing to be searched, she refused to budge from it. She claimed to have her period just then. That did it. Laban backed down. If he had touched her pack after she had been sitting on it, he would have become ceremonially unclean (Lev. 15:19). Rachel's secret was as secure as Fort Knox!

CHAPTER THIRTEEN

THEIR CULTURE

A reference to cultured people usually implies an appreciation for art, literature, and music. **These are the finer things in life,** which touch the very soul with their beauty. In ancient times, people used their creativity to add little bits of loveliness to their lives. Poems and songs were composed, household utensils were decorated, and joyful dances were kept in time by the beat of a drum. The Bible is filled with the mention of these joyful expressions.

CULTURE AND IDEALS

One could hardly discuss culture—the art, music, and literature—of the ancient world without a brief nod to the amazing Greek culture. The New Testament world was profoundly influenced by this society. The Greek people, led by Alexander the Great, had a deep love for all things beautiful.

ALEXANDER'S AMBITION

Alexander the Great wanted to conquer the whole world and transform it. He intended to use Greek language, thought, and culture to spread his ideals about kingship, government, learning, art, and beauty. He was a noble ruler, intending to bring peace and prosperity to all under his hand. He brought in Greek ideals as if they were a gift, improving the lives of conquered peoples. Cities were built for them, with public baths, gymnasiums, theaters, senates, political assemblies, feasts, philosophical discussions, and arguments. They were allowed to govern themselves. They were allowed religious liberty. They were allowed to keep their own languages, although Greek became the language of trade and learning. This introduction of all things Greek to a foreign people was called "hellenization."

ARISTOTLE'S INFLUENCE

Many people rave about a teacher they had that changed their lives forever. Oh, for an English professor who made you call him "O, Captain, my Captain!" Alexander the Great had a very inspiring tutor. At the age of fourteen, Alex studied under the great Athenian philosopher, Aristotle. Aristotle's work was so profound, that in the twelfth and thirteenth centuries AD, much of the Christian church regarded his teachings to be divinely inspired. His contemplations encompassed philosophy, geography, astronomy, botany, zoology, and art. Most likely, a school day under Aristotle's tutelage included the reading and discussing of Homer, the Greek tragedies, and politics. Under Aristotle, Alexander found his deep love for the Hellenistic culture, which inspired him to push out across the known lands, spreading it abroad. Tradition says that Alexander the

Great even carried a copy of Homer's Illiad throughout his Persian and Oriental campaigns.

FOR THE LOVE OF BEAUTY

The people of Greece, as a whole, were idealistic, and strived for perfection in every area of life. The Greeks had no room for ugliness; they worshiped beauty in all its forms—beauty of thought as well as body. Led by Alexander, who was a regular Adonis himself, they set out to beautify the world. Their intense love of games, athletics, drama, and pageantry led to the building of huge theaters and arenas, circular and tiered so that everyone could see and hear. Many of them were built in Palestine. Paul refers to the athletics when he urges

> **DID YOU KNOW?**
>
> • Alexander the Great made no objections to local deities, so under Greek dominion there was freedom of worship, even in conquered nations.

the church at Corinth to run for the prize. "Do you not know that those who run in a race all run, but one receives the prize. Run in such a way that you may obtain it" (1Cor. 9:24).

EDUCATION

Although the setting was different in ancient times, the three R's were still the basics to which every teacher adhered. There were no polished apples on the teacher's desk, nor a dunce hat in the corner. However, the quiet concentration we expect to find in the halls of learning reigned. Studious boys were set to work with a sharp reed and soft clay to practice their letters. Numbers were drilled, and respected writers were read. For those who could afford it, a classical education was available.

SUMERIAN EDUCATION

Abraham grew up in Ur in Sumer, and coming from a wealthy family, he was likely sent off to school. Ur was a great metropolis, and young

MOSES
Student in the Egyptian Schools

After being discovered in a basket among the bulrushes, baby Moses was adopted by a princess, but given back to his mother, who served as a wet nurse. When Moses was weaned and returned to Pharaoh's daughter to be raised, he didn't get to spend a lot of time exploring the royal palace. We are told in Acts 7:22 that Moses was instructed in all the wisdom of the Egyptians. This meant that he was whisked off to school at the tender age of four. Like many children of the extremely well-to-do, he was sent to boarding school. He became a "writer in the house of books," where students were flogged daily to encourage them to learn quickly. He was taught to speak Egyptian, although it was Hebrew he learned at his mother's knee. Moses learned to read and write the wise sayings of great Egyptians, and he learned to add and subtract. He used a sharp-pointed reed to do his lessons in soft clay tablets, which were then left in the sun to harden. As soon as he had completed his early education, he was sent to another school. Here he was taught advanced mathematics and philosophy. Moses would have also studied the stars, and learned about the arts of the magicians in the Egyptian court. His adopted mother made sure that young Moses learned to be a courtier, familiar with the niceties and formalities of palace society. As a privileged young man, he received training in such extracurricular activities as hunting. Along the banks of the Nile river, in the marshy backwaters, Moses learned to knock wild ducks out of the sky with a stick not unlike a boomerang. Instead of a dog to retrieve the fallen fowl, trained cats were sent after his catch. Since the Scriptures say that Moses "was learned in all the wisdom of the Egyptians, and was mighty in words and deeds" (Acts 7:22), it is likely that Moses was given military training as well, and was sent out on campaigns.

scholars were trained for religious, commercial, and governmental work. The bill for this schooling was footed by a boy's parents. The curriculum would have included geography, language, mathematics, botany, and drawing. The principal of these schools was called the "school father," and he had an assistant who prepared the daily exercises. Guest lecturers were brought in for special subjects. If any student became unruly, correction was administered by way of a cane. One boy's penmanship practice for the day tells what he did in school that day: "I read my tablets, ate my lunch, prepared my tablet, wrote it, finished it."

CLAY TABLETS

Paper allows us to jot down a to-do list, write out a check, sign up for the choir, and send Grandma a birthday card. There's loose-leaf, construction, typing, tracing, ten lb., twenty lb., parchment, and printer paper. All in all, it's pretty easy to come by. In the earliest days of writing, however, paper was still in the development stages. So, clay tablets were the popular means of writing. Lumps of soft clay were shaped into small square "pillows" about four inches across. A wedge-shaped stylus was then pushed into these tablets to write. Stacks of these little tablets have been found with everything from tales of victory to grocery lists on them.

SCHOOLS IN SUMER

In ancient Sumer, schools were rather vocational. Education was purely voluntary, and it cost an arm and a leg. Wealthy families could send their sons off to school in order to learn botany, geography, mathematics, grammar, and literature. This allowed the privileged to attain positions as secretaries in the temples, businesses, or in the palace itself.

EGYPTIAN EDUCATION

Adopted by an Egyptian princess, Moses had a free ride to the best education available in the ancient world (Acts 7:22). Early on, in the royal court, he learned from a tutor how to write in hieroglyphics with ink on papyrus. Cuneiform on clay was probably also taught, since Egypt had trade relations with Canaan. As he grew, he would have been sent to a school taught by temple priests. His curriculum would have included arithmetic, geometry, poetry, music, astronomy, and many other subjects. If a young man was headed into the priesthood, then medicine and religion were added to his class schedule. When Moses was told to teach the law to the people, he taught by repetition and example (Deut. 11:19), public reading (Deut. 31:10-13), and the use of song writing (Deut. 31:19). Since it was common in Egypt to sing lessons, this probably reflects the way Moses was taught.

DID YOU KNOW?

• Tablets from the city of Mari have been found with the children's exercises and the teachers' corrections in the clay.

• "I read my tablets, ate my lunch, prepared my tablet, wrote it, finished it." –description of a school day, found on a Sumerian boy's writing tablet.

• An important part of Egyptian education was familiarity with their wisdom writings; it opened doors to careers and privileges that were otherwise unobtainable.

BABYLONIAN EDUCATION

When King Nebuchadnezzar of Babylon descended upon the Jews and carried off their best and brightest, we begin to hear of the adventures of four young men. Daniel, Shadrach, Meshach, and Abednego were selected by the king for an education in all things Babylonian. Such an education would have included special training in the Babylonian arts of war, hunting, and leisure. They would have learned to speak Chaldean and how to read and write in cuneiform. They were given lessons in counting and mathematics. Etiquette and proper behavior in the king's court were also taught. Whatever they may have been taught of the Babylonian idol worship, however, they held to their own Jewish faith in God.

ASTROLOGERS AND ASTRONOMERS

Without the bother of neon lights and street lamps, the people of the ancient world had an incomparable view of the night sky. God even called Abram out into the night and showed him the view (Gen. 15:5). On a clear night, the stars' brilliance attracted the interest of men, who studied the paths of the stars and planets. Some thought that fortunes could be told from the stars, but many men gained a considerable understanding of the night skies as a science. In Babylon, scholars, sorcerers, and magicians were a part of the king's court, and they were expected to interpret the movements of the stars. Daniel would have been trained in reading the stars, as Moses and Joseph had been before him in Egypt.

ISRAELITE EDUCATION

The children growing up in Israel received a balanced education, split equally between religious instruction and vocational training. Since they were an agricultural people, very few Israelites ever learned to read and write. This was left to the scribes and leaders. In ancient times, children were taught at home, with no structured curriculum. The goal of parents was to have their child "increase in wisdom and stature, and in favor with God and men" (Lk. 2:52). As time passed, and towns and cities became more developed, more structure was given to the educational system. By New Testament times, the Jews had adopted a more formal approach to teaching. They set aside classrooms and qualified teachers to instruct all the children in the village.

PRESCHOOL

Education of both boys and girls was the mother's responsibility for the first three years or so—probably until the child was weaned and potty-trained. On their mother's knee, they heard the amazing stories of God, and of Father Abraham, and of faith and obedience. It is sure that Moses learned much of God from his mother before the time when he was returned to Pharaoh's daughter to be raised (Ex. 2:10).

EARLY RELIGIOUS TRAINING

Boys were taught the law from three years of age by their dads. This schooling was unorthodox by today's standards, but very effective. Essentially, a boy's education consisted of religion and heritage. Learning came as naturally as breathing, for it was woven into their everyday lives. These topics were made fascinating to the youngsters by way of stories and object lessons. Scripture was nailed to their doorposts (Deut. 6:4–9). It was tied onto their father's forehead (Deut. 6:8). It was repeated often and committed to memory. Their heritage was taught through exciting recounts of miracles and by games of questions and answers. A heap of rocks became an opportunity to retell the story of the crossing of a river (Ex. 14; Josh. 4:6–8). The festivals were steeped in traditions that taught them about God's promises and laws. Children were encouraged to ask questions (Ex. 12:26; Deut. 6:20-25). Children love to ask questions!

FOLLOWING IN FATHER'S FOOTSTEPS

Fathers were responsible for teaching their sons a trade. from the time a boy was out of diapers, he was given small tasks to do at his father's side. It was said that if a man did not teach his son a useful trade, he was raising the boy to become a thief. When a man had many sons, or if a boy showed interest in another field of work, dad might apprentice the boy to another man to learn a different trade. Since most trades were a family affair, over time an entire neighborhood might be given over to one particular profession. With all the brothers, uncles, and cousins living in close proximity, their corner of the city became the cloth-making district or the potter's street. Jesus was the son of a carpenter (Mt. 13:55), and he became a carpenter himself (Mk. 6:3). James and John, the sons of Zebedee, worked with their father in the fishing business (Mk. 1:19–20). Jacob was a shepherd, and his sons also tended the sheep (1Sa. 16:11). In ancient times, it made sense to follow in father's footsteps.

GIRLS' SCHOOL

Girls learned home-making skills—baking, spinning, weaving—from their mother. Making butter, yogurt and cheese, drying fruit, changing diapers, saving garden seeds, and packing fish were just a few of the things in which a girl must become proficient before she could manage her own household. In most cases, this was all that was needed. However some young women were able to take on professional jobs like midwifery (Ex. 1:15–21) or singing (Eccl. 2:8). Although often held back by their culture's expectations, girls with gumption were able to make their mark. In New Testament times, we hear of women who wielded great influence in their neighborhoods. Dorcas befriended many in her community, and worked as a seamstress, giving the garments she made to the poor (Acts 9:39). Lydia, a hospitable businesswoman living in Philippi, was a seller of purple dye (Acts 16:14). Wealthy women like Joanna were able to contribute financially to Jesus' traveling ministry (Lk. 8:3).

FURTHER EDUCATION

Even higher education for the Jews was religious in nature, since it was recognized that all knowledge came from God. Unlike other nations, knowledge was not sought for its own sake. Instead, people were educated so that they could use their God-given abilities to their fullest. Basic mathematics were needed, for instance, to calculate a harvest or survey land. Study of the sun, moon, and stars helped in working out a calendar. Still, God's Law was central. There were schools set aside for the serious students of the Law. Samuel established a school for prophets (1Sa. 19:18–21). Paul studied at the feet of Gamaliel (Acts 22:3).

GREEK EDUCATION

By New Testament times, all the known world spoke Greek and held to the Greek ideals. So quite naturally, Greek schools were famed from

one end of the Roman Empire to the other. The curriculum was very diverse. Body, mind, and soul, it was thought, needed room for expression. So the syllabus included athletics, philosophy, poetry, drama, music, and rhetoric. Boys would attend elementary school between the ages of seven to fifteen years, and would then go to a "gymnasium" for a wider education.

DISCIPLES

In Old Testament times, young men had the chance to become pupils of the prophets and priests. Samuel, for example, was given to Eli while he was a small boy, and trained by the priest. The prophet Isaiah gave private teaching to a group of disciples. These disciples lived with their masters, learning from them throughout the course of the day. They sometimes sat at their feet, learning by lecture and discussion. At other times they learned by their teacher's example, or from object lessons that presented themselves throughout the day. They would quiz their students, checking to see if any light bulbs were going on in their heads. This one-on-one relationship was the best way to instill learning in the next generation. In later times, the religious group known as the Pharisees appears to have organized a more formal school system. Still, when Jesus walked upon the earth, he called disciples to his side, and for three and a half years they lived at his side and learned from his teachings. Sometimes they sat at his feet (Lk. 10:39), or learned from his example (Jn. 13:15). Many object lessons were presented to them (Mk. 4:2), and Jesus quizzed them to see if they understood what was spoken (Lk. 9:20).

ART

Fine art in ancient times took the form of paintings, murals, carvings, and sculptures. However, there were pieces of art that became a part of everyday life. In ancient times, jewelry was a fine craft, and the women proudly wore one-of-a-kind pieces. Around the house, a water jug or urn might be beautifully painted with scenes from life and literature. Even the gateways of ancient cities were embellished with the stories and scenes of a people's triumphs as a nation.

JEWISH ARTWORK

Because of the prohibition from making graven images, there is virtually no sculpting or painting in Jewish culture. While a Grecian urn might be embellished with elaborately painted artwork, the same Jewish pot would be lucky to sport a stripe. When there was serious decorating to do, they called in foreign experts. Instead, the Jews found an outlet for their creative expression in other areas. For instance, gem-cutting seems to have been a specialty of their artisans (Ex. 25:7; 1Chr. 29:2).

BABYLONIAN ART

Babylonian art featured mythological creatures, war scenes, and religious rites. The Babylonians also had huge enameled brick panels on the gateways to their cities, and they built ziggurats. Babylon was the site of the ziggurat known as the "Tower of Babel" (Gen. 11:1–9). A description of the Tower of Babel that was found on a clay tablet described the tower as having two stories plus a tower of five stages, crowned by a sacred shrine at the top.

ASSYRIAN ART

Assyrians were a one-track mind kind of people. They were a race of warriors. They were proud of their many victories. They were ruthless, merciless, and bloodthirsty. This is reflected in their artwork. Much of

Assyrian art focuses on battle scenes showing dead and dying soldiers, or on hunting scenes depicting wounded and dying animals. How uplifting.

PERSIAN ART

Persian rulers loved their beautiful palaces, therefore much of Persian art reflected the life of the court. Royal carvings have been found cut into rocks that show foreign subjects offering tributes to their conquering king. Still, most of the great Persian artistry shows up in the lavishness of the palaces themselves. The whole Persian Empire was expected to contribute materials and artists to imperial projects. There was a great liking for animal themes in Persian art, and for creating life-like, three-dimensional carvings. One of Persia's contributions to the world of art was their refined touch in the creation of miniatures. This Persian flair shows up in some of the Jewish buildings after their exile under Persian domination. There is a synagogue in Capernaum (Mk. 1:21) that is beautifully carved in this way with animals and flowers.

COMMISSIONS FROM GOD

Many artists work by commission. Their patron tells them what they would like, say a portrait or a painting of their favorite poodle, and the artist is paid to create the piece. The Jews were given a commission from God himself when it was time to build the tabernacle. He gave them special instructions about everything from the tent pegs (Ex. 39:40) to the curtains (Ex. 26:1). Measurements and color schemes were laid out, and he expected the finished product to be "just so." Although the job was demanding, the resources were provided, for God gave the artisans special abilities to accomplish the task at hand (Ex. 28:3, 31:3).

MUSIC

Music was a part of life in Israel. String and wind instruments, as well as percussion instruments, were played for celebrations, funerals, and during worship. David wrote music, and some of his Psalms have notations to indicate the tune to which they should be sung.

WIND INSTRUMENTS

A few wind instruments are mentioned from Bible times. Some were simple pipes. They were bored out of wood or bone or cane, and their Hebrew name *halil* means "to bore." Anyone with a fondness for whittling could turn out a simple pipe or whistle, so these were common enough. More impressive were the *geren*, which were made from the horns of animals and used as trumpets. If the trumpet was made from the horn of a ram, it was called the *shofar*, which was used to call the people together on religious occasions. There were even metal trumpets in Bible times, which were crafted from silver.

These *hazozra* were used in Numbers to signal the people of Israel. One continuous call from the silver trumpet was sounded to call the chiefs of the tribes together, and a call from two silver trumpets was the signal for all to gather at the tabernacle (Num. 10:2).

BAGPIPES IN THE BIBLE?

The particular instrument translated as a flute in Psalm 150:5 and in Job 21:12; 30:31 was an ancient instrument that put in an appearance during celebrations. Some scholarly types have speculated that this instrument was more like the Scottish bagpipes. They say it consisted of two pipes fastened in a leather bag, one above and the other below. Through the upper pipe, which had a mouthpiece, the bag was filled with air, while the lower pipe had holes that were closed or opened with the fingers much like a flute. Air was forced through this bottom pipe by pressure on the bag. If this is true, then bagpipes were around long before plaid kilts! Of course, this is not a unanimous opinion. Other experts think that these musical pipes were more along the lines of a set of panpipes, which is also a very old instrument.

THE PIPES

A set of musical pipes could be made from reeds. The cane was hollowed out, and holes were positioned along the length of the tube. The bright and cheerful sound of a shepherd's pipes kept him company in the wilderness. The pipes were also used to add to the celebration of parades (1Kin. 1:40), or to warble a mournful tune (Jer. 48:36). These simple instruments were easily made and easily broken, so when a set of pipes became damaged, the shepherd would toss them aside and begin a new one. When it was foretold that "a bruised reed he shall not break" (Mt. 12:20), the prophet painted Jesus as a man who would not cast aside the broken. His way was to mend, restore, and make new.

DID YOU KNOW?

• Some of the instruments mentioned in the Scriptures were the cymbals, drums, dulcimer, harps, lutes, lyres, psalteries, reed pipes, sackbut, tambourines, timbrels, and trumpets.

• Jubal is credited with the creation of many ancient musical instruments. He is called the "father of all those who play the harp and the flute" (Gen. 4:21).

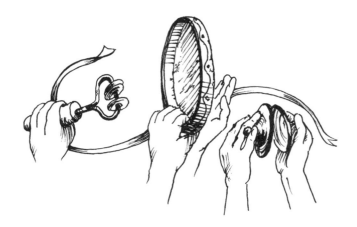

PERCUSSION INSTRUMENTS

The Jews used percussion instruments in their celebrations and in their worship. Although many other nations have pictures of their musicians playing tambourines, drums, and cymbals, the Jews were not allowed to portray people in their artwork. This would have broken God's Commandment against graven images. Still, there were three basic percussion instruments that were used in ancient times. One, called the *menaanim*, had metal rings that were set in a frame that jangled together. Basically, we're talking tambourine here. Miriam, Moses' sister, danced about with the other women, shaking their tambourines as they praised God for their safe passage through the Red Sea (Ex. 15:20). Another type of instrument, the *meziltaim*, were copper cymbals. Though they didn't provide the crash-bang finish to a rousing march, they were used by the Levites during worship in the temple. The gentle clanging of these cymbals marked the opening, closing, and pauses in the singing of the psalms. The other percussion instrument, the *tof*, was like a drum, with a stretched membrane on its frame. This instrument set the rhythm when accompanying singing and dancing.

STRING INSTRUMENTS

Two different stringed instruments are mentioned in the Old Testament, and David was apparently able to play them both. One was the *kinnor*, which was a small lap harp or lyre. The eight- or ten-stringed instrument had a wooden frame and was easy to transport. Perhaps this is the very sort of harp that David took with him out into the pastures while watching over his father's sheep. Plucking its strings made a sweet, soft sound. The other stringed instrument was also a sort of harp. It was the *nebel*, which is sometimes called a psaltry. This would have been a larger instrument with a soundbox.

WORSHIP TEAM

Just like today, music in Bible times had an important place in the worship service. The Old Testament describes how King David organized the temple choir and orchestra to sing and to play joyful music. David's Psalms became so popular that most Jews had them memorized. In the temple, the singing was often in parts—one line of a section being sung by one group, and the next sung in response by another. These choirs were composed of both men and women; Levites whose full-time job was to fill the Temple with joyful song. When the walls were rebuilt at Jerusalem, Nehemiah helped to organize two large thanksgiving choirs to sing during their celebrations (Neh. 12:31). Dancing, too, was often part of the people's joyful expression of worship. When the sacred ark of the covenant was brought to Jerusalem, "David and all the people danced with all their might to honor God" (2Sa. 6:16).

POETRY AND LITERATURE

The life of a culture is clearly reflected by its literature. What we know of the earliest people groups on the planet comes from their writings. All of Egypt was covered in hieroglyphics. The Sumerians left behind their dictionaries. The Jews had literature that was divinely inspired.

SAMSON, THE RIDDLER

Ask any child to pretend that they are Samson, the hero from the Book of Judges in the Bible, and they will grimace and make muscles for you. Indeed, Samson is remembered best for his great strength. Samson's parents dedicated him to the Lord before he was even born, and so he was subject to the rules surrounding a Nazarite vow from his birth. This meant that he couldn't eat or drink anything "from the fruit of the vine." No grape juice, grape jam, grape jelly, grape kool-aid, or wine made from grapes. During his toddler days in the finger-food set, this also meant no raisins. His hair was never cut, so he probably kept it in long braids down

JOSIAH
Literature Lover

Josiah became King over Israel at the tender age of eight. During a time when kings didn't last long in this world, he was set upon a precarious throne. Advised by a godly mother (2Kin. 22:1–2) and a royal court, he set about to lead a nation. Now, like most children, Josiah liked someone to read to him. The best scrolls in the palace had all been read aloud to him over and over in the early years of his reign. He was learning to read and write himself, and his love of literature must have been great. When King Josiah was eighteen years old, he gave the order that the Temple was to be renovated. His stewards were set to cleaning out all the dusty corners and its storage rooms. In the process, they stumbled upon some stone jars that hadn't been opened in ages. The High Priest gave the scrolls to the king's scribe. They were brought before the young king, and low and behold, it was the first few books of the Old Testament (2Kin. 22:8). They were read aloud to him. Imagine the young man's pleasure at hearing the great stories of Genesis for the first time, the stories of Adam, Noah, Abraham, and Joseph. Then came Exodus, and the thrilling tale of Moses, and God's rescue of the children of Israel from a life of slavery. Then the Books of Leviticus, Numbers, and Deuteronomy, which spoke of God's love for his chosen people and of holiness. Josiah was captivated and enthralled. Josiah was convinced that the whole kingdom should hear these stories. Not only that, they should hear and obey. And so the command went out, and scribes were set to copying and sent out to read aloud to all the people. The Law of God was put back into practice. Idols were suddenly illegal, and temples were torn down. The countryside was cleaned up, and God's people practiced holiness again. All this from a youngster who loved the literature of his people: the Scriptures.

his back. He wasn't allowed to touch anything dead either. For as long as he obeyed these restrictions, God gave him great strength. Now Samson lived in a time when there was little available by way of entertainment. Conversation was the centerpiece of a good time, and a storyteller was never at a loss for an audience. Poetry was read aloud, a good joke was appreciated, but best of all was a tricky riddle. A riddle was crafted to capture the interest and stimulate the mind. It usually described something familiar enough, but veiled the item in puzzling words. The best riddles posed a question in the form of a rhyming verse. Samson was fond of a good joke, and his quick wit and way with words are recorded in the Bible. He's a regular funster! He jests with Delilah when she pesters him about the source of his strength. He makes up wild stories of sheer nonsense about strength-sapping techniques. Delilah is not amused. As part of the entertainment during a wedding feast, he posed a riddle that stumped his friends for three days. Samson's riddle is in fact the oldest one on the books: "Out of the eater came something to eat, And out of the strong came something sweet" (Judg. 14:14). Even after he battled the Philistines, outnumbered one thousand to one, he glibly states "With the jawbone of a donkey, Heaps upon heaps, with a jawbone of a donkey, I killed a thousand creeps" (Judg. 15:16, slightly paraphrased). Samson the strong man was a poet at heart.

JEWISH LITERATURE

For the Jews, literature was mostly religious. Thanks to the childhood training of Moses in the court of the Pharaoh, the "Books of the Law" were written down and preserved. Moses penned the first five books of the Bible. Later books were recorded by kings and scribes and prophets. In fact, just about everything the Jews had in writing has ended up as a part of our Old Testament Scriptures. These scrolls were the ones read by Nehemiah at the dedication of the rebuilt temple (Neh. 8:4–8). These were the scrolls discovered almost by accident and read to Josiah, the boy king (2Kin. 22:10). These were the famous Dead Sea Scrolls, discovered in a cave in the desert by a shepherd boy.

"JOT AND TITTLE"

Penmanship was important when learning Hebrew, because all those rows of letters, running from right to left in an unbroken stream, were similar. A slip of the pen could change the entire meaning of a sentence. What's more, there were all these little dots and dashes, over and under the letters, which helped to indicate proper vowel sounds and pronunciation. These were the "jots and tittles" referred to by Jesus. He promised "till heaven and earth pass away, one jot or one tittle will by no means pass from the law till all is fulfilled" (Mt. 5:18).

> **DID YOU KNOW?**
>
> • Scrolls could be made of a number of materials: linen, cotton cloth, animal skins, or even strips of tree bark.

OSTRACA

Sometimes we tease our oldest relatives, who lived through the Depression and, therefore, save everything. They are the penny-pinchers and pack-rats who never waste a thing. To throw something away would be foolish, for you never know when it might come in handy! People were much more like this in ancient times, when personal belongings were few and precious. One item that people didn't have a whole lot of was paper. Scrolls were only owned by the wealthy, and even children were made to practice their letters in the sand, on the ground, or in soft clay. So, when a bit of information just had to be written down, the frugal had an ingenious solution. Pieces of broken pottery, called *ostraca*, were saved for just such occasions. When a recipe, song lyric, or receipt had to be written, a likely shard of smooth clay was brought out. Ink was blended from ready ingredients, and a written record was laid out. Archeologists have found thousands of these ostraca in the homes and businesses of the ancient world.

ALLUSIONS

Nowadays, the learned are admired for their ability to quote Shakespeare, Longfellow, and Keats in everyday conversations. When it comes to the great literature in Bible times, the hands-down greatest was the Bible, written over a period of centuries, by many different authors, in several different languages, and inspired by God Himself. If there had been such a thing, it would have hit the top of the best-seller lists for decades. Peter and Paul quote the Scriptures as easily as breathing, and make frequent references to the great men and women whose lives are recorded there. Jesus quoted from the Old Testament repeatedly. The gospels are riddled with allusions back to the Law and the Prophets and the Psalms. They were Jews, and their upbringing and education was so steeped in God's Word, that they referred to the Scriptures without batting an eye.

CHAPTER FOURTEEN

THEIR WORSHIP

Everyday life was inseparable from worship for the Jews. They understood very keenly that **they had been chosen** and that they belonged to God. They were careful to know and obey all of his commandments for them. It was the practice of every family to "talk of them when you sit in your house, when you walk by the way, when you lie down, and when you rise up" (Deut. 6:7).

SURROUNDED BY PAGANS

Surrounded by people whose superstitious observances were intended to appease false gods, the Israelites stood out, set apart by their faith in the one true God. This section offers insight into the worship practices of the other nations in the Bible.

THE GOLDEN CALF

The calf was a central idol in Baal worship. He started out as your average false god, believed to have power over bountiful crops and multiplying flocks. Later, he evolved into "Master of the Universe" and was thought to rule over all the other Canaanite gods. Baal worship involved prostitution (1Kin. 14:24), human sacrifice (Jer. 19:5), and self-torture. Suppliants also would kiss the idol itself (1Kin. 19:18; Hos. 13:2). Aaron fashioned a calf from gold, using an engraving tool (Ex. 32:4). However, when faced by the hot anger of his brother, Aaron hedged a bit. His fumbling explanation is almost laughable. Aaron says, "They gave the gold to me, and I cast it into the fire, and this calf came out" (Ex. 32:24). Jezebel is famous for reintroducing Baal worship into Israel. She lured her husband into idolatry (1Kin. 16:31), and attacked the prophets of God throughout Israel. She was quite a patron of the cult.

DAGON'S DEFERENCE

The Philistines were a seafaring people, and so naturally, their God was related to the sea. Dagon was one of their main gods, and he was half man, half fish—a merman, if you will. Dagon actually appears on the pages of Scripture, but he doesn't fare very well. You see, the Philistines managed to capture the ark of the covenant from the Israelites. They brought it home with great pomp and set it up in their temple to Dagon as a trophy of war. They partied all night in front of Dagon's statue, and went home happy. However, when they returned to the temple in the morning, they found poor Dagon flat on his face in front of the ark. This wasn't dignified for the conquering god, so his priests set him back upright. The next morning, they were stunned. Not only had Dagon hit the floor again in the presence of the Israelite's God, but their idol had lost his head (1Sa. 5:3–5)! Dagon had hit the threshold with a good deal of force, and his head and hands were destroyed. Since God had been so "harsh" towards Dagon (1Sa. 5:7), the Philistines opted to get rid of the ark, and brought it back to the Israelites voluntarily.

HOUSEHOLD IDOLS

Jacob decided it was high time to make a break from his father-in-law. He had poured fourteen years of his life into Laban's hands just to repay the privilege of marrying two of his daughters. After that he stayed on for a while, but Jacob soon tired of the family tensions. He came to his wives with a plan to leave. The women were willing to move on, saying that they were treated as strangers in their own father's home. In a spiteful move, Rachel took along the household gods of her father (Gen. 31:19). Some think that possession of these gods was a claim to inheritance, which is why Laban followed in hot pursuit. At the very least, they may have been made from precious materials. One's household idols were representations of the various gods who were supposed to control the wind and the rain and the fertility of the flocks. Yet even Laban understood that God was blessing him for Jacob's sake (Gen. 30:27). By losing both Jacob and his idols, he felt bereft of supernatural blessings!

> ### DID YOU KNOW?
>
> • Rachel took along the household gods of her father (Gen. 31:19). Since possession of these gods was a claim to inheritance, Laban followed in hot pursuit.
>
> • Jezebel made the worship of Baal and Asherah so common in Israel that four hundred and fifty prophets of Baal and four hundred prophets of Asherah dined in the castle with her every day (1Kin. 18:19).
>
> • The early Christians faced so much persecution. "They were stoned, sawn in two... slain by the sword...being destitute, afflicted, tormented" (Heb. 11:37).

STEPHEN
Waiting on Tables

In the early church, the new Christians depended heavily upon the apostles. They seemed to know just what to do in every situation, and the preached with a fire of conviction. When they stood up to tell of the Messiah and salvation, thousands dropped to their knees in repentance. However, all of life was not spent on a soapbox. Many needs had to be met, and the apostles spent much time in acts of mercy. The poor needed to be fed. The widows and orphans needed to be cared for. Communion suppers had to be planned. There was much that needed careful administration and oversight. Sometimes, Peter would run his fingers through his hair in frustration, for what did a fisherman know of such things? He wished to tell the entire world about his dearest friend, Jesus, not organize church suppers! Soon Jerusalem would be filled with visitors, Jews on their way to celebrate the next Feast day. What a chance to evangelize! Something had to be done. And so, the office of deacon was created. Stephen, along with a handful of other men, were chosen for their administrative gifts. While the apostles stood up and spoke as the Spirit led, the deacons waited on the tables and kept the ministry organized. They handled the offerings, and the distribution of funds. They made sure that widows had enough to eat and that orphans were cared for. Their ministries freed up the leaders to lead.

THE SILVERSMITH

Not everyone in a city could afford the beautiful work of a silversmith. Silver tureens, bowls, basins, cups, and spoons were luxury items, purchased by the wealthy. So how was a silversmith to make ends meet? One way was by making and selling little trinkets that the common person could afford. The silversmith's most popular items in the markets were miniature carvings of false gods. These were idols that people carried around with them like good luck charms. Paul spoke out against such practices when he moved from city to city. When the people turned to Christ, the silversmiths lost all their business. The enraged guild of silversmiths took it into their hands to put Paul out of business. A riot started in Ephesus over the whole situation (Acts 19:25–30), but the mob was dispersed and the silversmiths were instructed to take Paul to the courts if they really thought they had a case against him (Acts 19:38).

DID YOU KNOW?

• A man named Obadiah hid one hundred of the prophets of God in the caves, feeding them bread and water and keeping them safe from the massacre that Jezebel initiated (1Kin. 18:4).

• Rome's national religion was emperor worship, and they found Christianity to be "strange and unlawful" according to a Senatorial decree in AD 35.

HIGH PLACES

People in general figured that the best way to be heard by their gods was to get as close as possible to them. In many cases, this meant going up. This is first seen in the construction of the Tower of Babel. Folks wanted a tower whose top was in the heavens (Gen. 11:4). Throughout the Old Testament, kings were going back and forth between building up and destroying the altars upon the highest hills. "They built for themselves high places, sacred pillars, and wooden images on every high hill and under every green tree" (1Kin. 14:23).

Though King Solomon loved God as his father David had done, he traveled around to the various high places and offered incense (1Kin. 3:3). It wasn't until the reign of Josiah that many of the high places were completely destroyed (2Kin. 23:19).

SOLOMON'S OTHER TEMPLES

Solomon gets a lot of credit in the Bible for being a wise man. The wisdom of Solomon and the wealth of Solomon are unparalleled throughout history. Solomon was the son of David who was given permission by God to build for him a Temple in Jerusalem. The details of its construction and the beauty of its adornments are discussed in great detail. However, we rarely hear about Solomon's other temples. It comes and goes so quickly, you can easily miss it. 2 Kings 23:13 says that Solomon, king of Israel built temples for Ashtoreth, Chemosh, and for Milcom. These three false gods are called "abominations," and yet Solomon raised up their places of worship.

VERY HUMAN GODS

The gods of the Greeks and the Romans were downright dangerous. They were like superheroes run amok! Here were these immortals, allegedly imbued with incredible strength and magical abilities, but full of incredible character flaws. Unlike the one true God, they were not good. According to the stories of mythology, the gods had very human emotions. These supposedly powerful deities would get angry, throw fits, pout, commit adultery, hold grudges, plot revenge, ignore prayers, demand human sacrifices, and change their minds on a whim. No wonder the people tried to beg, borrow, and plead to stay on their favorite gods' good side! The gods weren't trustworthy, and so people learned to appease their gods and hope for the best. Worshipers depended upon flattery and bribery to get them through another year. Just to be on the safe side, the people of Athens even set up an altar to an unknown god (Acts 17:23). They didn't want to suffer the repercussions of leaving somebody out.

STANDING UPON CEREMONY

God was pretty specific when He laid out the program that His priests were to follow. Their way of life was set in stone. As time passed, more traditions were added to the initial laws, and so a great number of religious customs became part of the ceremony of worship.

CONSECRATED

In order to consecrate something to God's service, it was anointed with oil. The implements that were designed for use in the Temple were all anointed with oil in order to dedicate them to the Temple. People could also be consecrated—prophets (1Kin. 19:16), priests (Lev. 8:12), and kings (1Sa. 16:13; 1Kin. 1:34). They were anointed to separate them for service before God. The prophet spoke God's words to the people, the priest stood before God representing his people, and the king established God's Laws throughout the land. A person who had been anointed had authority and was to be obeyed (1Sa. 24:6).

BAR MITZVAH

A twelve-year-old Jewish boy waited for his next birthday with the same anticipation that teenagers have, waiting to be old enough to get their driver's permit. When a Jewish youth turned thirteen, he had achieved manhood. Up until that time, he had not been expected to observe all of the obligations of the Law. He had been taught by his parents, and encouraged to learn of his responsibilities before

God. This rite of passage was marked by the bar mitzvah. No actual ceremony was required in ancient times, but the young man was recognized by his community to be grown up. He was counted as a member of the synagogue. He could form binding contracts. He could testify before religious courts. He could marry! Also, he had the right to take part in leading religious services. This is how a young man announced his new status to the community. On a Saturday shortly after his thirteenth birthday, he was called up during the Sabbath services to come up front, read from the Torah, and recite a blessing over the reading of God's Word.

FASTING

In Bible times, fasting was a time of repentance. It wasn't hard to spot a faster. You only needed to look as far as the closest ash heap. Those who were grieved by their own sinfulness would often tear their clothing, put on sackcloth, and throw dust and ashes onto their heads. The sorrowful would let their hair become messy, and they stopped taking baths. Fasters often went barefoot, and would neither eat nor drink. Nehemiah fasted in his sorrow over Jerusalem (Neh. 1:4), and

> ### DID YOU KNOW?
>
> • When a man threw himself down at Peter's feet, he urged him to stand to his feet again (Acts 10:26). Only God was worthy of such worship.
>
> • Only a priest was to sacrifice before the Lord, which is why Saul was in such big trouble for rushing ahead and starting without one (1Sa. 13:8–13).

Esther called for the people to fast before she went before the king (Est. 4:16). The Bible makes it plain that these outward signs of fasting were not enough. In fact, Jesus urged fasters to wash their faces and put on a smile so that no one else would know of their fast (Mt. 6:17). It was not the show of sorrow that counted, but the change of heart!

THE SANHEDRIN

The Jews were allowed to maintain their own government in religious matters, and so even under Roman dominion, the Sanhedrin held sway over the lives of God's people. They were a kind of religious nobility, with pedigrees that traced back to Zadok, the high priest in Jerusalem during the reign of Solomon. By Jesus' time, though, the lineages had become muddied, and money figured greatly into appointments. This was a group of seventy-one men, being chief priests, elders and scribes, and presided over by the High Priest. In theory, these men were representatives of the whole Jewish nation, and served as liaisons between the masses and the Roman government. However, the ruling body was torn by partisan politics, with Pharisees and Sadducees quibbling over interpretation of the Law and attitudes towards Rome. The most famous member of the Sanhedrin was Nicodemus, who came to Jesus privately to ask him some questions. Nicodemus apparently became a believer, for he defended Jesus and his followers in front of the assembly (Jn. 7:50–52), and in the end provided the myrrh and aloes for Jesus' burial (Jn. 19:39).

BAPTISM

The Jews had been baptizing people for centuries. Long before Jesus made his way down the banks of the Jordan River to be baptized by his cousin John, baptism was a way to show a change of heart. It was called proselytizing! Foreigners who became familiar with the Jewish people

and were drawn by their God often became worshipers of the One True God. Ruth, though a Moabite, made Naomi's God her own. The Roman centurion who came to Jesus in order that his servant might be healed was a worshiper of God and had even built a synagogue for the Jews in Capernaum (Lk. 7:5–10). Lydia had been a worshiper of God before she heard Paul's message in Thyatira (Acts 16:14). Those who wished to make a public declaration of their faith and take up the obligations of the Jewish lifestyle became proselytes. They were circumcised and baptized to signify their belief.

TITHES AND OFFERINGS

The first mention of worship is found in Genesis, when Cain and Abel bring offerings before the Lord (Gen. 4:2–7). Noah also made offerings to the Lord once he and his family were safely off the ark (Gen. 8:20). The patriarchs erected altars across the land, wherever their nomadic wanderings led them (Gen. 8:20; 12:7–8). Abraham tithed a tenth of all he had to Melchizedek, the mysterious priest and king of Salem (Gen. 14:18–20). Tithes were required of the nation of Israel, to support the tribe of Levi. They had no inheritance in the land, but the tithe of the people was to be their inheritance, to support them as they dedicated themselves to the worship in the Temple (Num. 18:21). In New Testament times, offerings were taken up to provide for the needs of missionaries, church planters, the poor, widows, and orphans (1 Cor. 16:1).

PSALTER

The Jews had a kind of hymnal, even in ancient times. It survives today as our book of Psalms. David's songs and poetry were a big hit in ancient times, and all God's people were humming his tunes. Some were sung aloud by the groups of pilgrims who made their way each year to Jerusalem to celebrate the Passover festival. Others were a part of the worship services, sung by the temple singers. Most all Jews had committed the Psalms to memory by the time they were grown. If they heard just the first few lines, they couldn't help but follow the verses through in their minds to the end. Perhaps that is why Jesus cried out "My God! My God! Why have you forsaken Me?" on the Cross (Mt. 27:46). Those were the first few words of David's twenty-second Psalm, which predicted much of what the people had witnessed that day.

MEZUZAH

The Jews couldn't help but take God literally. When He said "you shall write them on the doorposts of your house," (Deut. 6:9) then they did it. A Mezuzah is a bit of special parchment on which is written two different sections of the Old Testament. One is Deuteronomy 6:4–9, and the other is Deuteronomy 11:12–21. It figures out to be twenty lines of seven hundred thirteen letters, and a certified scribe must write each letter properly. Just one mistake nullifies the Mezuzah. The parchment is then rolled from left to right so that the first word to appear when the Mezuzah is opened is Shema. The roll goes into a protective case that is then affixed to the upper third of the doorpost of the front door. This case is tilted so that the top slants towards the house. When coming and going through the door, the mezuzah is touched to show respect and to act as a reminder of God's commands.

DID YOU KNOW?

- Jacob took the stone that he had used for a pillow and "set it up as a pillar and poured oil on it" (Gen. 28:18–22). He renamed this sacred place Bethel, or "God's house."

- The pool of Bethesda was said to have healing virtues when an angel would come and stir the waters. Excavations in the area revealed this pool with five porches and a faded wall fresco depicting an angel and water.

- According to tradition, the reason that the Mezuzah is placed at an angle on the doorpost is that the rabbis couldn't agree whether to affix it horizontally or vertically. The angled mounting is their compromise!

COMMUNION

"Remember me!" During the Last Supper, Jesus raised up the bread and the cup and started the Christian tradition of the communion service (Lk. 22:19). The unleavened bread and the wine were a normal part of the

Passover meal, and so when the early Christian church began to practice communion, it was a part of a meal for them as well. Paul had to settle a squabble over the communion meal in Corinth. They would gather together for a meal, but food was served on a first come, first served basis. The greedy first comers would eat until they were both full and drunk. The last ones to arrive found only crumbs and dregs left on the buffet table (1 Cor. 11:21). That is why Paul commanded that the people wait until everyone had gathered and all had been served, then partake of the communion meal together.

ICHTHUS

So why do Christians drive around with little fishies glued to their bumpers? There is actually a very good reason. Back in the days of early Christianity, persecution ran rampant (2 Cor. 4:9). The Romans had taken to crucifying them, using them for torches in their gardens, and throwing them into the battle dome to face gladiators and wild beasts. The early Christians refused to stop meeting together, but found it prudent to keep their activities a secret. They used secret codes and symbols to mark rendezvous points. If the symbol was carved into their doorpost or worked into the pattern of their floor tiles, other Christians recognized that they were in the presence of a brother. Some of the most popular symbols were the cross, the anchor, the crown of thorns, and the fish. The Greek word for fish was *ichthus,* and the letters provided an acrostic of their faith, meaning "Jesus Christ, Son of God, Savior."

FEASTS AND FESTIVALS

Though the restrictions placed upon the Jews might seem severe, they were not designed to limit freedom. God's commands really were for the good of his people. He even worked in plenty of time for rest and refreshment during a time in history when life was very hard. Feasts and festivals came regularly throughout the year, breaking up the monotony of daily living.

THE HIGH PRIEST
Representing the People

The role of the High Priest carried a solemn obligation. Once a year, he was to enter the Holy of Holies and pray for the forgiveness of all the people of Israel. Preparation for this awesome duty began a week before Yom Kippur, for it was vital that the High Priest be mentally and spiritually prepared for the day.

The week before the Day of Atonement, the High Priest would move into the Temple and perform all the temple duties himself— making sacrifices, lighting the menorah, and burning incense in the Holy Place. He stayed up at night praying and reciting psalms and scriptures. If he dozed off, younger priests would gently wake him. Throughout the week, he took ritual baths. When the big day arrived, the High Priest changed from his ornate robes into a simple garment of white linen. He took a young bull and prayed for himself and his family, that all sin would be forgiven them. It was important that he be blameless before continuing with the day's activities. In his prayers, the High Priest spoke the name of God aloud. The people fell on their faces, for this was the only day of the year when it was uttered. Next, the High Priest approached two identical goats. By the casting of the holy lots, one goat was chosen to be sacrificed to God. The other became the scapegoat. A piece of red wool was tied around its horns. Then, the young bull was sacrificed, and its blood was collected in a basin. The people watched in silence as the High Priest walked to the altar, filled a gold pan with coals, gathered some incense, and approached the inner sanctuary. This was the only time that any man was permitted to enter the Holy of Holies. There, he was in the very presence of God, and every breath was held as he offered incense and prayers. If all went well, he would emerge unharmed and the people

would know their prayers had been heard. Just in case, though, a rope was tied around the High Priest's ankle, to drag him out if he dropped dead or fainted! The blood of the bull was sprinkled on the curtain of the Holy of Holies. The goat for sacrifice was slaughtered, and its blood was sprinkled on the curtain and around the base of the altar. The Day of Atonement was nearly finished. The last event was the leading out of the scapegoat. A priest was assigned to take the goat to a spot about ten miles outside the city walls. Stations were prepared along the path in case the weary priest needed to break his fast to continue his walk. At the final station, the goat was pushed off a cliff. Then the stations served as relay stations, and a system of flag signals sent word back to the Temple that the sins of the nation had been forgiven.

SABBATH

The Jewish day of rest set them apart from all other nations. Lots of other countries celebrated the New Moon or the harvest. God's people were the only ones with a day set apart for worship and rest every week. The Sabbath belonged to God, and was treated as sacred. It was to be honored by not traveling, working, or talking idly on that day. One man was stoned for gathering sticks on the Sabbath day (Num. 15:32–36)! By New Testament times, the Sabbath had been subjected to pharisaical rules and regulations.

The rabbis were able to distinguish thirty-nine categories of forbidden acts:

• Sowing	• Plowing	• Reaping	• Binding sheaves
• Threshing	• Winnowing	• Selecting	• Grinding
• Sifting	• Kneading	• Baking	• Shearing wool
• Washing wool	• Beating wool	• Dyeing wool	• Spinning
• Weaving	• Making two loops	• Weaving two threads	• Separating two threads
• Tying	• Untying	• Sewing two stitches	• Tearing
• Trapping	• Slaughtering	• Flaying	• Salting meat
• Curing hide	• Scraping hide	• Cutting hide up	• Writing two letters
• Erasing two letters	• Building	• Tearing a building down	• Extinguishing a fire
• Kindling a fire	• Hitting with a hammer		
• Taking an object from the private domain to the public, or transporting an object in the public domain.			

FEAST OF THE PASSOVER

The Passover was a weeklong festival, which was kicked off by a special meal called the *Seder*. At this meal, traditional foods with symbolic meanings were placed on the table—a sweet concoction of fruit and honey, parsley dipped in salt water, bitter herbs, an egg, and a shank bone. A place was set at the table for Elijah, and the door was opened for him in case he should come. This Seder meal was designed to pique the curiosity of children, and to encourage them to ask questions about everything they saw. There was even a game for them. A piece of the unleavened bread was hidden, and all the children tried to find it. The one who discovered it first was given a prize! In Bible times, every family sacrificed a lamb for their Passover meal as a reminder of that night in Exodus when God passed through the city, killing the firstborn sons of the Egyptians. Because the Israelite houses were sprinkled with the blood of the lambs, God "passed over" them, and they were spared (Ex. 12:23).

FEAST OF PENTECOST

Pentecost was called the Feast of Weeks, for the people counted off seven weeks after Passover to designate their celebration day. Pentecost took place on the fiftieth day, and was the start of the harvest season. Pentecost marked the offering of the firstfruits at the Temple. Farmers would form a parade, marching to the tune of many instruments, as they brought wheat, barley, grapes, figs, pomegranates, olive oil, and honey to the priests in the Temple. To help celebrate this festival, there were

> **DID YOU KNOW?**
>
> • During the exile in Babylon, two special fasts were held to mourn the destruction of the temple and the murder of the governor of Judah.
>
> • Passover is also called the Feast of Unleavened Bread, for the household was cleared of all leaven, and only unleavened bread, called matzo was eaten.

traditional foods that the Jews prepared. Milk products were popular, bringing to mind the whole "milk and honey" thing, and because it was said that only dairy foods were eaten on the day that Moses brought the Ten Commandments down from Mount Sinai. Challah, an eggy bread was baked in the shape of a ladder, reminding the Jews of the tradition that Moses used a ladder to climb into Heaven to receive the Law. The third "must" for Pentecost celebrations was kreplach, a three-sided Jewish pasta. Its three sides were said to represent the patriarchs—Abraham, Isaac and Jacob.

Feast of Tabernacles

While the Feast of Pentecost initiated the harvest season, the Feast of Tabernacles celebrated the end of the harvest. It was similar to Thanksgiving. To give the festivities a historical flavor, the people all camped out during the week. They ate and slept in booths or tents as a reminder of the time when Israel had lived in tents in the wilderness. Songs and dancing lasted well into the night. The whole city was illuminated by huge candelabra, which young men kept filled by scurrying up ladders with their pitchers of oil. Special sacrifices were offered in the Temple (Num. 29:35–39). Water was carried from the Pool of Siloam in gold pitchers and poured over the altar. This was to thank God for the rain of last season, and was offered as a prayer for rain in the year ahead. In another ceremony, a citron (the "fruit of the beautiful tree") and some branches were gathered and bound together—a palm branch, two willow branches and three myrtle branches (Lev. 23:40). The last day of the Feast of Tabernacles is called "the Great Hosanna," when the people marched around the Temple, waving branches and crying "Hosanna! Please save us!"

Happy New Year

In New Testament times, Rosh Hashanah was celebrated as the Jewish New Year. Trumpets announced the first day of the seventh month, and the people were called to a special celebration. Sweet foods were on the menu, like apples dipped in honey, in the hopes that the year to come would be filled with good things. Customarily, the Jews tried to avoid sleeping on Rosh Hashanah. Also, on this day, they were to bow, kneel down, and to prostrate themselves before God in worship and in thanksgiving. It was a day of reflection and repentance, for in just ten days, Yom Kippur would come. The Jews believed that God planned out the upcoming year based upon the deeds of the people. However, those fates would not become fixed until Yom Kippur. The ten days that intervened were an opportunity to influence God's rulings in favorable directions. The saying went "On Rosh Hashanah it is inscribed, and on Yom Kippur it is sealed." Rosh Hashanah signaled their freedom from the power of sin.

ON THIS DAY IN HISTORY

Rosh Hashanah is one of the most eventful days in history. Traditionally, it was the day on which Adam and Eve were created, so it's a kind of birthday party for all of mankind. Rosh Hashanah was also the day when it was decreed that three different barren women would be allowed to bear children—Sarah, Rachel, and Hannah. It was also the traditional day on which Joseph was released from his long term in an Egyptian prison. Rosh Hashanah was also the day on which the Israelites were released from slavery and allowed to leave Egypt for the Promised Land. According to the Jewish traditions, the month of Rosh Hashanah will also mark their final redemption as a people.

SOUND THE TRUMPET

When the shofar was blown on Rosh Hashanah, there were three different sounds made. The first was one long continuous blast. The second consisted of a series of three shorter blasts. The third was a set of nine short staccato notes. These two latter sounds were supposed to be the sounds of sorrow—sighs and short piercing cries. In contrast, the long continuous note was a sound of joy and triumph. The trumpets were blown throughout the month before Rosh Hashanah, but not on the last day. The silence was to prevent Satan from noticing the arrival of this holy day, which was "The Hidden Day" and therefore to be concealed.

DAY OF ATONEMENT

Yom Kippur was the Jewish Day of Atonement. The High Priest offered sacrifice for the sin of all the people on this day. He prepared himself carefully for the rituals of the day, for a mistake could cost him his life and the nation's atonement. It was the only time that he entered the Holy of Holies. There, blood was sprinkled from the sacrifice. It was the only time during the year when he uttered God's name, which was so holy that it was never spoken. During the Yom Kippur services, the High Priest spoke the name "Yahweh" ten times. The Jews fell to the ground in reverence of his name. The closing event of the Day of Atonement was the selection of a scapegoat. After laying his hands on its head, it was sent off into the desert as a sign that the sins of the people were taken away from them. At the close of services, seven times it is said "The Lord is our God." Then the shofar sounds and all the people proclaim "Next year in Jerusalem." At that, Yom Kippur is over.

DID YOU KNOW?

• Weeks before the Feast of Tabernacles arrived, the Jews would work to repair all the roads and bridges for the many pilgrims who would come to Jerusalem for Yom Kippur and the festival that followed.

• Solomon sacrificed one hundred and twenty thousand sheep at the dedication of the Temple (1Kin. 8:63).

DEFINITE DON'TS

On Yom Kippur, several things were definitely not done. It was a full Sabbath day, so no work could be performed. It was also a fast day. No food or water could be taken for a complete twenty-five hours. Also, there were to be no marital relations on Yom Kippur. Washing was not allowed, so baths and showers were out. Anointing with perfumes or lotions was prohibited, and today that includes all the deodorants and cosmetics. The wearing of leather shoes was also prohibited on Yom Kippur.

NEW MOON FESTIVALS

Along with the weekly Sabbath day of rest, the Jews of Bible times celebrated a New Moon Festival. This was the beginning of each month, when the new moon made its appearance. Trumpets were blown (Ps. 81:3) and special sacrifices were made (Num. 29:6). No work was done on this holiday (Amos 8:5), and special meals were prepared. David's absence from the king's side during the New Moon banquet enraged Saul, and sent Jonathan hurrying to warn David to head for the hills (1Sa. 20:27–30). There were times of special teaching as well. The arrival of the new moon was understood as a reminder that God had created an orderly world. Not one of these things would pass away (Ps. 148:6).

FEAST OF PURIM

Purim is such an excessive and noisy celebration, that it has been called the Jewish Mardi Gras. The Feast of Purim commemorated how the Jews were saved from massacre thanks to the bravery of Queen Esther. Purim means "lots" and refers to the lottery that Haman used to choose the date for the massacre. The feast is celebrated with a carnival-like atmosphere. Plays, parodies, beauty contests, games, and feasting are all a part of the festivities. The Book of Esther is always read during the celebrations of Purim, and it is customary for the listeners to boo, hiss, stamp their feet, and rattle noisemakers whenever the name of Haman is mentioned. This is an effort to blot out the name of Haman.

THE TABERNACLE
AND THE TEMPLES

In the earliest days of history, altars of earth or stone were used for sacrifices (Ex. 20:24–26). Then, God gave Moses the plans for a new kind of worship site. A Tabernacle was raised up in the wilderness that was a dwelling place for God. Later, when the Israelites had settled in the land he had promised them, they built for God a beautiful Temple in Jerusalem.

TABERNACLE

The Tabernacle was considered to be the dwelling place of God. It was a mobile Temple, which could be broken down and moved about with the children of Israel during their wilderness wanderings. Put most simply, the Tabernacle was a tent. However, it wasn't just any tent. The framework of the Tabernacle was draped with linen tapestries, goats' hair curtains, rams' skins that had been dyed red, and a weatherproof covering made from animal skins. Some say this outer layer might have been made from the skins of porpoises, whales, or manatees. Inside the tent was the Holy Place, and the Holy of Holies, where the ark of the covenant was kept. In the courtyard around the Tabernacle, sacrifices were made and the people offered prayers.

DID YOU KNOW?

- The seven-branched golden lampstand was the only source of light in the Tabernacle. It was hammered out of one piece of gold, weighed sixty six pounds or more, and was decorated with flowers, and buds, like almond blossoms.

SOLOMON'S TEMPLE

David had greatly desired to build a Temple for God in his capital city, but God had said no. His Temple was not to be built by a warrior with blood-stained hands, but by a man of peace. Solomon, David's son, was that man. Solomon's wealth and connections provided him with the finest of building materials. With the help of the precious metals and jewels stockpiled by his father in preparation for that day, Solomon began construction. The huge limestone blocks that formed the outside walls were cut in a nearby quarry, and were trimmed to size outside the city walls (1Kin. 6:7). This way, there wasn't a lot of construction noise for the citizens of Jerusalem during the years of construction. The Temple was the domain of the priests, who went about their business barefoot. The Holy Place was furnished with the incense altar, the table of showbread, and the lampstands. The inner room was curtained off from the rest, and this Holy of Holies held the ark of the covenant.

THE SECOND TEMPLE

When Cyrus of Persia told Nehemiah and the other Jews that they could return to their homeland, he gave them permission to rebuild Solomon's Temple. He even gave back to the Jews some of the sacred implements that Nebuchadnezzar had taken from the Temple when they had been captured. The Jews worked on and off, becoming discouraged and needing some pushes by the prophets to finish the job. The second Temple stood for about five hundred years, but it was a pale imitation of Solomon's glorious workmanship. The oldsters who remembered back to the day's of the first Temple wept when they beheld their pitiable replacement (Hag. 2:3).

HEROD'S TEMPLE

Herod the Great, an Idumean Jew who inherited his father's governorship of Judea, hoped to win the favor of his subjects. With that end in mind, he made plans to construct a new Temple in Jerusalem. Priests were specially trained for the work of building so they could be sure that the floor plan followed Moses' instructions. After ten years, most of the construction was completed, though the detail work continued for years afterwards. It is speculated that the Temple really wasn't even completely done when it was destroyed in AD 70. Herod's Temple was both a bribe for his subjects' goodwill and a chance to impress the Romans. It was a splendid building, twice as high as Solomon's Temple had been and covered in gold. The Temple literally glittered in the bright sun.

THE PRESENCE OF THE LORD

God had a few different ways of letting his people know that he was nearby. He appeared to Moses in a burning bush (Ex. 3:2). In the wilderness, he was the pillar of cloud by day and fire by night (Ex. 13:21). When Moses spoke with God in the Tabernacle, the people knew God was meeting with Moses because the "cloudy pillar" stood before the tent (Ex. 33:9). At Mount Sinai, darkness descended upon the top of the mountain, thunder crashed, and trumpets blared (Ex. 20:21). When the Tabernacle was dedicated, the Shekinah Glory of God's presence settled on the building as the people watched in awe (2Chr. 7:1–3).

ZECHARIAH
Taking His Turn

Zechariah was a priest of the tribe of Levi. He had lived on the outskirts of Jerusalem all his life, coming into Jerusalem whenever it was his turn to serve inside the Temple walls. He had a beautiful wife named Elizabeth, who had been his closest companion for decades. She was a faithful woman, but a shadow of sadness was always lurking behind her dark eyes. How he wished that God had answered their prayers and given them a child.

It was his turn to minister in the Temple again, so Zechariah made preparations for an extended stay in the small rooms reserved for priests within the Temple walls. Levites from across the nation had been put on a schedule, and they all took turns seeing to the everyday work—sacrifices, washing, dedications, special offerings and general maintenance. Once inside the Temple courts, Zechariah's days fell into a familiar swing. His days began well before sunrise, with the preparation of the Holy Place for the day ahead. The wicks of the lampstands in the Holy Place had to be trimmed. The lamps themselves had to be filled with oil. Ashes were removed from the altars, the floors were washed, the implements were cleaned and anointed with sweet smelling oils. The job assignments were determined by lot, so the priests gathered in the cool morning air to find out what the Lord had for them that day. When lots were cast to determine which priest would take incense into the Holy Place, Zechariah received the honor. It was a once in a lifetime event for a priest to enter the Holy Place. Zechariah moved to wash himself at the laver and donned fresh linen robes. With other priests offering prayers at the door, he took the incense in hand and moved through the imposing doorway. All was quiet and dark within the

Holy Place. The lampstands gave off enough light to reveal the table of showbread and the altar of incense before the heavy curtain that veiled the Holy of Holies. Awed in the silence, Zechariah moved to place fresh incense on the altar. With a start, he realized that he was not alone!

Outside, the priests began murmuring amongst themselves, for Zechariah was taking far too long inside the Holy Place. Yet none dared enter to check on him. Then came the gentle swish of fringes on flooring and the pad of bare feet. Zechariah, slightly dazed, stood before them. Unable to speak, he motioned furiously. The other priests realized that he had seen something wondrous within the sanctuary, and it had left him completely speechless.

HORNS OF THE ALTAR

The altar of incense inside the Holy Place of the Temple had raised points at the four corners, and these were known as the horns of the altar (Ex. 37:25). This was where incense was burned in the presence of God. It was rather small, just eighteen inches square and three feet tall. The priests were instructed to dab the blood of the sacrifices on the horns (Lev. 4:7). This Holy Place must have been considered a place of safety, for twice, men have fled there for sanctuary. Adonijah scooted into the Holy Place of the Temple and seized the horns of the altar. Clinging there, he pleaded for mercy from his brother, Solomon (1Kin. 1:51). Shortly thereafter, Joab, the turncoat general, tried the same tactic (1Kin. 2:28). He had betrayed the king, and had murdered innocent men, so Solomon ordered that he be killed. Since he wouldn't let go of the altar of incense, he was struck down right there in the Holy Place of the Temple (1Kin. 2:31, 34). So much for sanctuary!

INSIDE THE ARK

The ark of the covenant was a kind of treasure box. It held sacred things, which the children of Israel wanted to keep safe for posterity. Inside the ark were several items: the two tablets on which God had written the Ten Commandments, a golden pot of manna and Aaron's rod which had blossomed (Heb. 9:4).

OFFERING BOXES

The people of God were to bring their offerings to the Temple regularly. They paid a temple tax, to assist in the upkeep of the building and as wages for the tribe of Levi. To assist in the collection, the Levites monitored thirteen collection boxes, which were placed in accessible spots around the Temple. They were nicknamed "the trumpets" because of their funnel-shaped openings. When coins were thrown into them, it could raise quite a clatter. This made it easy for the onlooking priests to know that the people were paying up. The poor widow could probably have slipped her few coins down the side of the trumpeted opening without much notice (Lk. 21:2), but the pompous Pharisee liked to rattle his money around a bit to draw attention to the size of his contributions.

SYNAGOGUES

By New Testament times, the children of Israel had multiplied greatly, and they had been scattered across the known world. Many were too far from Jerusalem to make the regular journeys to celebrate the annual festivals there. So, a new system was developed, and local synagogues sprouted up across the world. The Jews in Capernaum were pleased to tell Jesus of the kindness of a Roman centurion in their neighborhood, who had built a synagogue for them (Lk. 7:5). These were places of worship, prayer, and learning. The Law was read, as were the prophets. Jesus taught in synagogues (Mt. 13:54), as did Paul (Acts 13:15). Jairus, whose daughter was raised from the dead, was a ruler in his synagogue (Mk. 5:22).

DID YOU KNOW?

• Solomon's temple was not large by today's standards, but it must have been the largest building the Israelites had constructed up to that time. It measured about 30 by 87 feet and was 43 feet high.

• God provided the recipe for the incense that was used in the Temple. It was a secret recipe that included sweet spices and frankincense (Ex. 30:37). This was the aroma of worship!

• The Holy of Holies was separated from the Holy Place by a beautiful embroidered curtain. This is the curtain that was ripped in two at the moment Jesus died (Mt. 27:51).

• The walls of each room in Solomon's temple were paneled with cedar, carved with flowers, palm-trees and cherubim, and overlaid with gold. No stonework could be seen from inside the building.

CHAPTER FIFTEEN

THEIR WARFARE

T he world of the Bible was a world of conflict. **The nations were in constant turmoil,** vying for control over the choicest bits of land. Abraham armed himself to rescue his nephew Lot, who got caught in the crossfire of warring factions (Gen. 14:14–16). Saul spent his whole life fighting the Philistines (1Sa. 14:52). Daniel was taken into captivity by the Babylonian Empire (Dan.1:3–4). Jesus was born into a world under Roman domination (Lk. 2:1). Even though people longed for peace, the Lord warned that the future held more struggles. "Nation shall rise against nation, and kingdom against kingdom" (Lk. 21:10).

405

RANK AND FILE

The Bible is full of military men—from Joshua, who commanded the attack on Jericho to the centurion who spent his days chained to Paul in Rome. The armies of ancient times were peopled with scouts and spies, cavalries and infantries, mighty men and mercenaries.

THE ARMY OF ISRAEL

A king of Israel had his regular troops. These were full-time army men—professionals, if you please. Then the king had a ring of elite fighting men who served as his personal bodyguards, at home or on the battlefield. David had a group of "mighty men" who were never far from his side (2Sa. 16:6). The king also had the ability to draft citizens to serve during times of battle. Should the numbers be needed, every able-bodied man in the nation could be conscripted for war. Samuel had warned the children of Israel that this would be so if they crowned a king (1Sa. 8:9). The professional army and the draftees had separate commanders, both of which reported directly to the king.

> **DID YOU KNOW?**
>
> • Robin Hood had his merry men, and King David had his mighty men (2Sa. 16:6).
>
> • The tribe of Benjamin had trained seven hundred slingers who were left-handed and never missed (Judg. 20:16).

REGIMENTS ON ROTATION

Since all the men in Israel were considered a part of the nation's army, King David had an enormous task setting up his militia. Twelve became the magic number. The population was divided into twelve groups of 24,000 men each. Each of the twelve divisions served on active duty for one month every year. The divisions were made up of a blend of men from each of the twelve tribes. Each tribe tended to specialize in a particular weapon (1Chr. 12), and it would send its trained units to serve their country. For instance, the tribe of Benjamin was famous for its slingers (Judg. 20:16). The king's home office would notify outlying tribes how many units they needed to supply the militia each month. Then the local authorities would decide whose turn it was to go into active duty (1Chr. 27:16–22). Men on duty headed into the capital city to be trained for battle by the professional soldiers (1Chr. 27:1–15).

CREDIT WHERE CREDIT IS DUE!

The king of a nation couldn't always be bothered to lead his troops into battle. David posted generals and captains over the army of Israel. He had advisors and strategists to help him plan his campaigns against the enemy. Then he minded the palace while his underlings waged war. After all, siege warfare could take months and even years. That was a long time away from house and harem! When a conquest neared victory, though, the generals notified the king that it was time to put in an appearance. As the Ammonite capital was about to fall, Joab sent for David to join him and take the proper credit for winning the war. He was to bring the militia with him to take the city (2Sa. 12:28–29).

MILITARY CENSUS

David was the leader of an immense army. Every man in the nation of Israel was a potential soldier. King David decided to find out just how many men he had under his control, and he called for a census. This would have been a military census, to find out the age and location of all the potential draftees throughout the tribes (2Sa. 24:2–9; 1Chr. 21:6; 27:24). This would give him a fair idea of the size of his standing militia. A military census was not an unusual thing. Others had been taken (2Chr. 17:14–18; 25:5; 26:11–13), but God said that David's motivation in calling this particular census was wrong, and David's heart condemned him (2Sa. 24:10). He pleaded with God for forgiveness, but not before a plague swept through the land.

MIGHTY MEN

Robin Hood had his Merry Men, and King Arthur had his Knights of the Round Table, but before them all was King David and his mighty men. Under David's leadership, the army of Israel began to take shape. Within the ranks of the enlisted men, there were a few good men who were recognized by their peers as being exceptional. These were mighty men of valor, according to the Scriptures. They had proved themselves in great feats of battle. One man, Shammah, had defended a field against a troop of Philistines. A man called Benaiah had gone down into a snowy pit with a lion and came away the victor (2Sa. 23:20). The most renowned of the mighty men was Josheb-Basshebeth, who had stood in battle and killed eight hundred of his enemies in one day. Another of the mighty men had defied the Philistines even after the rest of the Israelites had fled from the field. When the time came for him to lay his weapons aside, Eleazar found that his hand had frozen around the hilt of his sword, so fierce was his grip (2Sa. 23:10). These mighty men served King David faithfully throughout his reign, and then pledged their loyalty to King Solomon when he took his father's place on the throne (1Chr. 29:24).

ARMOR-BEARERS

An armor-bearer was more than a caddy. He was the original sidekick. He was a soldier's right-hand man and trusted friend. They kept an eye out for each other, watching each other's backs in the confusion of battle. David spent some time as Saul's armor-bearer (1Sa. 16:21). Jonathan and his armor-bearer took on a Philistine garrison by themselves (1Sa. 14:1). They worked as a team and fought their way through the courtyard, Jonathan knocking down the enemy left and right, and his armor-bearer coming behind him, finishing off the fallen enemies. Even Goliath had an armor-bearer who carried a huge shield before the champion into the battlefield (1Sa. 17:7).

COURIERS

In the heat of a battle, the king needed to know the latest news. He was not always on the front lines, so couriers were sent to keep him apprised of the latest troop movements. Young men were used as runners to bring messages to the king from his generals. King David depended upon couriers to inform him of General Joab's efforts on the front lines (2Sa. 11:19). All news was not good news, and wary was the messenger who brought ill tidings. "Don't kill the messenger" was their credo. King David killed the man who brought news of Saul and Jonathan's deaths (2Sa. 2:5, 15).

SPIES

Armies never went charging into a foreign land without doing a little reconnaissance first. The general needed to know the lay of the land and the state of the enemy's defenses. When the children of Israel prepared to cross into Canaan, they sent twelve scouts ahead (Num. 13:2). These men took notes on the number of people in the land, their strength and size, and the fortifications of the Canaanite cities. The spies brought back both good news and bad news. The land was indeed "flowing with milk and honey" as God had promised. However, God had left out a minor detail—namely that there were giants dwelling in the land. When Joshua was preparing to attack the walled city of Jericho, he sent two of his spies ahead. These two men were successful in their information gathering, but were nearly captured by the local authorities (Josh. 2:1).

POLICE

Since the local law enforcement in Roman cities didn't include bobbies or coppers or boys in blue, the local bigwigs hired lictors. A Roman magistrate was attended by a staff of lictors. The higher the rank of the ruler, the larger his staff. These lictors carried rods or axes to symbolize their authority—kind of like a billy club, badge, or side arm. They are called, literally, "rod-bearers" in Acts 16:35. Since there was no true citywide police force, these lictors handled the policing duties and escorted their magistrate.

> ### DID YOU KNOW?
>
> • The Roman army spent five centuries completing a road system that extended to every corner of their empire and eventually covered a distance equal to ten times the circumference of the earth at the equator—50,000 miles of first-class highways and 200,000 miles of lesser roads.
>
> • Even before they had a king, the recruited army of the tribes of Israel numbered some 400,000 men (Judg. 20:17).

JONATHAN'S ARMOR-BEARER

Fearless Follower

Saul had been king over Israel for two years now, and he had raised an army of 3,000 men. He himself commanded two thousand of them, and he had given the command of the remaining thousand over to his son, Jonathan. Saul had planned an attack on the Philistines, who had a fortress in a nearby pass, but he had been soundly rebuked by Samuel, and so retreated a little to sit under a pomegranate tree to lick his wounds. Saul still had six hundred men with him, and Jonathan was among them. Now, Jonathan looked back at his pouting father, and then looked away at the sharp rocks that surrounded the pass, in the direction of the Philistine garrison. Then he looked over to his companion—his armor-bearer. "Come with me! Let's go see if God will use us against these heathens!" he challenges his friend. Jonathan's armor-bearer was a skilled warrior, a sparring partner, and a trusted friend. The glint of excitement twinkled in his companion's eyes. "If you go, I am with you!" he replied. As they made their way towards the fortress on the hill, they made their plans. They would stand out in the open, showing themselves to the guards on the walls. If the guards called "freeze!" and started to make their way down the hillside towards them, then they'd boogie back to the camp. However, if the Philistines invited them to come up the slope to the camp, then that would be their sign from God that the garrison had been delivered into their hands. Making their way out from behind the rocks, Jonathan and his armor-bearer walked into the open. They were met with a bark of laugher and a taunt, "The Hebrews are coming out of the holes they've been hiding in!" To their amazement, the next words out of the Philistine's mouth were "Come up here! I have something to show you!" Jonathan and his armor-bearer began to crawl

up the steep slope on their hands and knees. At the top, Jonathon didn't waste any time, unsheathed his sword, and began to lay into the Philistines in the fortress. Jonathan and his armor-bearer fell into a kind of rhythm. Jonathan, who had a sword, would topple his foes and move on, while his armor-bearer followed behind, finishing off the wounded men. In the space of a few minutes, twenty men were scattered about the compound. The whole garrison began to tremble, and as fear mounted, the Philistines gathered up their weapons and turned on one another in their panic. The noise could be heard back where Saul sat under the pomegranate tree, so he did a quick roll call. Once they realized that Prince Jonathan and his armor-bearer were missing, Saul sent his forces to back up his boy. By the end of the day, the faith of one man, the fearlessness of his friend, and a miracle of God routed the whole Philistine race out of Israel.

IN THE NAVY

A few of the ancient nations had warships. Egypt commanded a large fleet, as did the Phoenicians. Even the dreaded Philistines of King Saul's day were said to have come across the sea from the island of Crete (Amos 9:7). For centuries, the Israelites maintained a safe distance from the unsettling sea. God had promised them a land, and they were content to stay on it. However, in the days of the kings of Israel, King Solomon saw the wisdom of providing oneself with a fleet of ships. He wished to secure his own trade vessels, and set about building up a merchant fleet. Now, other than paddling about on lakes in fishing ships, the Jews had no experience on the waves. Solomon knew he needed help to get his men afloat, and so he called on King Hiram of Phoenicia (1Kin. 9:27). He pulled a few strings and was able to borrow some of Hiram's expert ship-builders, as well as a few sailors. They helped the Israelites to learn the ropes.

> **DID YOU KNOW?**
>
> • The Praetorian Guard were the few, the proud. They were an emperor's elite task force, and he trusted them with his life. They were his personal guard, assigned as a team of bodyguards who traveled with their leader everywhere, keeping him safe.
>
> • Many nations hired mercenaries to serve as their initial striking force in a battle. This way these foreigners took the brunt of the defense's retaliation.

THE ARMY OF GREECE

Greece was not a large country, nor was it particularly impressive. Yet Greece ruled the entirety of the ancient world for a time, and transformed that world's culture and language to match its own. This was all due to the military way of life in Greece. The ancient Greeks were raised to be soldiers. From birth, children were taught what they needed to know to be good soldiers. Weak boys were thrown out of the cities to die in the hill country. Strong boys were adopted and educated by the state. They were taught to run, wrestle, endure pain without flinching, eat reduced rations, and obey commands. They were trained to dominate.

THE PHALANX

Alexander the Great's army was organized into phalanxes. These were groups of soldiers that marched in a tight formation together. They looked like walking tanks, and the sound of so many sandals hitting the ground in unison was enough to turn their opponents' knees to jelly. When it came right down to the details of things, there were actually nine thousand men in a single phalanx. These men were divided into squares with sixteen men on each side. Each man was protected with armor and a thirteen-foot spear. Standing about three feet apart, shields in position, they formed their own small fortress.

SOLDIERS OF ROME

The New Testament is full of stories about centurions. Centurions were officers within the ranks of the Roman army, charged with a command of over one hundred men. A centurion stood at the foot of the cross, and his words are etched forever on the pages of Scripture, "Truly this Man must be the Son of God" (Mk. 15:39). Cornelius of Caesarea was a centurion in Rome's Italian regiment (Acts 10:1). He and his whole household came to faith after being visited by Peter (Acts 10:44–47). Julius, a centurion assigned to escort Paul to Rome, was in the Augustan regiment (Acts 27:1). He prevented Paul from being put to the sword after their voyage was interrupted by stormy seas and a shipwreck (Acts 27:43). A centurion is a source of amazement for Jesus, "I have not found such great faith, not even in Israel" (Mt. 8:10).

ROMAN LEGIONS

The army of Rome was the most organized, best-trained bunch of soldiers in the ancient world. A Roman legion included about six thousand men. At the peak of Rome's domination, there were twenty four legions of men, or a half million men. The legions included Britons, Spaniards, Germans, Greeks, Slavs, and even Jews. Part of the reason behind these incredible numbers was the wonderful package deals offered by the recruitment offices. The government offered immediate citizenship to army volunteers, and paid them a pension upon retirement. Troops were drafted from all over the Empire, both to expand the borders further and to police the existing domain. In fact, native Italians usually avoided military service, for it could take them away from home and off to some distant outpost.

CHAIN GANGS

Many sturdy young men were drafted into the Roman army, for the army was always in need of new recruits. Some young Romans volunteered to serve their Empire, hoping to bring glory to their family and their hometown in their great exploits. They dreamed of battles, booty, and victory parades. Not one of those eager newcomers probably ever expected to be handed a shovel. The Roman army provided the sheer number of workers needed to accomplish Rome's ambitious building programs. That meant hauling rock for constructing bridges and aqueducts, laying sewer systems in large cities, and spending the day digging roadbeds through the farthest reaches of Rome's power.

"GO THE EXTRA MILE"

Being a Roman soldier, garrisoned in occupied territory, had its perks. In essence, he could boss around the locals. One of the laws on the books in New Testament times stated that a Roman soldier could call upon a civilian to carry his stuff for him. Anybody could be tapped for this indignity, and the chosen often complied with anger simmering barely beneath the surface. The only bright side was that the rule came with a limitation—a man could only be pressed into service like this for one mile. Then the Roman soldier had to take up his own baggage again, or find another sturdy-looking citizen. The Jews, who avoided contact with

Gentiles as a rule, were outraged by this law. That is why it came as such a shock that Jesus should say, "whoever compels you to go with him one mile, go with him two" (Mt. 5:41).

G.I. JANE

Battle was exclusively a man's domain, but a couple of military heroes in the Bible have been heroines. Deborah and Jael both had a part in the same decisive victory. God spoke through a judge named Deborah to tell the general named Barak how the Canaanites could be beaten. Barak agreed to attack the Canaanites, but he wanted Deborah to go with him into battle. She did so, and the Canaanites were thoroughly trounced. There was one loose end though. The Canaanite general, Sisera escaped on foot. A woman named Jael saw him, went out to greet him, and invited him into her tent. With the help of a warm glass of milk and a soft blanket, he soon fell asleep. As he was sleeping, Jael hammered a tent peg through his head, killing him (Judg. 4–5).

A MAN IN UNIFORM

PUT ON YOUR ARMOR

The soldiers in the Roman army were unmistakable, for they all wore the same uniform. Paul alludes to their get-up in Ephesians when he lists the "whole armor of God" (Eph. 6:10–11). Underneath the armor, a soldier had an undergarment to help pull him together. The armor itself consisted of a leather jacket and skirt, covered with metal plates. The strappy sandals that we see in pictures were not a military fashion statement. The official footwear of the Roman army was a hob-nailed sandal, which provided good traction. They also did a good deal of damage during battle, if a soldier planted his foot on someone.

BREASTPLATE

One of the most important pieces of armor was the breastplate. This was the bulletproof vest of Bible times. It covered most of the vital organs,

BENAIAH
Mighty Man of David

The mighty men were men of valor, proven warriors, like the Knights of the Round Table. When there were big battles or tough odds, General Joab called in David's mighty men to get the job done (2Sa. 10:7–9). Achieving mighty manhood was no easy task. A man had to distinguish himself above his comrades in an outstanding way. One of David's mighty men had killed three hundred men in one battle. Another could boast killing eight hundred men at one time. When that man's task was done, he found that his hand had frozen around the hilt of his sword so that he could not put it down (2Sa. 23:10)! Another had defeated an entire troop of Philistines in the midst of a field of lentils, killing every foe that entered that patch of ground. A group of three mighty men had broken into a Philistine garrison in King David's hometown of Bethlehem just to bring their king a drink of water from the well there. They risked their lives to give their leader a taste of home. One of the mighty men served as armor-bearer to the Israelite army's general, Joab. King David had more than thirty in the ranks of the mighty men. Of these, there were a few men who had achieved the greatest notoriety. They were called "The three." They were the equivalent of the three musketeers—unmatched in skill on the battlefield. The remaining men were called "the thirty."

Of these thirty, one man was recognized as their best. He was more honored than the thirty, but he didn't quite match up to the reputations of the three (2Sa. 23:23). He was Benaiah, son of Jehoiada. Benaiah was known for an event that had happened during the winter months. On a dare, he had jumped down into a snowy pit into which a lion had fallen. He faced the beast in close quarters, with his friends cheering him on from around the top edge. In the end, Benaiah came home with a beautiful lion pelt for his floor.

Benaiah's reputation went before him, and he was respected for his many deeds. In one battle, he had fought and killed two lion-like heroes from Moab. They had been broad men with flowing manes of hair. In another foray, he had faced a mighty Egyptian warrior. The opponent had been spectacular—tall, dark, and muscular. The Egyptian had come at Benaiah with a spear, and so Benaiah had taken his staff and met him in a great struggle. Many blows were exchanged before Benaiah managed to pry the spear from the Egyptian's hands.

Benaiah killed the Egyptian with his own spear. For his victories on the field of battle, Benaiah was granted a special honor. David appointed him as leader of the royal guard.

The mighty men were loyal to King David and accompanied him into the wilderness when Absalom stole the throne. They offered to kill King Saul for David when they found him sleeping alone in a cave (1Sa. 26:12). They protected him with their own bodies when a heckler followed their assembly, hurling rocks and insults (2Sa. 16:6). They were as loyal to the king as they were to each other. They were his constant companions, and his nearest friends. Even as David neared death and one of his sons declared himself to be the next king, Benaiah and the other mighty men stayed by the side of their king until he named his own predecessor (1Kin. 1:18). Then they submitted themselves to the leadership of David's heir, King Solomon (1Chr. 29:24). The mighty men were faithful until the very end.

protecting a soldier from mortal wounds. Some breastplates were made from leather, while later pieces were fortified with pounded brass. One detail worth noting is that the breastplate was only useful to soldiers who were on the offensive. When a man was suited up to face his worst opponent, he was protected from the darts of his enemy only as long as he faced his enemy. You see, the breastplate only covered the front of the body. When a man turned to run, he was left vulnerable to the assault of the men in pursuit. A man in armor was expected to stand (Eph. 6:1). Even the best armor had its chinks, though. After all, a man had to move! Openings were left at various joints so that a soldier could walk and swing his sword. Ahab was regaled in full armor on the field of battle, but he was hit by a stray arrow just where there was a little gap between the plates. Although he managed to stay in his chariot, Ahab's wound was mortal, and he died later that day (2Chr. 18:33).

> **DID YOU KNOW?**
>
> • According to the Bible, Uzziah was the first king who equipped his entire army with helmets and breastplates (2Chr. 26:14). Previously, such equipment had been the possession only of kings and special fighters in Israel.
>
> • The quality of an army's armor depended entirely on the prosperity of its homeland. For many of the earliest battles that we read of in Scriptures, only the king and his princes owned armor.

DISTINCTIVE HEADGEAR

Helmets were a wonderful invention. They protected the head from nasty things like swords, arrows, and rocks. The blows from an opponent that might have been fatal would glance off of a well-made helmet. It was better to have a ringing in one's ears than to be dead! When men were called to battle, they were expected to grab their helmets and line up (Jer. 46:4). So, those armies that could afford them issued helmets to their men. King Uzziah was the first Israelite king to be able to issue uniforms to his troops (2Chr. 26:14). Some armies decided to make their helmets more distinctive by adding embellishments to them. This distinctive headgear helped differentiate friend and foe in the confusion of hand-to-hand combat. The helmets of the Philistines were bronze, and crowned with scarlet feathers. They made an impressive picture, marching across the land with their bright feathers waving atop every gleaming head. The Roman army had that whole bristle-brush thing going on top of their helmets.

SHIELDS AND BUCKLERS

Troops had two different kinds of shields. One was quite tall, and it was used by heavy troops to protect their entire bodies. For all practical purposes, they could hide behind it. This shield provided an army with its own cover on the open battlefield. The second shield was much smaller. It was called a buckler, and was carried by lighter fighting troops. It was strapped to the arm, and was perfect in hand-to-hand combat (1Kin. 10:17). These early shields were made of a wicker or a wooden frame covered with leather. Leather shields needed regular oiling to prevent them from cracking. Different nations had slight variations on the general theme of these two shields. For instance, the Egyptian shields were rectangular with a rounded top. Other shields were slightly convex, meaning they curved outward. The Hittites carried a more ornate shield which bore a figure-eight pattern.

A CRIMSON TIDE

Uniforms were important for the success of an army. Not only did a unified theme in the clothing department help the men to identify each other on the battle field, but it helped them make a good first impression on their enemies. Nothing was more intimidating than seeing a mass of soldiers all dressed alike and moving as one. The unity and preparedness of the oncoming forces stirred up a real sense of dread in the men who watched their approach. The Assyrian army painted all of their armor red. This made their approach seem like a wave of blood washing across the horizon. The red armor served a second purpose, too. If a soldier became wounded in battle, his injury was well-hidden by the crimson clothing, and his opponents would not realize that he was weakened in any way.

WEAPONS OF WAR

The weapons used in war depended on the type of combat. In hand-to-hand fighting, clubs, axes, and short and long swords were used. There were darts, spears, and javelins for throwing. And there were many missiles, from stones and boulders to bows and arrows.

SLINGERS

Most of the time, we picture a slingshot as a two-pronged stick with an elastic band, dangling out of the back pocket of a youngster's overalls. It was a harmless boyhood toy, used more for mischief than anything. In ancient times, the slingshot was also a child's plaything. Boys could spend hours in target practice, improving their aim. But a sling was also a weapon of deadly force, carried proudly by ranks of military men. The tribe of Benjamin boasted seven hundred slingers, able to come within a hair's breadth of any target (Judg. 20:16).The slingshot could be considered the ancient missile launcher. A sling was deceptively simple in appearance, constructed from two leather thongs and a pouch to hold a rock. A slinger didn't stand spinning his sling overhead like a cowboy's lasso. The motion of the sling was more like fast pitch softball. A couple of deft turns, then zip! When one end of the leather straps was released, the rock could be hurled with terrific speed and deadly accuracy.

ARCHERS

In the armies of the ancient world, archers were specialists. They wielded one of the only long-range weapons available during the early periods of history. The bow of an archer began as a long piece of springy wood strung with sheep's gut. As weaponry improved, soldiers constructed their bows from laminated wood and from the horns of animals. Such bows were powerful, and allowed arrows to penetrate their targets more deeply. Since finely constructed bows like these were very expensive, few nations could equip their entire armies with them. The fierce Assyrians issued them to every man, however, and for decades, the Assyrian army was superior to any other. The arrows were made from reeds or wooden shafts fitted with horn or metal heads. These arrowheads were flat, and sometimes barbed so that they couldn't be pulled easily from a wound (Ps. 38:2). Sometimes the arrows were feathered. We see Prince Jonathan with his bow in hand, doing target-practice in the fields beyond the palace (1Sa. 20:35–37).

EGYPTIAN CHARIOTS

In the Egyptian army, there were leather-clad spearmen and even lighter clad bowmen who accompanied their captain's chariot. They often used mercenaries to bolster their ranks. An Egyptian leader might have had a company of Sardinians as his own guard, wearing armor and carrying two-edged swords. An Egyptian

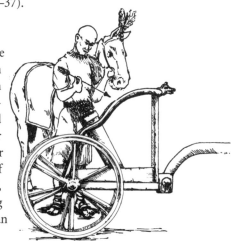

SAUL

Head and Shoulders Above the Rest

The children of Israel were dissatisfied. All the surrounding nations had kings, palaces, royal parades, theme songs, and really cool logos. Why shouldn't they have a ruler that would boost their image among the other nations? It was so hard to explain that an invisible God was their leader. They wanted a man to lead them into battle, and to defend them from the encroachments of the Philistines. So they began to pester Samuel, the prophet of God. "Give us a king!" Samuel conferred with the Lord, and then God conspired to deliver the future king right to Samuel's doorstep.

Now Saul was reckoned to be the most handsome man in all of Israel. He was the classic tall, dark, and handsome hero a full head and shoulders taller than anybody else in the neighborhood. However, Saul didn't get a lot of press because he was from the smallest tribe in Israel, and his family was relatively insignificant. He was the tribe of Benjamin's best-kept secret. So, when dad's donkeys got loose, Saul was sent with a household servant to retrieve them. After wandering around for a while, looking for hoof prints in the dust, the servant suggested paying the local seer to tell them where the donkeys had gone. Saul shrugged his shoulders and said that would be fine. Upon entering the city, they were met at the very gates by Samuel. After assuring the two men that the donkeys had been found, he took Saul aside and announced to him that God had chosen him to be the king over all of Israel. Saul blanched and back-peddled. However, he agreed to have dinner with Samuel. Afterwards Saul sent his servant home ahead of him, and in a private ceremony Samuel anointed Saul with oil. At this point, God gave Saul another heart (1Sa. 10:9) Then Saul headed homeward, keeping all that Samuel had told him to himself.

A few days later, the prophet Samuel called all of Israel together to announce that God would give them a king, chosen by

sacred lot. The twelve tribes were put to the test, and the tribe of Benjamin was chosen. Of the families within the tribe of Benjamin, Saul's family tree was chosen, then his father's household. When the lots were cast to determine which of Kish's sons were to be king, Saul's name received the perfect lot. The people were jubilant! What a perfect leader! He was regally tall and quite handsome. He would look great in a crown! Their new king was a rival for that of any other nation. But, where was he? After a good deal of searching and calling, Saul could not be found. The priests had to inquire of the Lord again. He pointed out the hiding spot, and Saul was discovered behind some piles of equipment. They brought him out before the people, and the glad cry resounded throughout the gathering, "Long live the king!"

war chariot was light and it took skill and strength to control. It was pulled by two horses, which strained its very framework with their fierce speed. Egyptian charioteers tied the horses' reigns around their waists in order to leave their hands free for fighting. These were the chariots that bore down upon the children of Israel as they scampered across the divide in the Red Sea. All six hundred chariots and their soldiers were bogged down in the soft sands of the seabed, and when the water returned to its rightful place, every Egyptian soldier was drowned (Ex. 14:28).

PEACE AT A PRICE

Solomon had the rest of the world at a standoff. It was an ancient cold war. The army of Israel was equipped with an unbelieveable number of chariots. Chariots were the pinnacle of ancient weaponry. And with every new conquest, Solomon's men captured more chariots from their vanquished foes. These were simply refurbished and added to the Israelite force. The presence of all the chariots was enough to make outsiders think twice before planning an invasion. Solomon reigned in peace because nobody wanted to get his dander up. However, this peace came at a high price. The citizens of Israel were taxed to help pay for the upkeep of the army of chariots (1Sa. 8:11–18). Horses were expensive to feed and house. Entire cities were equipped to care for the horses that pulled them.

THE CATAPULT

The most famous of the "engines of war" was the catapult. It was used to vault objects up and over the city walls of an enemy. Alley-oop! Where an arrow had a range of about three hundred yards, the catapult could easily fling things be-

tween three hundred fifty and five hundred yards. This gave the catapulters an advantage, for they could operate outside of the range of enemy archers. Your basic catapult was made like a giant crossbow, and was usually mounted on a wagon. Later, a more complicated type was invented, which used an arm to hurl large stones or racks of arrows. A city under siege could never be sure what might come hurtling over their walls. Flaming bundles of oil were often thrown over walls in order to set a city on fire. The bodies of the city's slain defenders were often tossed back into the city, frightening and demoralizing the people within its walls. It is no wonder that catapults were dreaded as the most horrible of weapons.

DEFENDING THE WALL

The walls of many Old Testament cities were casemented, which meant that they had that notched look that is usually associated with castles. From the narrow notches in the wall, archers would send down a rain of arrows. The higher portions of the wall created cover for the defenders as they walked along the top of the wall, surveying the attackers. Battering rams were used to attack fortresses, but the Canaanites thickened the walls of their cities so that they were useless. From the tops of these walls the defenders would shoot arrows, throw spears and javelins, and drop stones and anything else that was movable on the attackers who might be climbing up scaling ladders, seeking to undermine the walls, attacking the walls and gates with battering rams, or trying to burn or hack through the

DID YOU KNOW?

- Soldiers, especially those in the Roman army, wore hobnailed boots to steady their footing on the battlefield.

- Spears and javelins were standard equipment in armies from the time of the patriarchs. These weapons were sometimes tipped with metal so that it could be stuck into the ground when not in use. The blunt edge could be used as a club.

- Rectangular shields that were body length and curved at the top protected siege warriors. They covered the backs of the men who crouched at the base of the wall doing the undermining.

city gates. During one Old Testament altercation, a man named Abimelech got too close to a wall, and he was killed when a woman dropped her millstone on his head (Judg. 9:53).

ASSYRIAN BATTERING RAMS

Assyrians were warriors at heart, so when it came to inventions, all their creativity went into improving and refining their weaponry. The Assyrians routinely went up against the impressive fortresses of their enemies, so they had developed battering rams to break through their defenses. One kind of Assyrian battering ram had six wheels and was surrounded by a wooden framework supporting wicker shields. Several men could wheel it up to the gates of a city, protected by the wicker from every side. A metal dome topped its length, giving the men enough room to stand upright beneath it. This protected the siege soldiers from the spears and arrows that were being flung at them from atop the walls. Inside this protective shell, ropes from the framework suspended the huge battering ram. It was rocked back and forth on the ropes like a pendulum, with each swing delivering a shattering blow.

SWORDS

There was actually a time in Israel's history when there were only two swords in the entirety of the kingdom. Those two belonged to King Saul, and to his son Jonathan. The Philistines were oppressing the land back then, and they wouldn't allow the Israelites to have their own blacksmiths. That way they knew the Jews couldn't make weapons for themselves. Even farmers who needed to have their plows sharpened before tilling in the spring had to pay a Philistine blacksmith to do the job. Later, the number of swords in the land increased, because David took Goliath's sword from him when he defeated the giant. He actually carried this weapon with him when he and his men were on the run from Saul (1Sa. 21:9).

WAR GALLEYS

The war galley was the battleship of the ancient Mediterranean world. To begin with, these galleys were long slender boats powered by a row of oars on each side. Some armies developed galleys with two decks and two rows of oars. During the time of the Roman fleet, galleys became huge, with three decks and three rows of oars. Originally, each oar only required one rower, and being a rower was considered honorable. As the ships increased in size, the oars required more men to pull them. Some oars were up to fifty feet long and required six men to pull them. This backbreaking task was left to slaves or prisoners of war. One of the most important features of the new and improved war galleys was its battering ram. A long timber was overlaid with bronze and mounted to the front of the galley just under the waterline. During a battle, galleys would try to ram each other, and soldiers would swarm onto the crippled ships to overpower the crew.

WHIP OF SCORPIONS

One of the most common punishments handed down by a Roman judge was to send an offender to the whipping block. Being scourged was a humiliating experience, for the offender was stripped naked and

DID YOU KNOW?

• "Grieves" were shin guards that protected the front of a soldier's legs from the odd arrow or slingstone. Goliath wore them (1Sa. 17:6).

• The cumbersome war galley was not exactly a seaworthy vessel. During their heyday, more galleys were lost in storms than in battles.

tied with hands overhead to a post. The number of lashes was always prescribed, with more given to the worst offenders. Paul says that five times, he was given thirty-nine lashes (2Cor. 11:24). The soldier carrying out the punishment had a few different instruments at his disposal. First, there was the basic rod (Acts 16:22; 2Cor. 11:25). Then, came the whip, which could raise some pretty mean welts. Then came the cat-of-nine-tails style of whip, which had several strips of leather bound together on one handle. This efficiently delivered nine lashes with one swing, minimizing the efforts of the punisher and maximizing the pain of the punished. The ultimate scourging tool was the whip-of-scorpions. This fiendish device had bits of metal or glass embedded into the ends

GOLIATH
Philistine Champion

Goliath of Gath was the undisputed champion of the entire
Philistine army. Standing just over nine feet, nine inches, he was a
giant of a man. This wasn't so unusual, mind you! His whole family
looked down on most people. Some of his uncles were well over ten
feet tall! His folks were descended from the Rephaim, and some said
that they were the children of the gods. That is how their countrymen explained their stature, their prowess, and their superiority. It
was more difficult to explain the fact that many of their family had
six fingers on each hand and six toes on each foot. It was an unusual
characteristic, indeed.

Goliath's upper body strength was impressive. His spear was
nearly as tall as he was. It was really just a young tree that had been
smoothed and tipped with a metal spearhead that weighed fifteen
pounds all by itself. The sword he wielded was a good six feet long,
giving him a twelve-foot reach in the field of battle. During combat,
Goliath's foes couldn't get close enough to do any damage. All of
Goliath's armor was specially made for him. Actually, most everything
Goliath owned had been designed for his use. His clothes needed vast
amounts of woven cloth. His shield was as tall as the houses of the
Hebrews. His armor weighed more than some men, and had cost him
a fortune. And his hobnailed war sandals had to be special ordered.
Good footwear was especially important. He was too large to be carried by any of the horses or camels found in the land. Thankfully,
successful soldiering was a profitable business, and he stood with an
undefeated record. Goliath could afford his 9XLT garments, his super-
sized house, and his king-sized bed. Such things were usually reserved
for royalty (Deut. 3:11). So Goliath, the Philistine champion in hand-
to-hand combat comes to his last battle. Faced with a boy who doesn't

even carry a sword, Goliath laughs. The Israelites might as well be surrendering to send such a puny champion. But Goliath is not familiar with the slingshot, nor does he understand the power of God. Almost before his last insults are past his sneering lips, Goliath falls to the ground. The champion of the Philistines ends his days in humiliation, beaten by a mere boy, and beheaded by his own sword.

of the clustered lashes. With a firm grip, the wielder could bruise and bloody a man's back, but by adding a twist of the wrist, he could tear someone's flesh to shreds.

CRUCIFIXION

Crucifixion was the ultimate in corporal punishment. When the judge wanted a criminal to truly suffer for his crimes, he was sentenced to crucifixion. Generally, it was a sentence handed down to slaves and rebels. It was the most painful death the Romans had devised. A criminal's hands and feet were pinned to rough beams of wood with long spikes. Archeologists have unearthed skeletons with nine-inch spikes still embedded in their anklebones. When the cross was dropped into a hole to suspend it's victim in an upright position, death came very slowly. With arms outstretched, breathing became difficult, and a man had to push up on the spike in his feet to draw a breath. Sometimes a man would hang for more than a week before he was released from his suffering. To hasten death, a criminal's legs were broken, so that he could not catch a breath

DID YOU KNOW?

• If a Roman citizen was found guilty of a crime, he was spared many of the indignities suffered by non-citizens— including the ultimate death by crucifixion. Membership definitely had its privileges, even in Bible times!

(Jn. 19:31). A Roman citizen was exempt from the humiliation of death by crucifixion, which is why Peter was eventually crucified, but Paul was beheaded.

STRATEGY

In the strategy rooms of ancient times, kings and their generals discussed war. They analyzed enemy fortifications. They improvised attack patterns. They dictated troop movements. They laid ambushes. They deliberated over sieges. They made alliances. They hired mercenaries. Would they put the city to the sword, or did they need more slaves for their mines? The strategists decided the fates of whole cities.

DECLARATIONS OF WAR

There was a certain etiquette to declaring war against someone in the Bible. A messenger was sent to the border of an enemy's territory and shouted out "I wage war against you!" It was preferable that this be done near an enemy encampment, to be sure that someone heard the declaration. After this verbal declaration of war, the messenger would then shoot an arrow or throw a spear over the border (2Kin. 13:17). This was considered fair warning of a coming invasion. Thirty days were allowed for peace negotiations. If no reconciliation was reached, then on the thirty-first day, hostilities would commence.

PREPARATIONS FOR WAR

The kings of Israel prepared for war by seeking God's advice. This was usually through the prophets or through the priests who carried the sacred lots. If God gave the king the green light, the army received its marching orders. The Israelite army always brought sacred objects with them into the battle fray—the ark of the covenant often accompanied them (Josh. 6:8; 1Sa. 4:3). Before the actual command to attack was given, priests offered a sacrifice. On one occasion, King Saul became impatient waiting for the priests to show up, so he offered the sacrifice himself (1Sa. 13:8–11). This got him into trouble with the prophet Samuel and with God. Saul didn't learn his lesson, though, for he even attempted to get advice by consulting a medium (1Sa. 28:7).

ARMY ORGANIZATION

Very little is known of the ins and outs of army life in Israel. The Scriptures mention that the troops were divided into fifties and thousands under their captains (1Sa. 8:12). For a very long time, an army was just a large group of men on foot. Some of these men were highly skilled with the bow and arrow or with the slingshot, but most were used in hand-to-hand combat. They didn't really miss some of the innovations of other nations, for their battles often took place in the hill country. The treed slopes of Canaan didn't lend themselves to chariots. The people of Israel were not introduced to the finer points of strategy until David's era. King David expanded their borders like no other. Later, under King Solomon's rule, the Israelites were further equipped with horses, giving them a mounted cavalry and thousands of chariots to strengthen their ranks.

CONQUEST OF CANAAN

In the small land of Palestine, there was no unexplored territory available for colonization. If a nation wished to expand its borders, it must conquer lands belonging to others. The children of Israel were faced with this when they reached the Promised Land. God had given the land to them, but first they had to drive out its current inhabitants. Joshua used every strategy he could come up with to vanquish the Canaanites in their fortified cities. With the intention of dividing and conquering, Joshua marched right through the middle of the Promised Land, and then turned south and finally to the north. He tricked the defenders of Ai into leaving the shelter of their city (Josh. 8:3–22). He had the entire city of Jericho standing in wonder as a silent army marched around their city on a daily basis (Josh. 6:3). In the end, the conquest of Canaan was left incomplete. The tribes of Israel couldn't manage a clean sweep, and the Canaanites still held on to several strongholds.

OPEN COMBAT

In open combat, the two armies stood apart, facing each other across an open plain. Sometimes the opposing forces each stood upon high ground, with a valley between them (1Sa. 17:3). A trumpet usually signaled the command to attack, although sometimes there was a prearranged war cry. Then, the two lines of men would rush towards one another. The first line of men carried large rectangular shields and lances. Behind this protective hedge, the archers would send up volley after volley of arrows. This was the cover fire for the advancing troops. When the two armies finally met in the middle, there was a great clash as hand-to-hand combat erupted. Sometimes two opposing forces avoided the bloody confrontation by deciding the battle in a contest between their two champions. This was the proposal offered to King Saul by the Philistine champion, Goliath (1Sa. 17:8–9).

THE DUEL

Battles were costly—uniforms, weapons, and supplies were required to outfit troops that might never come home again. Some armies used a unique strategy to circumvent the carnage of a full-scale confrontation. One army would challenge the other army to a duel. Each side would choose a champion as their representative, and the outcome of their duel determined the outcome of the whole war. This cut down on expenses. The champion was under a lot of pressure to win his match, for the lives of his entire nation depended on his performance. Goliath, the Philistine champion, challenged King Saul to send out a champion for him to fight. Saul was in a quandary, because the forces of the Philistines outnumbered him, and their champion appeared unbeatable. It was a lose-lose

GIDEON

The Cautious Hero

The Israelites had sinned, and so God allowed them to be oppressed by the Midianites. For seven years, the children of Israel lived in caves and hid in the hillsides. The crops that they planted every spring never made it to their own supper tables, for the Midianites would come in and steal the harvest. The Israelites were hungry and miserable and eventually repentant. So, God decided to raise up an unlikely hero. Gideon is found during the harvest, trying to hide the grain he has picked from the Midianites by winnowing it down in a winepress. With one eye on the horizon and one on the task at hand, he is startled by the approach of a stranger. "The Lord is with you, you mighty man of valor!" What an ironic greeting, for Gideon was at that moment hiding in a pit! But the stranger is the Angel of the Lord, and he has come to tell Gideon that he will defeat the Midianites. That night, Gideon is told to tear down the local altar of Baal, which he accomplishes under cover of darkness. Next, Gideon is instructed to prepare for battle. Still uncertain of God's hand in his life, Gideon puts out a fleece—literally, to test God, just to be sure he's receiving his messages clearly. So Gideon, the cautious leader, calls up the troops. Twenty-two thousand men stand ready for battle. However, God demands some cutbacks, and the men are whittled down to a mere three hundred. That very night, God tells Gideon to go down against the Midianite encampment, for he will deliver them into the hands of the Israelites. But, Gideon wants to be certain again. He and his servant sneak down and listen in on the talk around the tents. Assured by what he hears, Gideon heads back up the hillside and rallies the men for battle. Gideon and his men surround the enemy camp and sound the battle cry. The Midianites are completely routed. Against impossible odds, Israel is freed.

situation! When David finally offered to defeat the giant, the army of Israel looked on with uneasy hearts. If Goliath defeated their puny champion, Israel faced slavery to the Philistine nation (1Sa. 17:9). Instead, the nation of Israel raised a roar of victory and chased the Philistines all the way home!

BANNERS

In ancient times, banners were used to help organize the forces during a military battle. These standards were embellished with unique devices, and by looking over the field, a soldier knew where the rest of his division was. In the heat of battle, if the tides were turning against them, the soldiers would sound a trumpet. This was the signal to rally around the banner in order to regroup and renew their efforts. The banner-bearer was vital to the troops, and if he was cut down in combat, the standard had to be retrieved and lifted quickly. If not, the other soldiers were thrown into confusion. The absence of a banner under which to fight could cause an army to lose their battle. Traditionally, each of the tribes of Israel had a standard that was the same color as the stone that bore their name on the breastplate of the high priest.

TRICKS AND TACTICS

During the time of the judges, the tribes of Israel developed new tactics. They were beginning to learn the art of warfare. Assassination was becoming popular, and Ehud made plans to kill the current tyrant, Eglon the Fat. This ancient hit man concealed a short double-edged sword on his right side to throw off the bodyguards. Most men were right-handed, and wore their swords on their left for the traditional crossover draw. Ehud ran

Eglon through and was away before anyone suspected anything (Judg. 3:21). Barak managed to lure the army of Sisera in all their chariots onto a muddy plain. They got stuck in the muck, and Barak destroyed them all (Judg. 5:21). Gideon, with a small raiding force, was able to surprise and defeat the army of the Midianites by way of a night attack (Judg. 7:16–22). Gideon's small band used special effects—lights on the hillsides and the blaring of hundreds of trumpets—to confuse their groggy foe.

TUNNELS AND TRAITORS

Sometimes the difference between an impenetrable fortress and a smoking ruin was the integrity of one of its citizens. When the fortress city at Bethel was under siege, the Israelite army spotted a man coming out of the city. The man was captured and interrogated. The Israelites forced the man to give them the location of a secret tunnel that led into the city walls. Such tunnels were often used by cities as a means of escape or as a launching point for attacks on invading forces. Armed with this information and their swords, the army entered the city. Bethel's citizens were caught completely off guard, and everyone in the city was killed. The only survivor was the man who had betrayed his comrades (Judg. 1:22–26).

> ### DID YOU KNOW?
>
> • Decaying animals and dead bodies could be thrown over city walls to cause disease among its population. This was the earliest form of germ warfare.
>
> • Kings defending their cities tried to stock up and assure adequate food and water supplies if they were expecting a siege. Hezekiah's engineers dug a tunnel through almost six hundred yards of solid rock to give him a water supply (2Chr. 32:30).

DISABLED DEFENDERS

Most of the ancient nations from Bible times were ruled by strongly-held superstitious beliefs. Just as some people will never open an umbrella in the house or walk under a ladder, the Hittite people would never lift their hand against the blind or the lame. To kill a disabled person was to incur the wrath of the gods. With this in mind, some nations would set up their defenses so that the blind and the lame were guarding the gates. Superstitious attackers shied away from these cleverly placed defenders. The dread of a curse from on high was enough to turn away the bravest of soldiers. When David set about to conquer Jerusalem, the Jebusites tried this tactic (2Sa. 5:6-8). Unbeknownst to them, David didn't give a fig for heathen curses. He marched into the city and took it for his capital.

BATTLE AFTERMATH

The blood and gore of battle did not end on the battlefield. When the army of a city was conquered, it was considered quite normal to go inside the walls and kill, mutilate, or enslave all the men who remained there. Women and children were taken captive. The city walls were broken down, and all the buildings were burned to the ground. There was a free-for-all of looting, and the conquering soldiers were allowed to take whatever plunder they could find. The most valuable findings were reserved for the king. If a city submitted to the invading forces before the battle began, then the slaughter was averted. Hostages were still taken, but the city remained standing. A heavy tribute was demanded as a token of their continued submission to their captors.

SOWING WITH SALT

When a man wished to lay a city in total waste, there were a few things that were traditional. First of all, every man, woman, and child in the city was put to the sword. Not one soul was left alive. The livestock were either hamstrung or butchered. Then, all the buildings were burned. The walls of the defeated city would be tumbled down so that not one stone

DID YOU KNOW?

• When a people were defeated, and led away into captivity, sometimes they were put on parade in the victor's city. Treated like animals, they were led through the marketplaces in cages or chains, or with hooks through their noses (Eze. 38:4).

• Entire nations of people were taken into captivity. This was a military tactic to prevent the rebellion of captured peoples.

stood upon another. The crops in the fields surrounding the city were burned. Trees were put to the ax. Wells were filled with sand and rubble. And as a final measure, to ensure that no city could ever be built upon that same spot in the future, the land in every direction was sown with salt, making it useless for agriculture ever again (Judg. 9:45).

CAPTIVITY

When one nation conquered another, there were usually two options when dealing with survivors. Everybody was either put to the sword, or taken away as captives. It was a sound military practice to remove large groups of people from their homelands. It prevented them from causing any more trouble in the future. In this way too, great nations provided themselves with slaves and workers for menial tasks. The people of Gibeon were made the servants of Israel, assigned all the woodcutting and water carrying tasks (Josh. 9:21). The Israelites became familiar with captivity, for they were carried off twice. Both the Assyrians and the Babylonians had a turn at making the Jews their slaves. The relocation program was so successful that many Jews living in Persia chose to remain there, even when given the chance to return to Jerusalem. It wasn't until the days of Ezra and Nehemiah that the children of God returned to their Promised Land to rebuild their cities.

PROOF OF VICTORY

In ancient times, when alliances were shaky and a man had to be taken at his word, a little hard evidence was appreciated. Kings were notorious for gently embellishing their victory sagas. A little exaggeration did wonders for a nation's reputation. So, occasionally men required proof. The men of Succoth asked Gideon if he had really defeated the army of Midian. To prove that Gideon and the Israelites weren't pulling their legs, they wanted a show of hands (Judg. 8:6). It was customary in those days for the victors to amputate the hands of their enemies as proof of their victory. It was also a "handy" way to tally up how many of the enemy had been killed. Before the men of Succoth would accept Gideon's claim of victory and feed his army, they asked to see the hands of the two Midianite kings (Judg. 8:6).

Siege Warfare

Siege warfare was both a full-scale attack and a waiting game. The invaders used a combination of weapons in their campaign. Battering rams, siege towers, scaling ladders, flaming arrows, catapults, ramps, and even tunneling were used to break through. Siege towers were rolled into position, and archers used them to get a better vantage point. Their arrows provided cover fire for the advancing ground troops. These ground troops carried battering rams and scaling ladders, hoping to break through the wall or get over it. When the walls of a city were high on a steep hillside, the army would often build dirt ramps up the sides so that they could reach the walls. These daily assaults would wear down the determination of a city on the defensive. Another key to siege warfare was to surround the city completely. By trapping the city's inhabitants inside the walls and cutting off their supply route, the invaders hoped to starve their quarry into submission. If possible, the water supply was cut off as well (2Kin. 6:26–29). When this was accomplished, then the attackers had merely to wait for the city's stockpiles of supplies to run out. Some sieges took years to resolve.

Spread Too Thin!

The Assyrians loved war so much that battle scenes make up most of their country's artwork. The pictures found by archeologists which depict sieges show the enemy walls being attacked by battering rams, swords, spears, axes, fire, scaling ladders, and undermining all at the same time. This would have been an accurate depiction of siege strategy. It was divide and conquer. Often several battering rams would be concentrated on one section of the wall. Then, just around the corner, troops were rushing the wall with scaling ladders. On the other side of town, soldiers with shields on their backs were digging at the base of the wall, trying to tunnel into the city. The defenders were forced to spread out their men in an effort to keep all the attackers at bay. Meanwhile, the real danger continued unchecked, as the battering rams weakened the very structure of the wall.

Too Close for Comfort

One no-no of siege warfare was getting too close to the walls without proper protection. It was wiser for an army to stand back a ways, out of the range of the archers stationed on the walls overhead. In order to manage a foray up near the walls, the soldiers would huddle together and carry their shields over their heads. This protected them from the arrows that were raining down, and allowed them to make use of their battering rams against the gates. In one particular war, the army of Israel, under the command of General Joab, made the risky choice of moving in close to the walls. The defenses were relentless in hurtling them with stones and arrows, and many men were lost. In fact, one poor fellow by the name of Abimelech was killed when a woman dropped a millstone on his head from above (Judg. 9:53). The General had an ulterior motive for this assault, and had informed some of his trusted soldiers to betray one of their own. In the midst of this confusion, Joab ordered his men to pull back, leaving Uriah alone and unprotected on the front lines (2Sa. 11:16–17). Uriah was quickly killed by enemy fire. When word was brought to King David of the battle losses, he was furious over Joab's

DID YOU KNOW?

• Garrisons were established throughout Palestine by the Roman Empire. These were the peacekeeping forces. They were a preventative measure, to ensure that citizens behaved themselves, paid their taxes, and didn't plot any rebellions.

• Defenders often began their stand outside the wall, where they had greater mobility. They would then fall back into the city or be drawn up the walls by ropes if they were unsuccessful (Josh. 2:15).

• A common tactic in ancient times was to try to kill the king. Once a soldier's king was dead, the troops dissolved into confusion without leadership (cf. 1Kin. 22:31).

foolish bid near the walls of the city. The losses were needless. Then the messenger gave David the rest of Joab's message. Uriah the Hittite was also dead. At this, King David held his peace. He had asked Joab to arrange Uriah's death so he could marry the Hittite's young widow, Bathsheba.

CONDITIONAL SURRENDER

The Aramaean army sent word to King Ahab that they were coming to lay siege to Jerusalem, so they might as well surrender now and save everybody the hassle of a long standoff. Ahab looked over the numbers and sent word back to the Aramaeans that he was willing to give them a conditional surrender. He was willing to pay them tribute, so long as they left his people alone (1Kin. 20:4). Word got back to Ahab that the Aramaeans fully intended to get some looting in on this trip, and that his city, palace, and family were in grave danger. Threats were exchanged, and the Aramaeans mobilized a contingent of their troops to batter down Ahab's defenses and take the city. Ahab wasn't sitting on his hands waiting, though. He was mustering Jerusalem's militia! The men of Jerusalem chose a narrow valley and laid a trap for the advancing Aramaean army. Taken by surprise, the invading forces were completely routed. Ahab's men chased the fleeing Aramaeans all the way back to their base camp. There, the rest of the army had been throwing a little pre-victory celebration. The drunken men were helpless in the face of the Israelite militia, and their entire force was defeated (1Kin. 20:16–21).

> ### DID YOU KNOW?
>
> • Moses had been trained in the art of Egyptian warfare, and he must have passed on his knowledge to the children of Israel as they prepared to enter the promised land.
>
> • Fortresses were built to defend the borders of a kingdom. When the kingdom of Israel was divided, Solomon's son Rehoboam fortified fifteen cities to provide for his defense (2Chr. 11:6–12).

A TIME FOR WAR

War was something that came in and out of season. In Bible times and in Bible lands, spring was the season that made a soldier's heart beat faster.

It was a matter of practicality, really. Invasion forces were always sent off in the spring, because it guaranteed good traveling weather. Dry roads were important, especially for the great wagons that carried catapults and siege towers. Slogging through the mud dampened the spirits of man and beast alike. Also, the spring travel put them in enemy territory right around harvest time, when the farmers who served as a city's militia were busy in the fields. They hadn't had time to brush up on their combat skills, and were caught unprepared for battle. Spring also made foraging for food easier for a large army. There were a lot of mouths to feed. When the family farms evacuated to a walled city in face of invasion, their fields and produce were left at the mercy of hungry troops.

SOMETIMES THE BEST OFFENSE IS A GOOD DEFENSE

The kings of Israel and Judah studied the construction and defense of cities carefully. In a land where conquests were frequent, it made good sense to plan ahead and be prepared. When trouble came, they liked to be able to hunker down and outlast the opposition. The walls themselves were built up and strengthened. Usually, a well-made wall was thick enough to withstand the efforts of a battering ram, tall enough to prevent the use of scaling ladders, and casemented to shield the defenders upon them. Casemented walls had jagged tops, giving soldiers cover while they shot arrows from the notches. Secret entrances into the city were hidden, to provide a point of attack against enemies camped outside the walls. These also allowed a means of escape when the city was about to fall. Armor and shields and weaponry were brought in, making ready to defend the city in case of a siege. Oil and wine and other foodstuffs were stockpiled, sometimes enough to last for years. Most important was a good water supply. Great cisterns were constructed to capture and hold rainwater. Wells were dug, tapping into springs deep beneath the city. One king even had an underground tunnel built to bring water from a nearby spring right into the city walls.

INTIMIDATION

Sieges were difficult and expensive to maintain, and so kings and their generals would usually try to trick a city into surrendering before hunkering down for a long assault. A frazzled and exhausted Jehoram wasn't quite willing to believe that the besieging Aramaeans had actually gone away (2 Kin. 7:10–12). He was sure they were watching from just around some corner. One very popular tactic was intimidation. Bold threats were hurled at the walls of a city in the hopes that the common people would get panicky and ask their king to give in. When Sennacherib of Assyria besieged Jerusalem, he verbally attacked everyone in sight (2Kin. 18:19–23). The king of Israel at that time was Hezekiah, and he allowed some of Sennacherib's negotiators into the city to discuss the situation. Hezekiah actually asked Sennacherib's men to stop speaking in the Hebrew tongue, and to revert to their own language. The city's defenders could eavesdrop in on the talks, and tension was mounting as the gossipers relayed information throughout the city. The Assyrian negotiators smugly replied that they were using Hebrew on purpose, hoping to make the defenders nervous. If they succeeded in lowering the morale of the city, the people might revolt against Hezekiah.

> **DID YOU KNOW?**
>
> • Assyria besieged many of the cities of Judah. The siege of Samaria took three years.
>
> • Fortress cities show evidence of wells, cisterns, complicated drainage systems, and underground tunnels to provide water for a city in the face of sieges or drought.

MIND GAMES

Psychological warfare was nothing new in ancient times. Some armies depended upon rumors and their exaggerated reputations to work for them. An army that could force a surrender before any blows were exchanged was both happy and wealthy. Alexander the Great was a master of propaganda. As the Greek army swept across the known world, Alex would send men ahead to get the rumor mills started. He used what might be called practical jokes, too. He loved to terrify foes by scattering enormous bridle bits where they could easily be seen. This gave the impression that he possessed super-sized horses! So the Greeks used shrewd psychology and mind games to their advantage.

TOPICAL INDEX

B

D

E

H

T

U

V

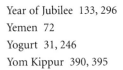